Honus Wagner
His Pittsburgh P......

9-12
5
9
22
35-36
52
123
132
134-135
138
162
167-170

Honus Wagner and His Pittsburgh Pirates

Scenes from a Golden Era

RONALD T. WALDO

McFarland & Company, Inc., Publishers
Jefferson, North Carolina

LIBRARY OF CONGRESS CATALOGUING-IN-PUBLICATION DATA

Waldo, Ronald T., 1961–
 Honus Wagner and his Pittsburgh Pirates / Ronald T. Waldo.
 p. cm.
 Includes bibliographical references and index.

 ISBN 978-0-7864-9667-9 (softcover : acid free paper) ∞
 ISBN 978-1-4766-1882-1 (ebook)

 1. Wagner, Honus, 1874–1955. 2. Baseball players—United
States—Biography. 3. Pittsburgh Pirates (Baseball team)—
History. I. Title.
GV865.W33W35 2015
796.357092—dc23
 [B] 2015008655

BRITISH LIBRARY CATALOGUING DATA ARE AVAILABLE

On the cover: John Peter "Honus" Wagner, Pittsburgh shortstop,
National League, ca. 1911 (Library of Congress)

Printed in the United States of America

McFarland & Company, Inc., Publishers
 Box 611, Jefferson, North Carolina 28640
 www.mcfarlandpub.com

Table of Contents

Acknowledgments

While I always strive in my books to give the best, most accurate representation possible of a particular player or time in baseball history, the efforts of others help make it possible for me to achieve that goal. This book about Honus Wagner and his era is no exception in that respect.

Securing permission to quote from articles that do not fall within the public domain is critical for baseball historians, since few things we can say about our subjects will bring it to life in quite the way that first-hand accounts can. I would therefore like to say thank you to Linda Parker, administrative assistant to the editors at the *Pittsburgh Post-Gazette*, and John Turner, deputy editor of *The Sporting News*, for their help during the permissions-gathering process. The coverage of Wagner and the Pirates in these two publications was indispensible to me, and the book is better for its quotations from them.

I would also like to thank photo archivist John W. Horne, Jr., of the National Baseball Hall of Fame Library for all of his assistance with the photos for the book. John always responded to my queries in a timely fashion, and the Hall of Fame's photo offerings were unfailingly good. The diligent efforts of Horne, Jenny Ambrose and Pat Kelly over the years have in fact made what can be one of the more onerous chores an author faces—finding the right photos and arranging for their permissions—a fairly straightforward and painless proposition. These photos have offered a vital visual component that beautifully complements the written word.

Lastly, I want to say thank you to all of the people who read my books and articles. I love writing about baseball history and am extremely happy that people enjoy reading about forgotten baseball eras that helped define the game.

Preface

One of the beautiful things about the game of baseball is that its rich history and abundant heritage remain relevant today, more than a century after a new era dawned when men like Christy Mathewson, Nap Lajoie, Cy Young and Ty Cobb rose to the level of diamond icons. These baseball greats and the teams they played for defined that era as the game experienced a grand transformation that allowed it to grow and thrive. Baseball quickly rose to the stature of America's Game as passionate fans across the country fell in love with this sport that was a combination of beauty and physical prowess. Players who performed on the diamond during the first two decades of the twentieth century were true pioneers who helped to build baseball into the great game that it still is today.

If men like Mathewson, Lajoie, Young and Cobb were the modern game's founders and builders, John Peter "Honus" Wagner was the necessary forged steel that was critical in this entity's construction. A native of the nearby municipality of Carnegie, Wagner was the undisputed top player in the National League while he played for his hometown Pittsburgh Pirates in the Steel City from 1900 through 1917. Many also deemed Wagner to be the eminent star in baseball when compared to other players from that era. Even today, Wagner is still considered the premier player in Pirates history, the greatest shortstop in baseball history and one of the top players who ever set foot on a diamond. The fact that Honus Wagner is still viewed in this manner almost a century after he played his final major league game in 1917 is due in large part to an enduring legacy that has continued to live and breathe for decades following his death in 1955.

There are many reasons why Wagner continues to have a lasting legacy during our generation. Statistics such as the eight batting titles, playing for four National League pennant winners and smacking 3,420

career hits certainly help him remain relevant today. Excellent biographies chronicling moments and events from his career have also contributed to keeping Wagner's memory alive. A third reason why Honus Wagner's legacy has endured is due to the time-tested practice of stories being related and passed down through the ages. Baseball has always been unique in respect to its history remaining vibrant due to tales that have been shared through generations from grandfather or grandmother, to father or mother, to child.

I believe it is important to present a narrative that examines Wagner not only as a ballplayer, but also as a man. Through the use of a large collection of stories from Wagner's time as a player and coach, which spanned 40 years, I decided to paint a picture that focuses on the climate of that baseball era as well as his personal achievements. Stories related to Wagner, his teammates and opposing players are presented in order to chronicle both that baseball era and that time period in American history.

Many of these stories are Honus Wagner's reflections about baseball during his illustrious career, while some are the words of teammates and others who knew him. While a large majority of this material examines the interaction between Wagner, his teammates and other players on the diamond, baseball is not the entire subject probed in this work. I went to great lengths to include many examples of Wagner's other pleasures in life such as fishing, hunting and going for long rides in an automobile. The underlying points regarding his selfless approach to life and the unique camaraderie that existed during that baseball era also come to the forefront in this book.

My approach in this book differs from others I have written. As someone who is fascinated by the little-known tales surrounding baseball, I wanted to immerse myself in a project about Honus Wagner, but not by writing a biography. Wagner is the subject of a couple of good ones already. The idea was instead to focus on events from the great player's career as described by Wagner and his contemporaries. Since reporting players' anecdotes about the game was one of the best advertising methods that existed when Wagner played, a wealth of information was at my disposal. Although Wagner often tried to avoid the limelight, he did become more comfortable talking about the game as the seasons went by. He transformed from a man who was reluctant to talk about

baseball into an avid storyteller who wrote or co-authored many newspaper articles.

Because some of the stories Honus Wagner told during his lifetime were embellished a bit as he grew older, I made a concerted effort to research these incidents in order to prove their veracity or correct any discrepancies. Some anecdotes did not make the cut when evidence pointed toward their fitting more into the category of yarn rather than fact. For many stories, I was able to identify the dates and places referred to, while some were too general for this to be feasible. While it's possible that Wagner and others used poetic license in some instances regarding these tales, this was a prevailing method from that time period as writers who chronicled baseball tended to romanticize the game. The chronology of baseball, much like other points of interest related to history, tended to become more popular because of the folklore which added some spice to numerous narratives.

Some unexpected minor roadblocks did occur from time to time during this project. Having already written books regarding baseball history, I certainly did not expect to spend time searching issues of theater magazines in an effort to pinpoint the show schedule for stage sensation Fritzi Scheff. New challenges arose that I relished tackling and overcoming throughout this process. Research was done using various tools such as books, magazines and newspapers in order to formulate this narrative regarding Honus Wagner and that time period in respect to baseball. Due to the fact that this story is about a local player from a municipality close to Pittsburgh, I was able to identify more closely with the sense of civic pride that existed when Wagner played for the Pittsburgh Pirates.

Honus Wagner is the premier shortstop in baseball history and one of the greatest players who ever played the game. While this is common knowledge for most baseball fans, many who love the game and its rich history are unaware of the underlying factors that made Wagner a great and a beloved player. This book is about more than the career of a baseball player. It is a story which looks at Wagner's life, his relationships with other players, and the uniqueness of the Deadball Era. Some of the tales contained in this book are humorous, while others are inspiring. Each anecdote was carefully selected in order to highlight Wagner, his Pittsburgh Pirates or that particular era of baseball history.

Greatness is not something that comes easily for those who have been fortunate enough to achieve that status in baseball. Hard work and dedication has been the recipe for many who are placed on this pedestal. While Honus Wagner was the true embodiment of greatness throughout his baseball career, he never approached anything in life using half-measures. Wagner truly was a baseball icon and a humble man who always adhered to the principles of honesty, dignity and utmost integrity in all of life's endeavors. Much like a kid on the local sandlots, Wagner loved playing baseball and always enjoyed having fun on the diamond with teammates he called friends.

1

From Carnegie to Pittsburgh, by Way of Louisville

Dedication, perseverance and tirelessness are just a few words that described the hard-working denizens of Pittsburgh who were responsible for helping that eastern city become one of the most important industrial metropolises in the United States during the late nineteenth and early twentieth century. The steel industry flourished as mills and plants in Pittsburgh and neighboring communities forged this vital metal that was central in the expansion of other American cities. Innovation and development were the theme as entrepreneurs such as Andrew Carnegie, Henry Clay Frick, Andrew W. Mellon and George Westinghouse built their fortunes due to western Pennsylvania's industrial boom. As a new century dawned in 1900, Pittsburgh truly was a blue collar city whose inhabitants believed that accomplishment and fulfillment were achieved by the sweat of one's brow.

Since the blue collar population from Pittsburgh and the surrounding area understood that hard work reaped success, baseball enthusiasts who followed the fortunes of the city's National League team expected those same character traits to be espoused by every player who wore a Pittsburgh Pirates uniform. This certainly was the case in respect to the Pirates' top player during the first two decades of the twentieth century. John Peter "Honus" Wagner truly embodied hard work and honorable behavior on the diamond during his long baseball career in Pittsburgh that lasted from 1900 through 1917. Over those 18 years, Wagner established his credentials as the best player from that era, the supreme performer in Pirates history, and one of the greatest stars who ever played baseball.

Honus Wagner certainly was well versed in the strong work ethic that existed in western Pennsylvania when he joined the Pirates follow-

ing the 1899 baseball campaign. "Honus" was a local boy from the municipality of Carnegie who fully understood the region's ideals and way of life. It seemed fitting that Wagner eventually ended up playing for his hometown team in Pittsburgh. A hulking man who was bowlegged, Wagner's massive, ham-like hands were compared to giant steam shovels scooping up dirt when he grabbed ground balls, with many cartoons depicting him in this manner. Wagner was an extension of every person who toiled for their weekly stipend in a Pittsburgh mill or factory. Wagner may have looked rough around the edges or lacked gracefulness on the diamond at times, but he was always willing to work hard and throw his body around in order to get the job done.

Johannes "John" Peter Wagner was born on February 24, 1874, in the milling and mining town of Mansfield, Pennsylvania.[1] Wagner's parents, Peter and Katheryn, were German immigrants who had arrived in America in 1866. Nine children were born into the Wagner family, but only six lived beyond infancy.[2] Johannes was the third-youngest of the six surviving children. Brothers Charles, Al and Louis were older than Johannes, while sister Carrie and brother Bill were younger.[3] Peter Wagner was a stern, old coal miner who instilled a strong work ethic into each of his children at a very young age.[4] It was while he was young that Johannes received the nickname of "Honus" from boyhood friends. For those friends who insisted upon calling him Johannes rather than John, it usually came out as "Honus" since these western Pennsylvania lads could not correctly pronounce his German first name.[5]

When Honus was 12 years old, he started to work alongside his father under the earth as a coal miner. Peter Wagner, whose particular athletic interest was track, put his boys through a daily regimen of road work after labor in the coal mines had been completed. Following these runs along Mansfield's dusty roads, Peter also had his sons do a set of calisthenics which were aimed at keeping them in top condition. This conditioning program was specifically beneficial to young Honus, whose fleetness of foot was destined to serve him well playing baseball.[6] Wagner always reflected on those days working in the coal mines with an air of pride, since such work was hard and tedious for a boy of his age.

"I seldom saw daylight in those days," Wagner later claimed, "except on Sundays and holidays. I went down into the mines when it was dark and when I came out it was the dusk of the evening. My pay was about

$3.50 a week. I received 70 cents for loading a ton of coal and it took me all day to do it. Baseball was in my blood even then but I knew I couldn't be a coal miner and a ball player, too."[7]

Honus quit working in the coal mines so he could focus his attention on playing baseball.[8] Wagner's first serious connection to baseball came as a 15-year-old watching his older brother Al play for a sandlot team in the Allegheny League. He constantly hung around his brother's squad, carrying bats, retrieving baseballs and generally picking up pointers watching these fellows play baseball.[9] When Wagner wrote an article for *Baseball Magazine* in 1915 which chronicled his life and baseball career, he harkened back to his days as a teenager in Mansfield. His reputation as a speedster was the result of those races father Peter Wagner oversaw near the family home on a street that was later named Railroad Avenue. Honus and others ran on that dirt street and thought nothing of participating in 15 or 20 sprints each evening.[10] According to Wagner, this blazing speed initially was not utilized on a baseball diamond for a host of reasons:

> I played baseball when I was a kid, but that didn't amount to much. There was no money in it. I went to school here in Carnegie and learned a few things. Then I had to go to work. It is mining country here and the coal mines are what they call surface mines. That is they don't sink a shaft as they do in some parts, but work into a side hill from the surface. I was a coal miner for about a year. I didn't do any breaker work like some of the other ball players, who have started that way. I was pretty husky for my age and did general work in the mine for pay. It was hard work, but good exercise. I did not work a whole year in the mine. Then I went into a mill and worked for about a year. That was also good exercise.
>
> When I was sixteen I started playing ball here in earnest. I began in 1891 and played that season, also in '92 and '93. In '94 I played with the St. Luke's Club of Mansfield, which was then the name of this town before it was changed to Carnegie. The latter part of the season of '94 I went away to play ball. That was on account of my brother Al. He was playing with a club at Dennison, Ohio and told the manager he had a brother who could play ball. They believed him and sent for me. I finished the season there.[11]

While Wagner's baseball career seemed to be on the rise in 1894, his hometown also saw changes that reshaped the history of that area. In late February, Peter Wagner and a majority of the local citizens voted in favor of merging the two municipalities of Chartiers and Mansfield. The new borough was named Carnegie in honor of western Pennsylvania steel

baron Andrew Carnegie. While Andrew Carnegie had amassed a vast fortune through steel manufacturing and other industries, he was also a charitable philanthropist who donated millions of dollars to support education and build free public libraries.[12] In return for this great gesture on the part of Chartiers' and Mansfield's populace, Andrew Carnegie agreed to build a high school and library in the new borough bearing his name.

By 1895, there seemed to be no doubt that Honus Wagner planned on following the same path as older brother Al toward becoming a professional baseball player. While brothers Charles and Bill took up the barber's trade, Honus did not seem destined to work in that profession since the desire to play baseball was burning inside his belly.[13] Honus Wagner was a busy man in 1895 as he was a member of five different baseball teams in three leagues. He played for Steubenville, Akron and Mansfield in the Inter-State League, Adrian in the Michigan State League, and Warren in the Iron and Oil League. Wagner's first stop during that 1895 campaign was in Steubenville, Ohio. Club owner and manager George Moreland had agreed to sign him on the recommendation of Al Wagner, who was playing for Steubenville.[14]

Honus Wagner was working in brother Charley's barber shop when the telegram arrived telling him to report to Steubenville. His first professional baseball contract called for him to earn $35 a month. On the advice of a railroad friend who didn't think that was enough money, Wagner decided to ask for more. He sent a wire to George Moreland requesting that he be paid $40 a month to play for his team. Moreland promptly dispatched another telegram which read: "Take the $35 or don't come." Wagner jumped on the next freight train for Steubenville.[15]

"Well, that night I was on my way via a coal train from Carnegie," said Wagner, "and had no extra clothes, but I knew the conductor. When I arrived in Steubenville and read over the contract, after signing, I noticed one clause which read: 'I agree to pay for my own uniform and shoes, cost to be taken out of my first pay.'"[16]

"I would have played for nothing," continued Wagner. "And I might as well have, too. They took out for two uniforms and my shoes, and my first month's pay check was about $3."[17]

Wagner's sojourn through various minor league outposts in 1895 quickly paid off for the young baseball player. During the off-season, his hometown Pittsburgh Pirates attempted to sign the Carnegie lad to

a contract that would pay him $100 a month.[18] Pirates owner William Kerr planned on farming out Wagner to the Western League's Kansas City Blues for more seasoning. During a meeting with Kerr in the team's office, the young player balked at going so far away from his Carnegie home. He had never heard of Kansas City and did not recognize any of the players who were playing for that club. In those days, players preferred if there was someone that they knew on a minor league team. Fearing he would become homesick, Wagner politely declined Kerr's offer to play for Pittsburgh and left his office.[19]

Wagner's decision to reject a contract offer from the Pittsburgh Pirates ended up being a huge stroke of luck for minor league owner Edward Barrow of the Paterson Silk Weavers. Barrow was fully aware of Wagner's ability from both the Inter-State League and the Iron and Oil League.[20] During February before Paterson's 1896 season opened, Barrow found himself in Pittsburgh on business. When he stopped in Johnny Newell's café on Fifth Avenue, he ran into Shad Gwilliam, who had managed Wagner when he played for Mansfield in the Allegheny County League. Gwilliam recommended that Barrow sign Wagner for Paterson.[21]

> "Charlie McKee, also of Pittsburgh, and myself had secured the Paterson, N.J. franchise, and I was in search of players," explained Barrow. "One day I dropped into Newell's Hotel, where I chanced to meet Shad Gwilliam, who knew I was mixed up in baseball. 'Say, Barrow!' exclaimed Shad, after we had been talking for a few minutes. 'I'll tell you where you can get a good young fellow who, if given the chance, will in a few years be the greatest ball player in the world. His name is Wagner—Hans Wagner, they call him—and he lives down in Mansfield (Carnegie). Take my advice and get him.'
>
> "I had seen this young Wagner in the old Iron and Oil League the previous summer, but his playing had not attracted much attention. However, I decided to follow Gwilliam's advice, and the next day found me in Mansfield searching for Wagner. Inquiry at the little pool room in the town elicited the information that Wagner had gone down to the railroad to have a long-distance throwing contest. I started down the track and soon came upon Wagner and his playmates. Sure enough, they were trying to settle between themselves the dispute as to which one could throw a heavy rock the greatest distance. Wagner won, and after congratulating him I told him the object of my visit."[22]

While it took some convincing on Barrow's part to persuade Wagner to hook up with Paterson in 1896, his timing in inking the Carnegie youngster's signature to a contract was impeccable.

"I asked him if he would play for Paterson," Barrow continued. "Wagner didn't know whether he wanted to play ball at all. As we talked he would stoop over every once in a while and pick up a lump of coal or a stone and heave it up the railroad tracks. I watched the rocks sail a couple hundred feet and I knew I had to have this fellow. I offered him $125 and he accepted.

"The day after I signed Wagner, Capt. William W. Kerr, president of the Pittsburgh club, called me and said he wanted the Dutchman for the Pirates. I told Kerr he couldn't have him but that if I ever sold Wagner he would be given the first chance to buy."[23]

Edward Barrow's sense of timing truly had paid off as he signed Honus Wagner one day before former Steubenville and Akron manager George Moreland attempted to land him for William Kerr and the Pittsburgh Pirates. Watching Wagner hurl a one-pound rock a distance of 360 feet along Carnegie's railroad tracks sealed the deal in Barrow's mind. From the moment that Wagner put on a uniform to play for the Silk Weavers, he became a fan favorite among Paterson's baseball rooters. His magnificent ability in the field and at the plate, his good nature, and his willingness to play any position on the field made him an idol among both his teammates and Paterson's loyal patrons.[24] In 1896, the right-handed-hitting Wagner batted .313 in 109 games, primarily at first base.

It took Barrow only a brief amount of time to realize that besides being a phenomenal baseball player, Honus Wagner was also a model young man. Wagner was a modest, retiring and gentlemanly young chap who was not capable of doing a mean or horrible thing if he had tried. The 1896 campaign certainly was an interesting one for Wagner and his teammates as Paterson, Hartford and Newark battled down to the wire for the Atlantic League pennant. In the end, Newark claimed the top spot as Paterson finished in third place, three-and-one-half games behind the Colts with a record of 74–60. Due to chicanery on the part of Newark manager George "Foxy Deacon" Ellis, who sometimes scheduled triple-bill exhibition tilts on their home grounds and counted any victories in the league standings, officials from the Paterson and Hartford organizations refused to recognize his club as the true pennant winner.[25]

Edward Barrow and Hartford manager Billy Barnie agreed to play a best-of-seven-game post-season series to determine the true Atlantic League champion, named the Soby Cup Series. Barrow and his Silk Weavers staked their claim to the Atlantic League championship when they defeated Hartford in six games. Although Honus Wagner was only

a young rookie playing at this minor league level, he had already established his credentials as a team leader after one season in Paterson. "Like all Germans," said Edward Barrow while discussing Wagner's leadership qualities more than a decade after he had debuted for Paterson, "Honus liked his glass of beer, but had no use for 'lushers' and 'called' more than one of the boys in his quiet way, when he thought a defeat had been caused by the bad effects of too much celebrating the night before. None of them resented this, however, for they all knew that his everlasting desire to win was the reason for his lectures."[26]

After his highly successful first season playing for Paterson, Honus Wagner took the Atlantic League by storm in 1897 and quickly established his credentials as a bona fide prospect. Wagner batted .375 during his partial season for the Silk Weavers in 1897 and reached double figures in doubles (18), triples (14) and home runs (10) before he made the next natural progression in his professional baseball career. During his two seasons with Paterson, he played with other men from the Pittsburgh area such as Homestead's Bill Armour, Pittsburgh's George "Heinie" Smith and Carnegie friend Patrick "Patsy" Flaherty.[27] While Wagner had become one of the Atlantic League's most dominant players in such a short time, his game certainly was not always the model of perfection. Edward Barrow remembered a diamond event from the 1896 campaign when Honus Wagner's huge hands betrayed him.

> Wagner had the best pair of baseball hands I ever saw and used them instinctively at the right time and place. Speaking of his hands reminds me of a laughable incident that happened one day when he was playing first base. He had dug down into his hip pocket for a chew of 'scrap' when the pitcher suddenly delivered the ball and the batter hit it sharply to the shortstop, who fumbled but recovered and hurried it over to first. In the meantime Honus was dancing up and down and yelling like an Indian for him to hold the ball, and making frantic jerks and yanks at something behind. But it was too late and the ball went like a bullet for the big Dutchman's bread-basket. He put out his glove hand in self-defense and, luckily for us, the ball struck it fairly in the middle and stuck there, retiring the side.
>
> Then everybody made a rush for the German to see what the trouble was, and found that in his hurry to get his hand out of his pocket he had failed to open it, and the pocket not being built for a ham, balked, and the more he pulled the tighter he became fastened, the pocket-lining holding his hand in a vise-like grasp. We finally cut the pocket and released him but the big fellow didn't hear the last of it for months.[28]

Due to the perception at times that the rawboned Wagner was awkward, good judges of major league baseball talent such as Patsy Donovan of the Pittsburgh Pirates and Boston Beaneaters manager Frank Selee initially passed on the player after scouting him once. To fully appreciate Wagner's skill and ability, he had to be viewed day after day making phenomenal fielding plays, taking mighty swats with the willow and stealing bases with daring precision.[29] While most National League teams were not actively pursuing Wagner, the Louisville Colonels and team president Harry Pulliam started taking an interest in his exploits. Pulliam and Colonels star left fielder Fred Clarke made the trip to New Jersey from New York to watch Wagner when Louisville had a scheduled Sunday off during an early June trip. While Wagner did not do too much that afternoon, Pulliam and Clarke were sufficiently satisfied that dickering for his services began.[30]

One week later, Pittsburgh Pirates manager Patsy Donovan and team ownership partner Phil Auten scouted Wagner at a game on Sunday, June 13. During the next few weeks, members of the Pittsburgh, Louisville and Paterson organizations postured as negotiations for Honus Wagner's services intensified. Pulliam finally gained the upper hand when he offered Edward Barrow and Paterson $2,000 to secure Wagner's services. Though extremely excited over this offer, Barrow remembered his promise to Pirates owner William Kerr to give him the first opportunity to purchase Wagner. Barrow wired Kerr to inquire as to whether he was willing to match Louisville's offer.[31]

While Kerr immediately answered that he would be receptive to purchasing Honus Wagner for $2,000, Harry Pulliam increased his bid to $2,100. When a second telegram from Barrow to Kerr was not answered, Paterson and Louisville finalized the purchase a few days later. On July 17, 1897, Wagner officially became a member of the National League's Louisville Colonels.[32] Although everything had been worked out between Pulliam and Barrow, Louisville's president was fearful that Wagner might change his mind about leaving Paterson. While Wagner and Pulliam waited for a train that would take the two men to Louisville, Pulliam stuck close to the Dutchman so he would not wander away looking for a place to eat dinner. Pulliam even offered to buy Wagner anything that he wanted to eat, from toast to terrapin, at a restaurant in the railroad station. Whenever he offered a suggestion from the menu's bill of fare, Wagner shook his head in the negative.[33]

12

"Isn't there something you would like to have?" Pulliam asked after he read each menu item out loud.

"Yes," Wagner bluntly replied. "I would like to have a bag of bananas."[34]

Harry Pulliam breathed a sigh of relief and secured a bag of bananas for Honus Wagner to eat during the train ride to Louisville. Two days after it was announced that Wagner had been added to Louisville's roster, he made his major league debut against the Washington Nationals on July 19, 1897. When outfielder Ollie Pickering was tossed from the game, Wagner took his place, rapping out a single and executing a sacrifice bunt during three trips to the plate. That first major league game immediately stamped Wagner as a fine fielder, a powerful, fearless batsman, and, despite his apparent awkwardness, a superb base runner.[35] Wagner's first two and a half months playing major league baseball in 1897 were a rousing success as he appeared in 62 games and batted .335. Used primarily as an outfielder that first year, Wagner also made nine appearances at second base.

Honus Wagner's versatility was more evident during his first full season with the Colonels in 1898. A man who had performed at every position but catcher during his minor league career, Wagner played third base, first base and second base for Louisville in 1898. He batted .299, smacked ten home runs and drove home 105 teammates during his second season wearing a Colonels uniform. While Wagner

Louisville Colonels president Harry Pulliam handled the negotiations to purchase Wagner from the Paterson Silk Weavers. After the deal was finalized, Pulliam accompanied Wagner on a train to Louisville. Before the locomotive left the station, Wagner requested a bag of bananas when Pulliam offered to buy his new player anything he wanted to eat on their trip (courtesy National Baseball Hall of Fame Library, Cooperstown, New York).

was serving notice that he had the capabilities of becoming a future baseball star, the Louisville team that he played for continued to languish in the National League's second division. After bottoming out in 11th place in 1897, Louisville could rise no higher than the ninth position in 1898.

One month prior to Wagner joining the Colonels in 1897, Fred Clarke had been named to replace Jim Rogers as Louisville's manager on June 16. Clarke had already established himself as a National League star after only three major league seasons when the 24-year-old was selected as Louisville's new pilot. Following solid seasons at the plate in 1895 (.347) and 1896 (.325), Clarke challenged Willie Keeler for the National League batting title in 1897 and finished with a mark of .390. Clarke started reshaping his squad in 1898 as second baseman Claude Ritchey and outfielder Dummy Hoy were acquired in a February deal with the Cincinnati Reds, while third baseman Tommy Leach, who had been purchased from Auburn of the New York State League in August, finally made his major league debut on September 28, 1898.

Hurler Deacon Phillippe was added to Louisville's roster during the 1899 draft, selected from the Western League's Minneapolis Millers. Phillippe, Leach and Ritchey were all major contributors to the Colonels' cause in 1899 as they finished two games short of the .500 mark. In spite of the marked improvement, Louisville placed ninth for the second consecutive season. Honus Wagner continued to terrorize National League pitchers as he batted .341, drilled seven home runs and recorded 114 RBI. Although their club had finished in the second division once again, Louisville's faithful fans were upbeat due to the young talent that Fred Clarke was stockpiling.

Unfortunately, these devoted Louisville baseball patrons were destined never to reap the reward for this shrewd player procurement on the part of Colonels management. Concerned over proposed contraction plans by the National League aimed at reducing the number of teams in the organization from 12 to eight, Louisville owner Barney Dreyfuss and team president Harry Pulliam began searching for a way to remain in baseball. They decided to use monetary capital and Louisville's best players in an effort to broker a deal with a viable partner from one of the National League's proposed eight remaining franchises. After many twists and turns, a deal was agreed upon between Dreyfuss and Pittsburgh Pirates owner William Kerr.

On December 8, 1899, one of the biggest deals in baseball history was finalized at William Kerr's office in the Arbuckle Building. Louisville sent Rube Waddell, Bert Cunningham, Patsy Flaherty, Walt Woods, Deacon Phillippe, Mike Kelley, Claude Ritchey, Tommy Leach, Chief Zimmer, Tacks Latimer, Fred Clarke and Honus Wagner to Pittsburgh for Jack Chesbro, George Fox, John O'Brien, Art Madison and $25,000 in cash. Barney Dreyfuss immediately became a stockholder in the Pittsburgh Pirates and was named team president. Fred Clarke was selected to manage the Pirates, while Harry Pulliam was named team secretary.[36] When Louisville officially folded along with Washington, Cleveland and Baltimore, Chesbro, Fox, O'Brien and Madison were returned to Pittsburgh.

After three previous attempts to obtain homegrown Honus Wagner had failed, William Kerr and the Pirates finally succeeded in bringing the rising star to Pittsburgh. With a new century beckoning, it seemed that everything was aligning perfectly for Wagner and faithful Pittsburgh Pirates baseball fans. Following a seventh-place finish in 1899, the Pirates contended for the National League pennant in 1900 and came home second, 4½ games behind the Brooklyn Superbas with a 79–60 record. The influx of baseball talent from Louisville, along with stellar holdovers such as Jesse Tannehill, Sam Leever, Jack Chesbro and Clarence "Ginger" Beaumont, turned Pittsburgh into a formidable foe to be reckoned with.

Honus Wagner also seemed to benefit greatly from the opportunity to play in his hometown before passionate fans that wasted no time giving their new favorite son adulation and adoration. In 1900, Wagner took the next step toward establishing himself as the top player in baseball by claiming his first National League batting championship. Wagner's mark of .381 easily outdistanced Elmer Flick of the Philadelphia Phillies, who placed second with a .367 average. Wagner also led the National League in doubles (45) and triples (22).

The 1900 season was bittersweet for Honus Wagner. While he and his teammates could be proud of their many great achievements that were truly appreciated by Pittsburgh's fans, Wagner and his family suffered a personal tragedy in 1900 that tempered some of the excitement. After contracting typhoid fever in June, Wagner's 62-year-old mother Katheryn passed away on September 10. Wagner immediately rushed home during the Pirates' final eastern trip to be with his family. Since

he was the family's wealthiest member, Honus took care of the funeral arrangements and purchased a plot which consisted of eight grave sites in Chartiers Cemetery. Funeral services were held on September 12 in the Wagner home on Railroad Avenue. A magnificent funeral arrangement was sent from the Pirates to offer condolences to Honus Wagner and his family.[37]

That winter, president Ban Johnson of the rival American League started raiding the older National League circuit for players in an effort to gain the status of an equal major league. Owners of American League teams were more than willing to offer players extravagant salaries above the National League limit of $2,400. Clark Griffith of the Chicago White Sox was turned down by Wagner on a snowy night that winter in Carnegie when he offered him 20 $1,000 bills to sign with the American League club. Over the next two years, Wagner was the upstart league's most targeted player. On one occasion, a meeting with Ban Johnson in Pittsburgh never transpired because Barney Dreyfuss found out the time and location of this conference with his star player. In another instance, two of Johnson's agents did contact Honus. When Dreyfuss found out, he hiked to Carnegie, found Wagner in a poolroom, pulled out a blank contract and told him to fill in the salary amount that he wanted.[38]

"I can't sign tonight," Wagner told his surprised and worried boss, who wanted to know the reason.

"Because I promised certain people I wouldn't sign tonight," continued Wagner, "and wouldn't sign with anyone until noon tomorrow."

The next day at noon, Honus Wagner walked into Barney Dreyfuss' office and said, "I'll sign that contract now, Mr. Dreyfuss." Wagner signed for less money than the American League had offered.[39]

Two things constantly worked against Ban Johnson and his emissaries from the American League in their pursuit of Honus Wagner. His loyalty was undeniable, and he thoroughly enjoyed playing near his hometown of Carnegie. It was quite understandable why Johnson was eager to bring Wagner into the American League fold. Wagner became the National League's undisputed best player as his Pirates claimed three consecutive pennants from 1901 through 1903. Wagner batted .353 in 1901 and led the senior circuit with 49 stolen bases and 126 RBI. He was also the day's hero when Pittsburgh clinched the National League pen-

nant on September 27, 1901. In the eighth inning, he smacked a two-run single that tied the game and scored the deciding marker on Kitty Bransfield's single as Pittsburgh defeated Brooklyn, 5–4.[40]

While Wagner was primarily an outfielder during his first two seasons in Pittsburgh, he did see some action at first base, second base and the hot corner. In the summer of 1901, he took over at the position where he would claim diamond glory throughout the remainder of his career. Regular shortstop Fred "Bones" Ely was released by the Pirates in July after ownership discovered he was working as an agent for the American League.[41] Wagner made his debut as a shortstop on July 27, 1901, after Lew Carr, Tommy Leach and even Fred Clarke had tried playing that position.[42] In 1902, Wagner split time between the outfield and shortstop due to an injury to right fielder Lefty Davis and the presence of infielder Wid Conroy on Pittsburgh's roster. Wagner officially became Pittsburgh's exclusive, full-time shortstop in 1903.

Pittsburgh cruised to the National League pennant in 1902 with a 103–36 record that established a new league record for most victories in a season. Honus Wagner batted .330 as teammate Ginger Beaumont claimed the National League batting title with a mark of .357. Wagner did pace the circuit in runs scored (105), doubles (30), RBI (91) and stolen bases (42). He claimed his second National League batting championship in 1903 with a .355 average as the Pirates won their third consecutive pennant. In spite of the defections of star hurlers Jesse Tannehill and Jack Chesbro to the American League after the 1902 campaign, Pittsburgh still topped the senior circuit with a record of 91–49. Due to the decision by owners Barney Dreyfuss of Pittsburgh and Henry Killilea of the American League champion Boston Americans to have their teams oppose each other in a post-season series, Wagner and his Pirates teammates had the privilege of participating in the first modern World Series.

This battle was viewed as a way to determine which league could claim baseball supremacy. Boston's roster was littered with former National League players who had jumped leagues to join the Americans. One, star hurler Denton "Cy" Young, had played for the Cleveland Spiders and the St. Louis Perfectos/Cardinals. One tale regarding a previous encounter between Honus Wagner and Young when he was with St. Louis indicated that Pittsburgh's star could not possibly be intimated by the veteran pitcher. During a game between Pittsburgh and St. Louis in

1900, Young was throwing hard and had the Pirates absolutely bewildered. Wagner stepped up to the plate and allowed two fastballs to whiz by for strikes. On Young's third pitch, Wagner reached out, caught the baseball bare-handed, and tossed it back to the mound. "Changeup, huh?" sneered Wagner. Although the umpire called Wagner out, the incident demoralized Young to the point that he was wild for the remainder of this game.[43]

Young and other former National Leaguers such as Jimmy Collins and Bill Dinneen were victorious in this first encounter between the two league champions as Boston claimed the 1903 World Series over Pittsburgh, five games to three. Pirates hurler Charles "Deacon" Phillippe gave a gutsy, heroic performance as he went 3–2, tossed five complete games and posted a 3.07 ERA. Phillippe was forced to handle the bulk of Pittsburgh's pitching duties since Sam Leever was ineffective due to an injury and southpaw twirler Eddie Doheny was home in Andover, Massachusetts, suffering from mental delusions. Honus Wagner was an absolute bust at the plate with a .222 average and committed six errors at shortstop. For many years, Wagner had to live with the humiliation surrounding this World Series performance as many baseball writers questioned his courage.

While the Pittsburgh Pirates' string of consecutive National League pennants ended at three, they remained competitive from 1904 through 1908. During those five seasons, Wagner claimed batting titles in 1904 (.349), 1906 (.339), 1907 (.350) and 1908 (.354). The 1908 campaign may have been the best of Wagner's storied career. In a season when pitching dominated both leagues, he also led the circuit in hits (201), doubles (39), triples (19), RBI (109), stolen bases (53), on-base percentage (.415) and slugging percentage (.542). What made this season even more remarkable was that Wagner had vowed to retire before the Pirates embarked for spring training. He had even sent owner Barney Dreyfuss a letter stating his intentions to walk away from the game for the 1908 season.[44] After Pittsburgh played their opening series in St. Louis, Wagner had a change of heart, signed a contract, and joined the team when they reached Cincinnati on April 19.[45]

The Pittsburgh Pirates, New York Giants and Chicago Cubs were involved in an exciting battle for the 1908 National League pennant that went down to the wire. Honus Wagner and the Pirates were eliminated

from contention when they lost their final game of the season on October 4 against Chicago at West Side Grounds, 5–2. There was no such race in 1909 as Fred Clarke's team claimed the bunting for the fourth time during the twentieth century's first decade. The Pirates set a franchise record for victories in 1909 as they posted a mark of 110–42. Pittsburgh needed nearly every one of those 110 wins as the second-place Cubs finished at 104–49. Wagner also added a seventh batting title to his resume that year as he topped the National League with an average of .339.

Pittsburgh's opponent in the 1909 World Series was the Detroit Tigers. Led by a young firebrand named Ty Cobb, Detroit claimed its third consecutive American League pennant. For the first time since the modern World Series was established in 1903, the batting champions from both leagues were slated to go head-to-head in the Fall Classic. Cobb had won the American League batting title by hitting at a .377 clip. While all of the hype before the World Series focused on the battle between Honus Wagner and Ty Cobb, it ended up being a rookie pitcher who stole the show. Charles "Babe" Adams was the World Series hero and became the darling of Pittsburgh when he won Games One, Five and Seven as the Pirates defeated Detroit, four games to three. Fellow hurler Nick Maddox secured the other victory for Pittsburgh in Game Three as staff mainstays Howard Camnitz, Lefty Leifield and Vic Willis faltered when they took the mound.

The 1909 World Series also provided sweet vindication for Honus Wagner six years after his courage and desire had been questioned following Pittsburgh's defeat against the Boston Americans in 1903. Wagner batted .333, drove home six runs and stole six bases against the Detroit Tigers. Star counterpart Ty Cobb had a tough Series as he checked in with a batting average of .231 and pilfered only two bases. Cobb did make his hits count as he led the Tigers with five RBI. Winning a championship in 1909 certainly was the pinnacle of Honus Wagner's baseball career. During his first 13 seasons, Wagner had carved out a reputation as a humble man who always placed team success above personal goals.

Following the glory of a highly successful season in 1909, disappointment quickly followed as Pittsburgh grossly underachieved in 1910. The Pirates came home in third place with an 86–67 record. In 1911, Wagner claimed his eighth and final batting championship by leading

the National League with a .334 average. After posting averages of .324 in 1912 and .300 in 1913, he failed to reach the .300 mark in 1914 for the first time since 1898. Trips to the World Series were also a thing of the past for Honus Wagner and his Pirates teammates as Pittsburgh lost the perennial contender status and transformed into a second-division team.

From 1901 through 1913, only three teams claimed the National League pennant. Baseball fans from the cities of Boston, Brooklyn, Philadelphia, St. Louis and Cincinnati were disappointed each of those years as the Pittsburgh Pirates, Chicago Cubs or New York Giants were crowned as the league's best team. During the Pittsburgh Pirates' successful run under the guidance of manager Fred Clarke from 1901

Longtime New York Giants manager John McGraw (left) believed Honus Wagner (right) had class that no other player possessed. Simply put, McGraw believed Wagner was "The most wonderful ball player who ever lived." In this photograph, these two old warhorses are quite possibly reminiscing about great baseball battles from the past (courtesy National Baseball Hall of Fame Library, Cooperstown, New York).

through 1909, games against John McGraw and his New York Giants were particularly contentious and ferocious at times. While New York's pugnacious manager was a throwback to the days when he played for the ruthless Baltimore Orioles who would cross any line if it helped ensure victory, McGraw understood baseball greatness when he saw it. McGraw never hesitated when a discussion arose regarding the greatest baseball player of all time. After a series between Pittsburgh and New York in the summer of 1912, John McGraw reiterated that it was Honus Wagner.

> I'll tell you, that big Dutchman played great ball against us. Players may come and they may go, but Honus seems to go on forever, and to keep getting better. His work on Friday was highly sensational. He did not hit today, but his fielding could not be improved upon.
>
> He has class that no other player possesses. You can have your Cobbs, your Lajoies, your Bakers and all the rest of them, but I'll take Wagner for my pick of the greatest. He is not only a marvelous mechanical player, but he has the quickest baseball brain I have ever observed. I have watched him many and many a time, trying to pick out one time when he would fail to grasp a situation like a flash, and I have never been able to catch him yet. He is never asleep, and he always knows what the other fellow ought to do.
>
> Pittsburgh ought to be proud of Hans. He is the greatest ever, and there is no mistake about that. He does everything better than the ordinary star can do any one thing.[46]

One year later, in 1913, Pittsburgh Pirates team secretary Leslie H. Constans went beyond McGraw's assessment of Honus Wagner as a player and talked about the man in an article he wrote for *Baseball Magazine*.

> With all this greatness as a star, Wagner is probably the most modest and unassuming player in the game today. Seldom can he be drawn into a conversation pertaining to baseball, and never can he be led into expatiating upon his own prowess. One of the surest ways for the poor fan who meets him to become persona non grata is to attempt to talk baseball. But few fans get such an opportunity, however, as Wagner is never a seeker of the spotlight, either on or off the field, and one of the rarest sights about a hotel during the stay of the Pittsburgh Club in any town is the person of the mighty Dutchman in the lobby; in this it has often been thought that Wagner was conceited, or, to use the more general expression, had an enlarged head, but nothing is further from the truth. It is only the result of modesty, and modesty, if we remember, seems to be one of the chief attributes of greatness.[47]

Honus Wagner's greatness went far beyond his accomplishments

on a baseball diamond. His relationship with teammates such as Fred Clarke, Tommy Leach, Sam Leever, Deacon Phillippe, John "Dots" Miller, George Gibson and others was nearly as important as getting hits and making great plays. Wagner personified the camaraderie and solidarity that existed during the Deadball Era, and as the National League's premier player, he had more than his peers' respect; he had their admiration. Even John McGraw, a man who seldom flattered the opposition, fawned over Wagner, calling him "the most wonderful ball player who ever lived."[48] One hundred years later, few historians would disagree.

2

Bilson Jack, a Louisville Hearse Ride and Wagner's Early Days in Baseball

On many occasions throughout history, the true greatness of a baseball player, or any person, has been measured beyond how well that individual performs his or her particular craft. In baseball, character, determination, positive temperament and dedication are just as important as being exceptional in the departments of batting, fielding and running. These particular traits also go a long way in defining the man as well as the baseball player. Having the proper work ethic at a young age is crucial during a player's formative years as he strives toward becoming a major league player, and quite possibly one of the greatest performers in the game's history.

For John Peter "Honus" Wagner, his formative baseball years acted as a springboard to greatness and baseball immortality. While Wagner did experience numerous growing pains during his early days playing baseball, one crucial component was prevalent at the outset. Wagner always preached and followed the team-first concept. Years before baseball became his passion in life, this philosophy was exhibited when he made a trip to downtown Pittsburgh with two friends.

When Wagner was a mere youth in the 1880s, he and his two companions were passing along Diamond Street in Pittsburgh's city district. The three youngsters, broke and eager to earn some money, were hoping to gain some kind of employment. Wagner and his buddies were drawn to a sign on a building which read: "Bilson Jack is meeting comers inside and $25 will be given to any man able to stay four rounds with the battler." Wagner's friends encouraged him to accept the challenge. In a spirit of defiance, Wagner agreed to go into the ring and then split the winnings

with his friends if he were triumphant. Although Wagner was not versed in glove snares and the pugilistic rites, he quickly knocked out boxer Bilson Jack. A solid right hand did the trick so effectively that the $25 was turned over by the event's promoter without so much as a whimper.[1]

Honus' parents, Peter and Katheryn Wagner, were largely responsible for him possessing a strong moral foundation at such a young age. Peter Wagner was a hard-working, proud man who was always devoted to Honus and his siblings. On one occasion when Honus was 18 years old, his father's proud demeanor came to the forefront after he misinterpreted a comment which was made by one of the players on his son's baseball team. In 1892, Honus Wagner was pitching for a sandlot team from his hometown. Following a game against a small-town team in the Pennsylvania Panhandle which Honus pitched and lost, he returned home to Mansfield (Carnegie) with a few of his teammates. Peter Wagner was sitting on his doorstep smoking a pipe, not paying much attention to any of the banter being tossed about, until one of Honus' teammates made what he perceived to be a disparaging comment.[2] "Well, Honus can't be blamed for our losing," he said. "If he had any decent support he would have won easily."

Peter Wagner sat on the doorstep for a few minutes with a stunned look on his face before he jumped to his feet. As Peter took the long pipe from his mouth and shook it at the speaker, he cried, "Don't you ever say that again. My boy had as good support and as fine a home as you ever had, and if you ever talk about his support again I will throw you into the creek."[3]

Although Honus' teammate was talking about run support, Peter Wagner's natural reaction was to stick up for himself, his family and their way of life.

◆　◆　◆

Catcher Pete Lavelle was Honus Wagner's teammate when the two men played for the Inter-State League's Steubenville Stubs and Akron Akrons in 1895. On a few occasions, Lavelle caught Wagner during his abbreviated career as a minor league pitcher. Years after these two men played together, a story surfaced which claimed Lavelle always had to use beefsteak in his glove whenever Wagner was on the mound bringing the heat. Lavelle refuted this tale, vowing that sirloin held another pur-

pose for him other than using it in his catcher's mitt.[4] Wagner always claimed that Lavelle was the first catcher he ever witnessed using the pitchout. One day at Akron, Lavelle explained to Wagner the idea of pitching out to assist in catching a player who was attempting to steal a base.[5] Besides being a great catcher, Lavelle possessed a beard that resembled barbed wire. Doubling as the team barber, Wagner would shave players from the Akron team every Sunday morning. Brother Al Wagner was always first in line before Honus tackled Lavelle's rough beard.[6]

> "Lavelle had the toughest beard of any man I ever saw," Wagner stated years later. "When I played with Lavelle and that old crowd I shaved the players and every Sunday morning there was a big rush and the Dutch barber had his hands full. Lavelle always wanted to be first, claiming that the kids with peach-fuzz on their mugs could wait. By the time I would get through with Pete's porcupines there wasn't much edge left for the others. I see where Pete denies that he used beefsteak in his mitt when he caught me. Well, I guess he is right, for if we ever caught sight of a piece of sirloin, tenderloin or plain round steak those days it went under the chest protector, and not in the mitt."[7]

Using beefsteak under the chest protector was a very prudent strategy for any receiver who was willing to catch the wild Wagner when he was on the mound. Shortly after he joined Steubenville in 1895, Wagner was asked to pitch by manager George Moreland. Before the game began, Wagner went over the signs with Steubenville's starting catcher and took his position on the mound. After only one inning, Steubenville's catcher started to complain and asked Moreland what kind of a Dutchman he had picked up.[8]

"I've given him signals for everything," the catcher said to Moreland, "but he just rears back and throws fastballs. If he ever hits one of those batters, you better have an ambulance ready."[9]

After the third inning, Steubenville's catcher had to leave the game with two broken fingers. By the time this contest ended, Honus Wagner had gone through three receivers who were brave enough to go behind the dish and expose themselves to bodily harm.[10] At one point, Wagner was so wild that players from the opposing squad refused to assume any kind of position at the plate for fear they would be maimed in some fashion.[11] Probably due to this fear on the part of Steubenville's opponent that afternoon, Wagner picked up the victory in spite of a pitching line that usually spelled doom for a hurler.

25

"I hit seven men, including Jack Schrader (a teammate of Wagner's in 1895 on the Warren baseball team), in that game," reflected Wagner many years later. "Then I got so wild that they threatened to get out an injunction against me to restrain me from pitching. Canton ordered our manager to take me out of the box, but he didn't, and although, in addition to hitting the seven opponents, I walked nine and struck out 15, I won my game. The manager decided, however, that I would not make good as a pitcher."[12]

Manager George Moreland astutely realized that Honus Wagner could best serve the Steubenville team playing in the outfield.

◆ ◆ ◆

Honus Wagner had received his big chance to play professional baseball with Steubenville in 1895 due to older brother Al recommending him to manager George Moreland. Since things had not been going well for the Stubs, Al suggested to Moreland that he sign little brother Honus to help out. When Moreland asked Al what position Honus played, he stated that his younger brother could play anywhere. Figuring that Honus fit into the jack-of-all-trades category of a baseball player who performed at many positions but was master of none, Moreland expressed skepticism over signing Wagner.[13] Moreland was also reluctant due to the perception that Wagner was too awkward ever to amount to anything on a baseball diamond. Needing to add a hurler to his pitching staff, Moreland finally agreed to sign Honus after Al Wagner assured him his younger brother could pitch and throw a baseball mighty fast. A wire was sent to Carnegie asking Honus to report immediately to play baseball for Steubenville at a salary of $35 a month.[14]

Honus Wagner also received a message asking him to leave on the first train for Steubenville, Ohio. When he arrived at the depot, the "first train" happened to be a freight train. Rather than wait for a passenger train that was scheduled to leave an hour later that would land him in Steubenville much sooner, Wagner opted to travel on the freight train. Due to his responsible nature, he believed in following orders to the letter. Since the message had stated to grab "the first train," Wagner boarded the freight carrying nothing more than a pair a baseball shoes that were tied together and slung over his shoulder. When Wagner arrived in Steubenville, he hunted up Moreland and reported for duty to play for his new baseball team.[15]

"I see you have your shoes all right," said Moreland upon meeting Honus Wagner, "but I fear that we have no uniform that will fit you."

"Oh, that's all right," Wagner replied, "I have my uniform with me."

"Good. Where is it?" asked Moreland.

"Here," said Wagner as he rolled up his trouser legs and revealed his baseball stockings and the uniform which bagged below the knees.

"You are a wonder," exclaimed Moreland, "Come in to dinner and we'll try you out this afternoon."[16]

Another version regarding this meeting claimed that Wagner arrived in the morning at Moreland's hotel after traveling on the freight train through the night. When Moreland came down to the hotel lobby for breakfast, Wagner was standing there with his uniform wrapped up in a newspaper parcel. Moreland decided to place Wagner in left field that afternoon only because he had to put nine men on the diamond.[17] The truth regarding Wagner carrying his baseball shoes upon his arrival in Steubenville is also a bit muddled. One tale forged in baseball folklore alleges that Wagner played that first game in his bare feet since it was impossible to find a pair of baseball shoes in all of Steubenville large enough to fit him.[18] Wagner himself shed no light on the stocking feet story when he reminisced in 1916 about that first game with Steubenville.

> I could not be induced to put on a uniform and my brother Al laughs to this day at the sight of the Steubenville (Ohio) gang trying to show me that baseball pants should be turned inside out and donned through the knee band and not the waist. My only real experience prior to that time was with a semi-pro team, led by Shad Gwilliam, and my only chance was when he was short a man for a trip and would say: "Oh, if some other fellow fails to show up, we'll take Al Wagner's brother."
>
> This is how I got to Steubenville. My brother was with that team and he was the real star of that period, while I was only a proud brother, glad at the privilege of sometimes making a trip and doing the trainer's duties or carrying water. I went there as a pitcher in 1895 and in my first game they played me in the outfield. I muffed three flies and hit a home run but the homer did not get back the runs caused by my muffs and I quit the team and went back to old Carnegie on a freight. Al came after me hot-footed and I rejoined the club.[19]

Although this first game may not have been a rousing success in Honus Wagner's mind, he quickly established his credentials as a deadly hitter playing for George Moreland in Steubenville and Akron.

◆ ◆ ◆

The 1895 baseball season was a whirlwind tour for Honus Wagner as he played for five different teams due to various franchises either folding or relocating. In Ohio, he played for Steubenville, Akron and Mansfield of the Inter-State League. He also spent time with the Michigan State League's Adrian Reformers/Demons and the Warren, Pennsylvania, entry in the Iron and Oil League. During his abbreviated time with Adrian, Wagner did fine work and helped the team climb into second place. Two black baseball players—catcher Vasco Graham and pitcher George Wilson—were briefly his teammates. Homesick for his Carnegie home, Wagner requested and was granted his release from Adrian by owner Rolla L. Taylor. He finished the 1895 campaign by appearing in 65 games at shortstop for Warren and batting .369.[20]

Besides playing on some of these teams with brother Al Wagner in 1895, Honus also shared the same baseball diamond with future major league teammates and friends from Carnegie. Claude Ritchey played with Wagner at Steubenville and Warren, while catcher Harry Smith was also a member of the Iron and Oil League team. Carnegie friend Jimmy "Toots" Barrett was Honus' teammate with Steubenville and Akron before those two organizations were dissolved and he landed with the Canton Deubers. Al Wagner also ended up being Barrett's Canton teammate after Akron folded. When Al received a second offer to play for Mansfield after he had signed with Canton, he told Honus to go in his place and play for the Kids.[21]

Honus Wagner arrived in Mansfield early in the afternoon before the team played that day. Mansfield owner William H. Taylor (father of Adrian magnate Rolla L. Taylor) recognized Wagner, having seen him play previously. Since the club was lacking a quality third baseman, Taylor decided to take a chance, placing his new arrival at the hot corner.[22] Wagner benefitted greatly by two things during his first appearance in a Mansfield uniform against brother Al's Canton team. Canton built up a huge lead during the early stages of the game and buddy "Toots" Barrett was on the mound pitching for the Deubers.

"It so happened that Mansfield played Canton that day," stated Wagner about his first game with the Kids. "My brother was in the lineup of the Canton team, and the pitcher, 'Toots' Barrett, was also from Carnegie, or Mansfield (Pennsylvania), as it was called in those days. They regarded me as pretty

much of a kid, and when Canton got away to a good lead early in the game, Barrett let up in his pitching when I went to bat. He wanted to see me make good, and figured that a couple of hits, more or less, would not affect his rating any. I made a couple of hits in this way, and then came the ninth inning. Never will I forget it. Mansfield was three runs to the bad when we went to bat. They needed four to win. We filled the bases and it was my turn to bat.

"Taylor was not 'wise' to the fact that Barrett had been easing up when I had been at bat before and made a couple of hits, as he might have sent in a pinch hitter. He let me stick. With the bases full, Barrett meant to strike me out. It was too ticklish a time for 'monkey business.' He shaved across a fast one and I knocked it over the fence for a home run and won the game. It was just a case of the luck of things. That's always the way. If the pitcher's lucky, he gets you. If you're lucky, you get him."[23]

Lucky or not, Honus Wagner was definitely able to get by with a little help from his friend on this occasion.

◆ ◆ ◆

Following a long 1895 season globetrotting throughout the eastern part of the United States, Honus Wagner almost signed to play for his hometown team that winter. He eventually balked when Pittsburgh Pirates owner William Kerr suggested that he play for the Western League's Kansas City Blues in 1896 to gain more minor league experience. Wagner refused to go there since it was too far from Carnegie. Eventually he hooked up with Edward Barrow's Paterson Silk Weavers of the Atlantic League. Wagner played the outfield and first base for Paterson in 1896 and batted .313. Two stellar performances late that summer impressed an interested big league scout who had been hot on his trail. In a game against the Newark Colts, Wagner banged out six hits against former National League hurler Cornelius "Con" Lucid. Shortly after that, facing Hartford, he hit for the cycle and recorded five hits off Joseph Frye.[24]

Wagner was even better for the Silk Weavers in 1897 as he hit a blistering .375 while appearing in 75 games before a major league baseball team secured the services of the 23-year-old, hot prospect. Claude McFarlan, an outfielder who played against Wagner for the Norfolk Jewels, was relentless in his efforts to convince Louisville Colonels president Harry Pulliam to purchase the youngster from Carnegie. While the Colonels had an off-day during an early June series against the Brooklyn

Bridegrooms, Pulliam and star left fielder Fred Clarke made the trip from New York to watch Wagner play for Paterson. On July 17, 1897, the announcement was made by Louisville management that Honus Wagner had been purchased by the Colonels from Paterson for $2,000.[25]

Two of Honus Wagner's favorite yarns described events that occurred during the three years he spent in the minors' bushes. The first tale focused on the time he was robbed of a home run by a locomotive. According to Wagner, he hit a monstrous drive that traveled over the center field fence. The opposing team's center fielder helplessly watched as he reached the boards of the outfield fence and saw the baseball sail out of sight. As the baseball began its descent to the ground outside the ballpark, it became engaged with a passing train and dropped into the engine's smokestack.[26]

Seconds after the ball fell into the stack, the train's engineer gave his locomotive some more steam. As the first puff of smoke exited the smokestack, the baseball was jarred loose and sent back into orbit. To Wagner's surprise, the baseball was launched back onto the baseball diamond where that center fielder who had felt distress seconds earlier caught it for one of the most beautiful putouts these fans had ever witnessed. Throughout his life, Wagner always insisted this truly did occur.[27] This statement does lose some veracity due to Wagner embellishing the tale as he grew older, later claiming the locomotive incident occurred during a game between the Pittsburgh Pirates and Chicago Cubs at Exposition Park. In this version, Wagner smacked the drive off hurler Mordecai "Three Finger" Brown while outfielder Frank Schulte was the beneficiary of the locomotive's generosity.[28]

Another favorite tale of Wagner's from his minor league days involved an outfielder who was temporarily incapacitated while attempting to catch a ball hit by Wagner. Wagner always claimed this play was the craziest thing that he ever experienced during his long baseball career.

I hit a drive to left field, and the left fielder jumped up to the screen to get the ball. The ball struck about two inches above his outstretched glove, and bounded back on the field. I looked up as I reached second, thinking the hit was good for a double, but I see that outfielder still on the screen as though he is nailed there. He's cussin' and shoutin' trying to shake himself loose. Well, before anyone else can recover the ball, I've stretched it into a home run. You wanna know what happened to that outfielder? When he jumped up for the ball, his belt caught on a wire, and there he stayed until someone pried him loose.[29]

In the end, everything balanced out as a home run lost because of a locomotive was gained back due to an encounter between a belt and a wire.

◆ ◆ ◆

When Honus Wagner joined the Louisville Colonels in July of 1897, his new team was buried in its customary place near the bottom of the National League standings. On June 16, 24-year-old Fred Clarke had been named to replace Jim Rogers as Louisville's manager. One of baseball's rising stars, Clarke was in the midst of a great season which would see him bat .390 and finish second behind Willie Keeler for the National League batting title. Although Wagner had been unstoppable playing for Paterson in 1897, Clarke was not overly enamored with his new recruit at the outset. Forced to give Wagner his first action on July 19 when outfielder Ollie Pickering was tossed from the game after he sassed the umpire, Clarke certainly did not give the Colonels rookie a ringing endorsement as he made the lineup change.[30] "This is a mess," moaned Fred. "Now I haven't got anybody to jam into that outfield but that clumsy, bowlegged rookie from Paterson."[31]

Wagner acquitted himself quite nicely in that first game against Washington as Louisville defeated the Nationals, 6–2. He recorded two putouts and one assist from his outfield position, smacked a single and pulled off a successful sacrifice bunt during three plate appearances. This game acted as the springboard for a sensational start to Honus Wagner's major league career. Wagner hit safely in his first nine games, going 14-for-33 for an average of .424. On August 27, he hit his first major league home run against Brooklyn Bridegrooms hurler Jack Dunn.[32] Although Wagner enjoyed much success during his first month and a half as a major leaguer, not showing enough tenacity during a September game almost placed his baseball future in jeopardy.

On September 8, Louisville arrived in Baltimore to open a three-game series against the defending National League champion Orioles, known as a group of ruthless players who sharpened their spikes before each game and were always willing to play outside the rules if a victory could be achieved. Contests against the Orioles were more like wars than baseball games. Honus Wagner immediately received his painful initiation to playing hard-nosed baseball, courtesy of the Orioles' infielders.

Wagner hit a long drive into right field that eluded Willie Keeler and seemed destined to be an inside-the-park home run. As Wagner neared first base, Baltimore's Jack Doyle was blocking the bag and Wagner was forced wide coming around the initial sack. He had to make another detour at second base since shortstop Hughie Jennings was standing in his running path. When he reached third base, John McGraw stopped him in his tracks as the ball was finally thrown in from the outfield. What should have been an easy four-bagger for the Louisville rookie ended up going for only three bases.[33] Wagner always used more colorful, descriptive language when he described this particular rite of passage during the early stages of his major league career. "I knew it should have been stretched into a homer," Wagner claimed, "but Jack Doyle gave me the hip at first, Heinie Reitz (Joe Quinn actually played second base that day) nearly killed me as I was rounding second, Hughie Jennings tripped me at short, and John McGraw was waiting for me with a shotgun at third. I had to settle for a triple."[34]

Settling for a triple was not a suitable scenario for Louisville manager Fred Clarke. "What the hell kind of ball playing is that?" stormed Clarke when Wagner returned to the bench. "If you can't do any better than that, you won't be with us when we leave here tomorrow."[35]

"Did you see how they blocked me off the bases?" replied Wagner in an effort to defend himself.

"Yes," shot back Clarke, "and if you keep on letting them block you that way, there's no place on this club for you."[36]

Once Louisville's manager calmed down, he counseled Honus Wagner, claiming that these guys would ride him out of the league unless he gave them a dose of their own medicine.[37] In his next at-bat, he bunted the baseball to McGraw, who grabbed the ball and tossed a wide throw to Jack Doyle as Wagner barreled toward first like a runaway freight train.[38] As Doyle stretched for the baseball, Wagner banged into him with his shoulders and bowled him over. McGraw's throw rolled past both men deep into right field foul territory toward the bleachers. Wagner came around to score before any Oriole could retrieve the baseball.[39]

After Wagner had knocked over Doyle to start this play, Hughie Jennings, sensing that trouble was ahead, stepped out of the determined Louisville player's way as he tore into second base. The pugnacious John McGraw attempted to hold his ground at third, but Wagner's slide almost knocked him into the bleachers.[40] When Wagner returned to the dugout,

he was greeted by a smiling Fred Clarke. "That's the way to play baseball in this league," said Clarke as he patted Wagner on the back.[41] From that point forward, members of the rowdy Baltimore Orioles understood it was best not to wake a sleeping giant by attempting to intimidate the great Honus Wagner, whose rock-solid, 200-pound frame could be used as a lethal weapon.

◆ ◆ ◆

While Honus Wagner may have realized during this encounter against the Orioles that baseball could be an ugly battle that involved more than just hitting and fielding, he was occasionally victimized through trickery by opposing players. From 1888 through 1896, first baseman Jake "Eagle Eye" Beckley had been a star player for Wagner's hometown Pittsburgh Pirates. After a short stint with the New York Giants, Beckley was playing for the Cincinnati Reds when Wagner debuted with Louisville in 1897. It was during Wagner's time as a Colonel that Beckley executed a play that made Wagner look extremely foolish during a game against Cincinnati that was umpired by veteran arbiter Tim Hurst.[42]

> I was on first base and saw Jake hide the ball under his arm. I told him several times that I was wise to such bush league stuff, but Jake pretended he did not hear. Finally, when Hurst was not looking, I grabbed the ball from under Jake's arm and threw it into right field. Then I started for second base, only to have the pitcher throw another ball to the second baseman, and I was run down between the bases. I felt so cheap I could have dropped clean through China. Beckley had been holding a dummy ball.[43]

While mistakes such as this by Wagner became more infrequent as he gained major league experience, Louisville's baseball fortunes remained bleak throughout his time with the Colonels. During Wagner's rookie campaign in 1897, Louisville finished in 11th place. Things improved slightly in 1898 as the Colonels moved closer to the .500 mark and jumped two spots into ninth place. During both seasons, Louisville was an abject failure playing on the road. After one particularly brutal trip that netted only a handful of victories for the Colonels, Fred Clarke and his players were greeted in a most unusual manner when the team's train pulled into the Fourteenth Street Station in Louisville. A howling, laughing mob met the players at the train station with hearses and a band that was playing mournful funeral dirges.[44]

Many of the Louisville players were upset over this reaction by fans they believed should be supportive during both good and bad times. Clarke was not offended by this public display. Louisville's manager ordered his players to climb into the hearses and participate in this cathartic event. The rowdy rooters were shocked that Louisville's players decided to join in this procession that was intended to ridicule them. Instead of being devoted to the club's humiliation, this parade turned into a festive, welcome-home celebration for the Colonels.[45] Fred Clarke, who realized that losing was just as tough on the fans as it was for his players, explained why he acted in this manner during such a rocky period for the Louisville club.[46]

Louisville occupied the second division in each of the seasons that Honus Wagner played for the Colonels. Louisville was absolutely horrible on the road in 1897 and 1898. After one particularly brutal road trip, the train carrying the Colonels players was greeted at the Fourteenth Street Station by a howling, laughing mob with hearses and a band that played funeral dirges. In this 1898 team photograph, Fred Clarke is fourth from the left, sitting in the middle row, while Honus Wagner is third from the left, standing in the top row (courtesy National Baseball Hall of Fame Library, Cooperstown, New York).

Oh, yes, there was a band at the station to meet us. That band played the weirdest dirges and the most discordant music you ever heard. They had a hearse there for us and the street was lined with carriages for the fans. One or two of the players got very sore over the thing, but I determined to go through with it. We all piled into their hearse and we gave them a good time of it anyhow. They paraded all over town with us and after they had enjoyed themselves to the limit, they warmed up to us again. It cured the fans of their grouches, and they pulled for us all the harder. We had other bad trips after that but they never worked the old hearse gag again.[47]

After Honus Wagner and Fred Clarke moved on to Pittsburgh and had great success playing together for the Pirates, the two always thought back to that Louisville hearse incident whenever they were traveling by train through the Kentucky city. In each instance, when the team's train reached the Fourteenth Street Station in Louisville, Clarke always grabbed Wagner by the arm and exclaimed, "Look, Dutch, there's the station where they met us with the hearse."[48]

◆ ◆ ◆

While Louisville's baseball fans sometimes found fault with the hometown boys, they were particularly rough toward opposing players and umpires who visited Eclipse Park. Making matters worse for National League arbiters was the fact that fireworks always seemed to erupt when certain teams rolled into Louisville for a series. One such team was the Cleveland Spiders, who had been runners-up to the Baltimore Orioles in both 1895 and 1896. On June 26, 1896, umpire George "Stump" Weidman incurred the wrath of numerous Spiders. Although Honus Wagner was not a member of Louisville's squad until the following summer, he always loved to talk about this game with any attentive writer who brought up the subject.

Having been told this story when he joined the Colonels, Wagner always talked about it as if he had been present when numerous Cleveland players and Fred Clarke verbally harassed Weidman throughout the afternoon. After Cleveland fell behind Louisville, harassment turned to physical abuse as the Spiders stepped on Weidman's feet and battered him around, almost precipitating a riot.[49] The Spiders were loaded with characters such as Patsy Tebeau, Bobby Wallace, Jesse Burkett, Cupid Childs and Jack O'Connor, who believed an umpire was never right.[50] When Cleveland clawed their way back into the game, Clarke started

adopting their methods and began to harass poor Weidman. Clarke insisted it was getting dark and demanded that Weidman call the game on account of darkness so the score would revert back to the previous inning.[51]

"Call the game," yelled Clarke, as he danced dangerously close to Weidman's bunions.

After several minutes of verbal abuse from Clarke, Weidman threw up his hands and yelled, "Yes, yes. I call the game on account of darkness."[52]

This decision did not sit well with Cleveland's players, who assaulted the arbiter and cursed him in front of the Louisville fans. While the Colonels' faithful baseball patrons had not been satisfied with Weidman's work that afternoon, they became incensed over the treatment he was receiving. The fans rushed the field and surrounded Cleveland's players. Before the Spiders were able to reach their omnibus that would usher them to safety, outfielder Jimmy McAleer was knocked to the ground when someone hit him in the face. After the players finally reached shelter, fans pelted their omnibus with rocks as it rambled up the street away from Eclipse Park. Louisville owner Dr. Thomas Hunt Stucky immediately had warrants sworn out for the arrest of the nine men who appeared in the game for Cleveland that afternoon. When no game was played the following day due to rain, these players were placed under arrest at the ballpark.[53]

Patsy Tebeau, Bobby Wallace, Jack O'Connor, Cupid Childs, Jesse Burkett and even the venerable Cy Young, one of the most well-behaved players that ever lived, were hauled away by police. Cleveland's players were forced to appear before a judge in a special session held in his Louisville courtroom that afternoon. The courtroom was packed by the time this hearing got under way.[54] Nearly 20 years later, Wagner explained the final outcome in respect to Fred Clarke, as told to him after he joined the Colonels in 1897. "The courtroom was crowded and in a corner stood Fred Clarke, snickering at the plight of the Spiders," said Wagner.[55] "Pat Tebeau made a fiery statement to the judge, and said, 'Fred Clarke started this by stepping on Umpire Weidman's toes. You ought to arrest him.' Clarke didn't wait around to hear any more. He dashed through the crowd, out a door and went down the street on a dead run."[56]

During the final stages of Honus Wagner's major league career, the

game was filled with fast men such as Ty Cobb, Fritz Maisel, Max Carey and Clyde Milan. While each of these players was categorized as a speed burner, their swiftness paled in comparison with Fred Clarke's phantom-like evaporation when he heard Patsy Tebeau's accusation on that day in 1896.[57]

♦ ♦ ♦

Honus Wagner and Fred Clarke were together for 19 seasons, from 1897 through 1915, with the Louisville Colonels and Pittsburgh Pirates. One of the greatest combinations to don a baseball uniform in major league history, Wagner and Clarke became close friends while making life difficult for opposing National League teams. When Wagner broke in with Louisville in 1897, Clarke was a two-fisted, scrappy young manager who was willing to do anything to secure victory on a baseball diamond. During those early days with the Colonels, Wagner had not yet learned to admire Clarke as he later would.[58] Clarke was also very subdued in his opinion regarding Wagner when the youngster reported to Louisville after his purchase from Paterson. As Wagner described it,

> Those days a youngster, on reporting, was not greeted with newspaper headlines of welcome, handshakes from fellow players and a lot of fussing. He went through a harrowing initiation. I went through the sprouts and soon had every man on the club calling me "the luckiest and most awkward Dutchman" they ever saw. Fred Clarke, during the first month, was the loudest in proclaiming that I was so lucky my diet must consist of horseshoes, but he was the first to change his opinion and inform the others that he really thought I was a good ballplayer.[59]

By 1899, Honus Wagner was one the National League's rising stars. During an early-season game against the Pittsburgh Pirates at Eclipse Park, Wagner took some initiative of his own to secure victory for the Colonels. In the fourth inning on April 25, Wagner smacked an offering from Pirates southpaw Jesse Tannehill over the left field fence to knot the score at one run apiece. In the bottom of the ninth frame, Wagner secured a 2–1 victory for Louisville when he led off, connected once again, and smacked the baseball over Eclipse Park's left field wall in the same spot.[60] What made this feat so remarkable was that Wagner had ignored the wishes of his manager during each of these at-bats. Since the Colonels were having trouble hitting Tannehill, Fred Clarke

had asked Wagner to bunt and use his impressive speed to reach first base.[61]

"So I told him to lay one down the third base line and to try to get on," said Clarke. "He selected a bat for the purpose and while we sat back watching for his bunt, he didn't do a thing but knock the ball clear over a distillery for a home run.

"The next time his turn came [it was actually two turns after the first homer] I asked him if he thought he could bunt another one like that. He never cracked a smile, but said he thought he could. He did. The first good one Tannehill served, Honus cracked it over the same distillery. They were two of the longest home runs I ever saw and on those two smashes over that old Louisville distillery we beat Tannehill that day 2 to 1."[62]

Months after Wagner's heroic accomplishment, Colonels catcher Malachi Kittridge offered an excellent descriptive narrative for baseball pundits who had not been fortunate enough to witness this event in person. This story for the *Washington Post,* as told by Kittridge, also appeared in the hometown newspaper back in Wagner's old baseball stomping grounds in Mansfield, Ohio.

Honus feinted at two out curves, and it looked as if Tanny had the Dutchman where Svengali had his Trilby. Honus tossed a dopey glance at Clarke and made a Sharkey swing at the air before Tanny delivered the next ball.

But Clarke was game and signaled Honus to try for another dump. Then Tannehill swung a high teaser, medium-paced, at Wagner. It was one of those toothsome, inviting, insinuating, come-tickle-me, round-house floaters, and Honus gathered himself for a right swing and injected Mauser action in Tanny's slow one. The ball winged merrily between Jack McCarthy and Tom McCreery, way down yonder in the corner of the lot, high over the fence, and with it went the game to the Colonels.[63]

Later in life, whenever Honus Wagner talked about the day he hit two home runs in a game against Jesse Tannehill, he always added that Fred Clarke had fined him $25 for disobeying his orders to lay down a bunt. Clarke always refuted Wagner's contention that he was fined $25 for hitting a game-winning home run on April 25, 1899.[64]

This incident was resurrected by Wagner and Clarke many years later during a four-game series that began on July 30, 1913, at Forbes Field against the Brooklyn Superbas. Heading into this series, Wagner was mired in an awful slump. His average was plummeting daily and he was unable to hit anything but pop flies and grounders. On July 31, Clarke was totally exasperated by the sixth inning since his Pirates were

doing absolutely nothing against Brooklyn. After Fred Kommers beat out a slow roller to Superbas second baseman George Cutshaw, Clarke selected the biggest, ugliest and thickest Cuban wood bat he could find and handed it to Wagner, who was due up next. In pleading tones Clarke said, "Now, Dutch, go up there and hit one. Doggone it, hit one like you used to. Take a reef at it and let me see you hit that ball as you have been hitting it all these years."[65]

Wagner grunted a reply and carried the ugly war club up to the plate. Wagner lunged mightily at Nap Rucker's first offering and came up empty. Brooklyn's infielders punched their gloves and chattered like monkeys, prepared to handle the hard drive they believed was coming their way. On the next pitch, Wagner bunted down the third base line and beat it out. Wagner's bunt single paved the way for two Pirates runs that helped secure a 3–2 victory. Fred Clarke couldn't help but laugh as he sat in the dugout.[66] Once again, Honus Wagner had managed to pull off the unexpected.

3

Rough-and-Tumble
Fred Clarke

It certainly comes as no surprise that any baseball team which has been fortunate enough to dominate the game for a number of years usually has been blessed with a stable of quality players. During the first three decades of the twentieth century, teams that were given legitimate consideration at being christened baseball dynasties always had a deadly combo that acted as the catalyst. Babe Ruth and Lou Gehrig were the New York Yankees' lethal combination. In Philadelphia, Jimmie Foxx and Al Simmons were the Athletics' dynamic duo. For New York Giants manager John McGraw, his great pitching combination consisted of one constant—Christy Mathewson—and a succession of other hurlers such as Joe "Iron Man" McGinnity, George "Hooks" Wiltse and Richard "Rube" Marquard.

From 1897 through 1915, Honus Wagner and Fred Clarke were one of baseball's top combinations. The stellar amalgamation helped lead the Pittsburgh Pirates to four National League pennants in 1901, 1902, 1903 and 1909. While both men adhered to the principles of hard work, dedication, commitment and devotion to team goals above personal success, Wagner and Clarke were quite different in methods used on the baseball diamond. Although Wagner did lose his temper on some occasions, he usually followed the gentlemanly path. Fred Clarke pursued the opposite philosophy. Clarke was a fiery, pesky player and manager who was willing to fight, kick with umpires over calls, and guarantee that opponents knew he and his players could not be intimated.

Fred Clarke exhibited this fervid personality that served him well throughout his long career when he made his major league debut for the Louisville Colonels on June 30, 1894. Facing Philadelphia Phillies hurler Gus Weyhing, he smacked four singles and one triple as Philadel-

phia defeated Louisville, 13–6. After the game, Clarke brashly chastised his older teammates who had mocked the youngster before the contest, claiming Weyhing would knock Clarke's little bat out of his hands.[1] Weeks after his major league debut, Clarke opposed the Chicago Colts and their brusque star, Adrian "Cap" Anson, for the first time. Clarke wasted little time showing Anson that he had no intention of cowering with fear when subjected to a heavy dose of intimidation which was the National League norm.

> When I broke in Pop Anson was just about ending his fine career. In my first game I slapped a long drive to the outfield, good for two bases any time, but Pop hooked my foot as I turned first. I went down on my face and was lucky to scramble back to the bag before the ball. The next time I aimed for Anson's foot with my spikes, and sliced the shoe so neatly down the side that his footwear fell off.
>
> "You fresh busher," roared Anson. "I'll swing at you!"
>
> "And I'll swing back," I yelled.
>
> But Pop was twice as big as me and a famed battler, so I took care that I had a good lead on him when I said that.[2]

Cap Anson did extract some revenge against Fred Clarke in 1897 for this incident. On June 29 at West Side Grounds, the Colonels suffered the worst defeat in major league history as Anson's squad demolished Louisville, 36–7. Pitches from Louisville hurlers Charles "Chick" Fraser and James "Sheriff" Jones were battered around the ballpark all afternoon. Although Anson was no longer connected with the team in 1898, Chicago ruined an important celebration for Clarke that summer. Before a contest between the Orphans and Louisville on July 3, a big crowd gathered at West Side Grounds to honor Clarke with flowers and other presentations. This celebration was the result of his upcoming marriage in two days to a Chicago girl named Annette Gray, who was the sister-in-law of Colonels teammate and best man Chick Fraser.

Fraser was the losing pitcher as Chicago failed to reach double figures in runs this time, winning, 7–4. While his squad had been savagely beaten by Chicago on that June afternoon in 1897, the bitter taste of defeat was more pronounced for Fred Clarke a year later when he was surrounded by flower bouquets and wedding presents from adoring fans days before the greatest moment of his life.[3]

◆ ◆ ◆

Two weeks prior to suffering a humiliating defeat at the hands of the Chicago Colts in 1897, 24-year-old Fred Clarke had been named to replace Jim Rogers as the Louisville Colonels' manager. Clarke did not fare very well in his managerial debut on June 16 as the Washington Nationals defeated Louisville, 4–2. While Clarke was a young fellow who knew nothing about managing a major league baseball team except what he had observed while playing for the Colonels, he seemed to possess the proper mindset and leadership qualities to succeed in this vocation.[4] Clarke explained how an embarrassing, stupid play he made that first day as Louisville's pilot helped initiate a management philosophy that became the major tenet in how he handled baseball teams throughout his career.

> I remember well the first day I managed the club. I was on the bases and I pulled a regular "bone"—one of the kind that would shame a busher. Well, I returned to the bench mad at myself and everybody in sight. I walked up and down in front of that bench several times, and not one of the ball players looked at me. They all wore straight faces, and were trying their best to look unconcerned. You see, they didn't think it would do to even notice a mistake made by the new manager—at least, they weren't going to notice while I was around.
>
> Well, I kept on walking up and down gritting my teeth and looking every player in the face. But not a whimper from them. Finally I shouted in their faces: "Say it, you boobs, say it! I know what you're thinking. I pulled the worst bone on record and I know it. Tell me about it and make it as strong as you like. I'll do the same for you the first time you pull a bone, so get it out of your systems."
>
> Well they said it, and they said it good and strong. They jumped on me with both feet. They felt better and I felt better, and I never had any cause later on to ask them to jump me when I made a mistake. They did it without me asking them. But I want to assure you right now that I jumped on them six times as strong when they did anything wrong.[5]

For the remainder of his illustrious career as a baseball manager, Fred Clarke never tried to make his players believe he was perfect. Clarke always admitted when he made mistakes and expected the verbal tongue lashing he received when this occurred.[6] Prior to his being named as Louisville's pilot, four men had managed the Colonels during his first three years playing major league ball. One was John McCloskey, who was responsible for developing Clarke into the star player that he became. Besides managing the Colonels in 1895 and part of 1896,

McCloskey also oversaw Clarke's minor league development as skipper of the Montgomery Colts (1893) and Savannah Modocs (1894). While McCloskey was highly unsuccessful as Louisville's manager, posting records of 35–96 in 1895 and a 2–17 mark before he was fired in 1896, he certainly was an interesting character.

On one occasion during his Louisville tenure, McCloskey showed his players that bats could be used for things other than hitting baseballs. As was usually the case whenever Louisville went to play Cincinnati at League Park, Reds fans gave the Colonels' players their standard reception when the team omnibus traveled to and from the ballpark. McCloskey and his troops were greeted by the usual barrage of pop bottles, eggs, tomatoes and rocks. These Cincinnati roughs always made sure they waylaid Louisville's players. McCloskey happened to be sitting on top of the bus with the driver one day. With missiles flying from every direction, Fred Clarke and some of the other players declared that they were going to get off the bus and chase these miscreants with their baseball bats.

"Oh, shut up," McCloskey yelled to his chattering players. "You fellows make me weary. If you would keep quiet and pay no attention to them they would not bother you."[7]

Seconds after McCloskey's words drifted from his mouth, Louisville's manager was nearly knocked from the box where he sat when he was hit behind the ear with a cucumber. Before he could recover his faculties, McCloskey was smacked flush in the face with an overripe tomato. He immediately took matters into his own hands. After having told his players to stop whining, McCloskey jumped off the bus and started running after the perpetrators like a homicidal maniac. "You ought to have seen him leap off the bus," laughed Fred Clarke. "He had a bat with him and I'll bet he chased that mob three blocks."[8]

While McCloskey may have influenced Clarke's approach, another famous baseball man was responsible for him getting started in the game. Growing up in Des Moines, Iowa, Clarke started to show his ability as a young newsboy playing baseball for a local newspaper's circulation manager. That circulation manager was Edward Barrow, the same man who was responsible for discovering Honus Wagner.[9]

◆ ◆ ◆

Honus Wagner never gave manager Fred Clarke a moment's worry during their 19 years together in Louisville and Pittsburgh. The same could not be said for a host of players who caused much consternation and anxiety for Clarke as skipper of these two teams. One such player was a talented and eccentric southpaw pitcher named George Edward "Rube" Waddell. While Clarke only had to deal with Waddell's escapades for parts of four seasons in Louisville and Pittsburgh, the childlike hurler constantly pushed his manager's patience beyond the breaking point. Wagner referred to players of Waddell's ilk as "nuts" or "bugs" who always received loads of publicity due to their outrageous stunts. Wagner claimed that Waddell framed up more wild and crazy schemes than any man who ever played major league baseball.[10]

Rube Waddell made his major league debut with the Louisville Colonels on September 8, 1897. The Colonels had signed Waddell as a free agent two weeks earlier after he built up quite a reputation that summer playing sandlot baseball in his hometown of Butler, Pennsylvania. His deeds of slinging greatness were so impressive that a fan from Butler, who was friendly with Louisville's owners, wrote and expounded upon the phenomenal exploits of Rube Waddell. Realizing that Louisville was interested, this Good Samaritan sent out a telegram that closed the deal for Waddell. "Sign him to a contract," wrote Waddell's self-appointed cheerleader. "Then tell him to report to Fred Clarke, manager of the club, at Washington."[11]

Waddell reported to the Colonels in Washington as they were nearing the conclusion of a long Eastern road trip that had started on August 14. He arrived at the team hotel around 2 o'clock in the morning. Every member of the Louisville squad was in bed, sound asleep. Waddell walked up to the night clerk and asked him for manager Fred Clarke's room number. "Really, I don't think you'd better awaken Mr. Clarke at this hour," the clerk told Waddell. "I'm sure he'd not welcome you, for he doesn't like to be bothered once he goes to bed. I'll fix you up with a room, and you can see him early this morning when he gets up."

"No, I'm positive he wants to see me tonight," Waddell replied. "He told me to look him up as soon as I reached Washington. I'm the new pitcher, and he wants to be sure I've arrived."[12]

Waddell was so persistent that the night clerk finally gave him Clarke's room number. Waddell trotted upstairs to Clarke's room and

hammered on the door for a few minutes with his fist.[13] Clarke, who had turned in around midnight, was eventually awakened from his heavy sleep due to Waddell's determined pounding. Wondering what the devil was going on, Clarke arose from his bed, struck a match, looked at his watch, and saw that it was 3:30 a.m.[14] Before he opened the door, he demanded in a loud voice to know who was disturbing his slumber at this late hour. Waddell shouted through the keyhole that he was Louisville's new pitcher.[15]

"Well, tell the clerk to give you a room and I'll see you in the morning," Clarke yelled.

"Not on your life," came Waddell's answer through the keyhole. "Must see you now, or I'll take the first train out of this burg."[16]

Not wanting to risk turning away a player who could possibly help improve Louisville's fortunes, Clarke lit up the room and opened the door. The big and lanky Waddell rushed through the door right at Clarke with hand extended and a wide grin on his face. "Hello Freddie, hello Freddie," Waddell chuckled. "How are you, old boy, how are you? Let me have $2, will you?"

"Doesn't seem as if we've ever met before," replied Clarke as he looked Waddell over. "Would you mind telling me who you are?"

"Say, ain't you Freddie Clarke, the manager?" demanded Waddell.

"Yes," replied Clarke.

"Well," responded Waddell. "I'm your new pitcher—Rube Waddell. Just got in town and I need $2."

"Well, well, I'm glad to meet you," responded Clarke. "I guess you haven't met any of the other boys yet, have you?"

"No," answered Waddell.

"Well, I haven't got $2 to loan you," said Clarke, "but I know some of the boys have. Furthermore, it is customary in the big leagues for a new player to visit all the older players on the team as soon as he arrives. So you duck downstairs, get the names and room numbers of all the boys from the clerk, and visit them."

"All right, Freddie, all right Freddie," answered Waddell as he exited Clarke's room and rambled downstairs.[17]

Waddell started on his journey and Clarke nestled himself back in bed. Clarke chuckled over the insurrection that was sure to follow when Waddell awakened the other members of Louisville's team. Clarke was

sound asleep once again when another terrible pounding on his door awakened him again an hour later. "Who's there?" thundered Clarke.

"It's Rube Waddell, your new pitcher," was the reply.

"Well, you go back to wherever you came from or get to bed, one of the two," responded Clarke gruffly. "I'm not going to allow any 'nut' living to wake me up all hours of the night, no matter how good he can pitch."

"Yes, Mr. Clarke," replied Waddell, "but I just wanted to tell you that I've met all of the boys except the one in Room 128, and I can't wake him up. I thought possibly something was the matter with him and you ought to know about it."[18]

Honus Wagner always claimed that there was no response in Room 128 because deaf-mute outfielder Dummy Hoy was its occupant.[19] Of course, this scenario was not a possibility since Hoy did not join the Colonels until 1898. The next morning, Clarke sat at a table by himself during breakfast. He made a concerted effort to avoid his teammates who were also kept awake all night listening to Rube Waddell's own stories concerning his greatness and pleas for the loan of two dollars.[20]

◆ ◆ ◆

Rube Waddell kept Fred Clarke very busy during their short time together. His best season pitching for Clarke was with the Pittsburgh Pirates in 1900, when he posted a record of 8–13 and led the National League with a 2.37 ERA. The following May, Clarke became so disgusted with Waddell's antics that he gave him away to the Chicago Orphans for virtually nothing. While Waddell had exasperated Clarke on many occasions, it was next to impossible for him to remain angry at the southpaw hurler for a long period of time.[21] Events that troubled Clarke when they happened usually seemed humorous later. One such incident involved Waddell and reserve catcher Clifford "Tacks" Latimer, who played for Louisville in 1899 and Pittsburgh in 1900.

> You know, Rube could frighten you pretty good. I know I almost blew my top when Latimer came to me one day and complained about Waddell. "I don't mind if he keeps that shotgun in his trunk," Tacks told me, "but when he puts it together and loads it and points it at me, that's going too far. It's liable to go off."
>
> I tackled Rube right away and gave him a long lecture about firearms, which intrigued him. He was always a sucker for a gun. Rube didn't say a

word until I had finished. Then he made an almost apologetic remark: "Sure, Fred, I know that's bad. I'd have a time explaining that, and I would quit doing it except that Latimer is always waving a razor around my neck."

Now I had to cross-examine Latimer. Sure enough, he'd been threatening Waddell with a razor. "I like Rube," Tacks explained, "and I want to keep on catching for him. So every morning I jump on him when he's in bed and I get my razor at his throat until he promises to let me catch him the next time." I don't know if there has ever been another battery like that.[22]

Thankfully for Fred Clarke's sanity, this particular battery was nothing but a distant memory by the spring of 1901.

◆　◆　◆

While Fred Clarke had to deal with many crazy characters who fit into Honus Wagner's category of "nuts" and "bugs," the highly successful manager also loved to drive opposing players and managers absolutely crazy. Clarke was always coming up with some new strategy or using a novel method of psychological warfare aimed at rendering his opponent powerless. In 1899, Clarke pulled off a brilliant stunt using mind games against manager John McGraw and his Baltimore Orioles that endured as one of Wagner's favorite stories. Clarke got the best of his long-time antagonist while managing Louisville during a game at Union Park.

Down by two runs late in the game, Louisville had not scored and Baltimore's pitcher was finishing them off with a tantalizing array of pitches. The Colonels finally got a rally going as they loaded the bases with two outs. Fred Clarke was standing on third, Tommy Leach occupied second, and Honus Wagner was at first. Clarke started kidding and heckling Baltimore's hurler as he took his lead from third base, trying to wreck his concentration.

"Why, you nut, you think you've got control," Clarke yelled. "You can't put the ball where you want to. You know you can't."

"Bet you a dollar I can put this ball anywhere you tell me to," retorted the flinger.[23]

John McGraw started going ballistic on the bench since his pitcher was paying more attention to Clarke's mouth than the baseball diamond. McGraw called time and ran out to the pitcher's mound to lecture the Orioles hurler about maintaining his concentration during this critical juncture. As soon as McGraw returned to Baltimore's dugout, Clarke

yelled something else just loud enough for the Orioles pitcher to hear it: "Bet you $2 you can't throw the ball behind the batter."

"You're on," replied the pitcher.[24]

The hurler wasted no time collecting on his bet with Fred Clarke as he tossed his next pitch behind Louisville's batter. Honus Wagner, who was standing on first base at the time, explained what happened next.

> It went so far behind him (the batter) and so far behind the plate that "Cap" and Leach had scored and I was on third before it was recovered. Well, you can bet McGraw yanked that pitcher out of the box in a hurry, and as he passed our bench he told Fred he would be around after the game for the $2. He was, but he didn't get it. We won the game, and McGraw was sore enough to murder the pitcher. He did "can" him, and the funny thing is that later the same pitcher came to Clarke looking for a job—which he didn't get.[25]

While Fred Clarke may have gained the upper hand against McGraw on this occasion, there was another incident that McGraw loved to share in which Clarke looked foolish in a game against the Boston Doves. McGraw was not on hand to witness Clarke's embarrassing moment, but only passed along the story that involved Honus Wagner's friend from Carnegie, southpaw Patrick "Patsy" Flaherty. During the December National League baseball meetings in New York following the 1920 campaign, McGraw described for writers this bizarre play which he believed was the funniest double play ever witnessed in a game. Before McGraw related this story with a sober face and fixed smile, he asked Pittsburgh Pirates owner Barney Dreyfuss if he remembered this yarn. Dreyfuss declined to respond, opting instead to leave the room for a bit of fresh air.[26]

> Patsy Flaherty, southpaw, with that wonderfully deceptive move to throw to first, quick return and wit, was in the box, pitching for Boston maybe, against the Pittsburgh Pirates. Ginger Beaumont was on first and Fred Clarke at bat. Patsy bluffs around with the ball, raises his arm, throws to first and Clarke swings his bat at the ball.
>
> "One strike," says the umpire.
>
> Flaherty bluffs 'round with the ball some more, raises his arm, throws one straight across the plate. Clarke lets it go by and Beaumont slides back to first.
>
> "Two strikes," says the umpire.
>
> Flaherty fools with the ball some more, raises his arm once again and throws to first base. Clarke makes another desperate swing in the air.

"You're out," says the umpire.

The ball got to first base before Beaumont could get back and he was tagged out for a double play.[27]

John McGraw always claimed this story in which the joke was on either the ball players involved, the umpire, or both, was accurate and true.[28] If this were the case, the identity of Pittsburgh's runner on first base had to be incorrect. Otherwise, the tale lacks authenticity since Ginger Beaumont was traded on December 11, 1906, along with Patsy Flaherty and Claude Ritchey from the Pirates to the Boston Doves for Ed Abbaticchio. Beaumont and Fred Clarke never opposed Flaherty together when he pitched for Boston.

♦ ♦ ♦

Besides being one of the greatest baseball players and managers of his era, Fred Clarke was also a shrewd businessman who accumulated substantial wealth through various enterprises. A second love for Clarke, almost equal to baseball, was ranching and farming during the off-season. Fred, his wife Annette, and daughters Muriel and Helen lived on a beautiful spread in Winfield, Kansas, that was named the "Little Pirate Ranch" in honor of the successful baseball team he managed. On many occasions, teammates and friends from the Smoky City were invited to spend time relaxing at Clarke's Kansas ponderosa.

Hunting was one of the activities that all visitors to the "Little Pirate Ranch" engaged in. Before Clarke left for spring training in 1913, his ranch foreman asked the Pirates manager to tell Honus Wagner that there were now some black pigs on the ranch. It seemed the foreman wanted to avoid future mistakes after Wagner's egregious blunder when he visited Clarke's Kansas ranch in 1908. After they broke spring training camp in Hot Springs, Arkansas, Clarke entertained his team at the "Little Pirate Ranch."[29] While Wagner still planned on remaining retired for the 1908 campaign, he did make the trip to Winfield to have fun and relax with his former teammates.[30]

Businesses throughout Winfield and the adjacent Walnut River Valley closed for the day when Clarke and his renowned team arrived on April 7. The Pirates played an exhibition game at the local fair grounds that afternoon. The following morning, Clarke's players boarded buggies that ushered them to the "Little Pirate Ranch" for a grand hunting expe-

dition that included a pack of his best bloodhounds. While owner Barney Dreyfuss missed a jackrabbit with the first shot, the excursion was a rousing success for everyone involved as a bounty of ducks, quail and rabbits were bagged. Honus Wagner exhibited his proficiency at handling a gun by shooting several wild ducks.[31]

At one point, Wagner set out to hunt by himself. While gliding on a skiff on a stream that traversed Clarke's property, Wagner spied two red pigs that were a few weeks old on the nearby shore. This section was a somewhat wild part of the ranch, and he had never seen pigs of that color in his life. Wagner did not know what they were, and assuming they had to be some kind of wild game, he fired his gun and killed one of the pigs. Hearing the shot, the second red pig scurried into the stream. It didn't get very far as Wagner subdued it with an oar and lifted it into the boat.

Having what he believed to be a successful hunt, Wagner reached dry land and began carrying his trophies toward Fred Clarke's house. He came upon Clarke and his ranch foreman near a barn with one pig held by its tail, while the other was alive and kicking under his arm. He proudly exhibited his catch to the two men. Even though Wagner had killed one of his prize red pigs, Clarke could not help but laugh uncontrollably for a few minutes. Once Clarke gathered himself, he instructed Wagner on the habits of this particular wild animal that usually provided such things as ham and bacon.

Clarke's foreman, an archetypical farmer who was rawboned and six foot, three inches tall, stood in open-mouthed amazement while Wagner proudly exhibited the red pigs. When the Dutchman's back was turned for a brief moment, the foreman turned to Clarke with a disgusted expression and offered up a quick comment. "And they call us rubes," said the foreman.[32]

While every member of the Pirates entourage had a grand time at the "Little Pirate Ranch," these festivities also had a positive effect in convincing Wagner to abandon the notion of retiring from baseball. Amid rumors that he was upset because second baseman Ed Abbaticchio was earning a higher salary, seemed miffed that management was reluctant to re-sign veteran catcher Harry Smith, and had a falling out with the team's manager, Wagner had a change of heart after a talk with Clarke during the trip to Winfield. "Jokes, just like the interview manager Frank

Chance gave out in the South, that Wagner and Clarke did not hit it off ever since a dispute on the field at New York last summer," declared Pirates team secretary William Locke when these rumors were brought to his attention once the 1908 season was under way.[33]

"I think that the last talk Clarke had with John won him over," continued Locke. "Fred told him that he was needed, and he felt that the long association should not be broken up. When we were at Kansas City we received word that it was all right. That meant the big fellow would join us if he could get into shape."[34]

Although Fred Clarke did lose a prize red pig due to Honus Wagner's overzealousness, he was able convince the great shortstop to return to playing the game he loved. While Clarke was fortunate to have a player of Wagner's caliber at his disposal for many years, he never had good luck when it came to incidents involving birds and animals in respect to Wagner and his ranch. Besides Wagner shooting his red pig, Clarke was also thwarted on another occasion when he placed a wager involving one of his teammate's pigeons. At his home in Carnegie, Wagner kept pigeon lofts which included some wonderful flyers that he constantly boasted about to friends and teammates. Wagner was particularly proud of one carrier pigeon whose instincts were impeccable.

Wagner made a bet with Clarke that his prize carrier pigeon, if taken to the "Little Pirate Ranch" and released, would find its way back home to Carnegie. Clarke agreed to place a little wager against the bird's ability and took the carrier pigeon with him from Pittsburgh to Kansas after the season. Before he set the pigeon loose at his ranch, Clarke tried to pull one over on his friend. He calmly clipped the bird's wings, without causing it any physical harm, and remarked, "Now, let's see you get back home!"[35]

Five months later, the carrier pigeon arrived at Honus Wagner's Carnegie roost. Wagner claimed the bird's feet were pretty sore, but it had arrived in spite of Clarke clipping its wings and won the bet for his master.[36] Clarke most likely did not welsh on this wager as he had with the pitcher from John McGraw's Orioles.

◆ ◆ ◆

Fred Clarke was admired and adored by most of the men who played for him on the Pirates from 1900 to 1915. As manager, Clarke always made sure his players were prepared for the long season ahead. As their

captain on the field, he displayed a willingness to stand behind them during both good times and bad. Pittsburgh's great manager always seemed to push the right buttons to get the best out of his players. During the 1909 World Series between Pittsburgh and the Detroit Tigers, Clarke adeptly used psychology to keep his team loose prior to Game Seven at Bennett Park on October 16. With Pittsburgh and Detroit knotted at three games apiece, both teams were tense.[37]

Pittsburgh's manager pulled off a maneuver that would have been illegal during the "Roaring Twenties" after the Volstead Act was passed. On the off-day prior to Game Seven, Clarke invited every member of the Pirates to his room that evening. He insisted that all of his players break any previous engagements due to the importance of this meeting. Once everyone had agreed to meet, Clarke pulled Honus Wagner aside and let him in on the secret. As each player arrived that night, Clarke and Wagner met him with a bottle of beer. "Drink up," said Clarke. "There's four barrels more on ice and we won't go home until it's finished."[38]

Years after Clarke's baseball career ended, he explained his philosophy behind having a party the night before the decisive game of a World Series.

> One of the big secrets in any sport is to know how to take the tension off athletes. Whenever any competitor is nerve-tight, he cannot play his game. I knew only one way. The night before the game I called the boys into my sitting room. I had a big table full of sandwiches in the middle of the floor, and tubs of beer and pop around it. We ate and drank, and told stories, and got up a good barber shop quartette. I brought Barney in and brought him a beer. At 10 o'clock I sent them to bed with this message: "If we do we do, and if we don't we don't, and to hell with it. Just have a good night's sleep."[39]

By all accounts, Pittsburgh's players should have been a woozy bunch the following day against Detroit. This was not the case, however, as Clarke's trick broke the strain these players had been preforming under and brought about total relaxation. The Tigers never stood a chance as rookie hurler Babe Adams tossed a shutout and Pittsburgh cruised to an easy 8–0 victory in Game Seven on October 16, 1909.[40] It was no secret that Clarke's players were always united with their manager when going into battle.

Such positive bonding certainly did not exist between Clarke and National League umpires. The relationship tended to be adversarial at

A master at using psychology, Pittsburgh manager Fred Clarke invited the Pirates players to his hotel room for a party on the eve of Game Seven of the World Series against Detroit on October 16, 1909. Clarke helped to alleviate the tension with this friendly gathering where players drank beer and pop, ate sandwiches, told stories, struck up a beautiful barbershop quartet and generally had a great time (courtesy National Baseball Hall of Fame Library, Cooperstown, New York).

best, judging by many incidents throughout his major league career. Disdain for the old tactic of kicking over calls forced players and managers to use more finesse when dealing with baseball's arbiters. They had to be quick with the tongue if they hoped to hold their own. Most of the time, Clarke was a master at getting his point across with umpires.[41] On one occasion in Pittsburgh, he had an interesting spat with revered umpire Bill Klem.[42] It seemed the arbiter was not flattered over a sly comment that Clarke made.

> I had attended a vaudeville show the previous night at which time one of the actors referred to the definition of the word "model." A "model," he said, "was an imitation of a real thing." The next afternoon we had a tough game with Klem in charge of decisions. Bill had any number of hard rulings to make. Several times I passed him on my way to or from left field. As I walked by, I played upon Bill's vanity by referring to him as a "model umpire." In the seventh or eighth inning, Bill gave a close one against us and I was sore. As I passed him on the way to left field, I remarked:
> "Yes, Bill, you're a model umpire, but when you get to the hotel tonight just get yourself a dictionary and see what it means."
> I had forgotten the incident when we went to the field the next day. I was just getting set and Klem had hardly called play when I saw him step out of the box. Bill was ordering somebody out of the game before it really started. From where I was standing I thought he was putting the third baseman out, so I ran in to see what I could find out.
> "No, not him, but you!" roared Bill as I came charging in. And then as I came to a stop, he bellowed: "I looked up the dictionary last night—now you can study it for the rest of the afternoon!" And I was out for the day.[43]

Fred Clarke had learned his lesson and never told a baseball umpire to use the dictionary as a reference point again.

◆ ◆ ◆

It is quite possible that Fred Clarke could not help himself when he referred to Bill Klem as a model umpire. Throughout his illustrious career, Clarke was a known trickster who loved to keep his players loose by pulling little pranks and engaging in harmless mischief. Brother-in-law Chick Fraser also enjoyed participating in this baseball initiation as well. After Fraser's playing career ended in 1912, he joined the Pirates organization as a scout and coach. Fraser was part of Pittsburgh's coaching staff in 1914 while Honus Wagner still played. That year, Wagner and Clarke were indirectly involved in a little joke that Fraser played on one

of the Pirates' young players. After a game in Chicago, Fraser told this fresh busher that he and the other players could get into any theater in the city without paying. "Just tell the manager that you are members of the Pittsburgh National League baseball club," Fraser said, "and he'll pass you in and give you the best seats in the house."[44]

Fraser soon forgot about this encounter. Following dinner, Fraser invited Fred Clarke and Honus Wagner to attend the most popular show in Chicago. When the three men reached the theater, Chick walked up to the box office and purchased tickets. Fraser, Clarke and Wagner walked into the theater, found their seats, and killed some time looking around the playhouse. They noticed eight of Pittsburgh's young players sitting together in a box, as large as life. Chick Fraser laughed and said, "Guess they got turned down, and to make good bought seats. Gee, but they'll be sore at me."[45]

After the show ended, the fresh youngster who had been told that he could get into the theater for nothing walked up to Fraser. Fraser, expecting him to be angry, received the surprise of his life as the kid started thanking him for the money-saving tip. "I sure am obliged for that tip you gave, Mr. Fraser. The manager of the theater told us he was tickled to take care of ball players, and insisted upon us taking a box."[46]

Fraser stood there, dumbfounded. He soon became peeved that he had been set back $4.50 for the three tickets he had purchased. Fred Clarke and Honus Wagner had a good laugh at their friend's expense since this joke ended up being on him.[47]

Moments such as this, filled with mirth and laughter, were the exception for Clarke in 1914. After winning four National League pennants and one World Series, and finishing in the first division each season since 1900, Pittsburgh came home in seventh place in 1914. Another poor performance the following year and health issues convinced Clarke to announce his retirement from baseball on September 8, 1915.[48]

Throughout his 16 seasons at the helm piloting the Pirates craft, Fred Clarke played the game on his terms, battled like a true warrior and never minced words with teammates, opponents, umpires and fans. Four years prior to his decision to tender his resignation as Pittsburgh's manager, he batted .324 in his final season as a regular player. On May 31, 1911, Clarke was presented with a German shepherd puppy from adoring Pirates fans. He smiled graciously as he accepted this token of their

appreciation, patted the dog and then took him to the Clarke home on Forbes Street.[49] The following day, Clarke explained to a member of Pittsburgh's press corps his intentions regarding this German shepherd.

> Got a great idea. You know these police dogs are the smartest in the world, and I'm going to train this fellow and bring him up in the baseball business. One of the first things I am going to do is to take him to the bench and make him acquainted with every member of the team, and if all goes well and he lives up to tradition, I guess the player who even thinks of swerving from the narrow path will find this puppy on his trail, night and day. Now, please don't mention this in the *Gazette Times,* for I don't want the boys to know that I have put a dog detective on the job.[50]

If Fred Clarke had only received a German shepherd as a gift years earlier, he might have been able to use that dog detective to keep a close eye on nuts like Rube Waddell.

4

Trains, Dining Cars, Theaters and the Stage

Baseball seasons were long, drawn-out affairs at times for men like Fred Clarke and Honus Wagner. Spring training usually started in late March or early April, while post-season barnstorming tours kept players busy until the end of October. During the first decade of the twentieth century, players spent more than seven months riding trains, sleeping in hotel rooms and eating meals away from home. They could not help but become more than just teammates to each other due to all of the time they spent together. Friendships were forged and a general feeling of camaraderie existed when Wagner played for the Louisville Colonels and Pittsburgh Pirates. Teammates who had each other's back on the diamond during a game were also a family away from the field of battle.

Filling idle time was not always easy for players as they traveled on monotonous train rides and spent countless days in foreign cities during a long road trip. Some men pursued vices for amusement. Most indulged in simpler pleasures together. While a small minority drank alcohol to excess, no one could fault a man for wanting to relax over a frothy beverage after a game in St. Louis' midsummer heat. Pittsburgh certainly could become very hot and humid during the summer as well. The Smoky City was filled with numerous gin joints where a player who lacked self-control could spend his free time. Some players ended up in the collective doghouses of Pirates owner Barney Dreyfuss and manager Fred Clarke. Although it was not done specifically to curb some of his players' drinking habits, Clarke did devise a plan on one occasion to help his teammates combat Pittsburgh's sweltering heat.

Clarke had the best of intentions when he decided one year to have a swimming pool constructed at Exposition Park. This personal swim-

ming hole built for Pittsburgh's players was a state-of-the-art tank walled with concrete and lined with copper.[1] Clarke believed that his men would benefit greatly from relaxing in the pool during Pittsburgh's hot and humid summer days. He perceived that relaxed bodies and focused minds would lead to better results for the Pirates on the diamond. He could not have possibly foreseen the negative consequences that came to light once his players started enjoying the serenity of this pool's cool water.

As soon as the blazing hot weather arrived in Pittsburgh, that swimming pool became a magnet for Clarke's players. Some of the Pirates arrived at Exposition Park early in the morning so they could splash around in the pool's refreshing water until noon. By that hour, almost every member of Pittsburgh's team was enjoying himself in the pool. Some players slipped into their clothes long enough to make food runs to the lunch counter, while others would either send the team batboy to get sandwiches or go without eating. Honus Wagner heartily enjoyed this summertime fun and possessed the swimming prowess of an eel. Wagner, Tommy Leach, Deacon Phillippe, Sam Leever and the rest of the gang spent every spare minute of their day in that tank playing water basketball, water polo and other popular aquatic sports.

From noon until game time, Clarke was kept busy trying to convince his men to leave the pool and return to dry land. Clarke usually had to order Exposition Park's groundskeeper to drain the tank before his players could be convinced to don their uniforms. What originally had been a good gesture on his part was now becoming a problem. He also became outraged when his team's performance declined due to the weakening effect his players experienced from soaking for hours in the pool. Although Clarke would rant and fume around the dugout in anger, every Pirate made a mad dash for that swimming pool once the game concluded each afternoon.[2]

Clarke's concerns eventually were alleviated with a little help from Mother Nature. Due to its proximity near the Allegheny River, flooding frequently occurred at Exposition Park. A heavy dose of rain and the rising river finally did the trick as the ball grounds became flooded, destroying the swimming pool. It was never rebuilt. Fred Clarke and Barney Dreyfuss certainly were not sorry over this turn of events. Pittsburgh's players, on the other hand, were devastated.[3]

◆ ◆ ◆

While Honus Wagner always enjoyed bonding with his teammates, Pittsburgh's star player also loved to spend time with his family in Carnegie. In some instances, these Wagner family get-togethers helped supply entertainment for his friends and teammates. Hurler Charles "Deacon" Phillippe even made sure that the boys in the press knew about one misunderstanding involving the Wagner family after the 1905 season. In November, Wagner gathered the family in their Carnegie home and proudly displayed the new and improved version of the phonograph. He also had a collection of up-to-date melodies that he intended to play for the whole Wagner clan. After he showed his father and brothers how this music maker worked, he selected a tune that had been recommended by some Pirates teammates.[4]

"Here's one that the gang says is the latest," remarked Honus. "'Everybody Works at Our House But Father.'"[5] When the tune neared the famous chorus, he noticed that his dad had a puzzled look on his face. It was evident to everyone in the room that Peter Wagner was not happy. He didn't think it was fair and took the shot about "everybody working but father" to heart. He was an industrious man despite the fact that all of his boys were excellent wage earners. Peter Wagner did not appreciate one bit the suggestion that he was perceived as being lazy. Peter imagined that his big boy was throwing it into him and took the stance that Honus had made the record on his own. It took a great deal of convincing on Honus' part to persuade his father that the song was not recorded by his famous son. When Phillippe finished relaying this story to baseball writer A. R. Cratty, he swore that it was no joke.[6]

This bad experience did not dampen Honus Wagner's enthusiasm in respect to this improved piece of technology. He looked forward to chronicling events at Hot Springs, Arkansas, during spring training in 1906. "I want to bottle the talk of one man ere I give up this business," said Wagner. "I'll give any man a dollar bill who can get Ritch [Claude Ritchey] to talk into the machine. I could sell that record for a fifty spot. Who would not give a wad to hear Claude roasting some fellow who thinks he is something."[7]

In a way, Wagner resembled his father in literally taking things to heart at times. Besides his love for music, he also enjoyed going to the

theater. A big fan of both comedy and drama, Wagner sometimes lost himself while viewing the latter. He became so engrossed watching the plot that he saw it in vivid and sometimes shocking realism. During the spring of 1914, Wagner and some of his Pirates teammates attended a performance of "The Bird of Paradise" one night in Chicago. The acting company was so brilliant that many of Pittsburgh's players declared the Hawaiian piece to be one of the finest they had ever witnessed. Wagner was the only dissenter among this group as he had not enjoyed the production at all.

Wagner hung his head in sorrow as the players walked back to their hotel. He had formed an unequivocal disdain for one character in the play—Dr. Wilson, the young American research expert who married and mistreated Luana, the beautiful Hawaiian princess. The boys insisted to Wagner that this man was a magnificent artist who performed all of his treachery using play acting. These reassurances proved futile as Wagner remained firm in respect to his dislike for the actor. "I don't care a darn," he growled. "Any guy who can treat a purty little thing like her so mean as that on stage, well, in my mind he can't be much good off the stage."[8]

Things certainly could have been difficult for the actor who played Dr. Wilson in "The Bird of Paradise" if Honus Wagner had ever become a theater critic.

◆ ◆ ◆

Taking in a play or a musical performance at the theater offered the perfect relaxing diversion for baseball players following a hard-fought battle on the diamond. Honus Wagner and his teammates gained much pleasure and enjoyment by taking in evening stage performances at playhouses in every National League city. Things did not always go as smoothly as expected when these men were drawn toward the thespian arts. In one instance during Wagner's early days with the Pirates, some players on the team believed a prank had been played upon them by a teammate who legitimately was only the victim of misinformation.

William Edward "Kitty" Bransfield played for Pittsburgh from 1901 through 1904 and was a member of National League pennant winning teams in 1901, 1902 and 1903. Regarded as a decent first baseman, Bransfield's best season with the Pirates occurred in 1901, when he batted .295

and drove home 91 runs. After three solid seasons playing for Fred Clarke, Bransfield was traded to the Philadelphia Phillies on December 20, 1904, after he had hit only .223 the previous season. Bransfield's nickname of "Kitty" was acquired in a most unique way. When he was a youngster in Worcester, Massachusetts, Bransfield was referred to as "Kid." Some of his friends expanded this to "Kiddy." One day, a buddy who had been bitten by the "Kit" Carson novel bug started calling Bransfield "Kit." It did not take long before these boys began referring to him as "Kitty."[9]

Bransfield believed he would shake that nickname once he reached the National League. However, Tommy Leach, who had played for the Eastern League's Worcester Farmers along with Bransfield in 1899, called the first baseman "Kitty" when he first joined the Pirates. Bransfield never liked the idea that a big fellow like himself was called a girlish name. Despite his displeasure, Bransfield was pragmatic about the moniker since he couldn't lick every person in a fight who called him "Kitty" or go before the legislature asking for a new nickname.[10] During his four seasons playing for Pittsburgh, Bransfield was well-liked by his teammates. On one occasion, his fellow players showed their extreme faith in him when they entrusted him with a very important task.

In 1904, eight members of Pittsburgh's squad decided they would like to attend a show in Chicago where famous comic opera singer Fritzi Scheff was performing. They chose Sunday evening since they reasoned that would be the best time to buy tickets for her show which was selling out in cities throughout the country. On behalf of the group, Honus Wagner asked Kitty Bransfield to buy the tickets. Pittsburgh's first baseman agreed to help out. Immediately after the game between the Pirates and Cubs concluded that Sunday afternoon, Bransfield went to the theater ticket office and had no problem purchasing eight tickets in the first row of the balcony. He was surprised that he was able to procure tickets so easily for a popular show featuring Fritzi Scheff.

After dinner, they left for the theater and arrived so early that they had plenty of time to find their seats and kill time by observing the hall's late arrivals. Wagner was the first to notice that most of the people gathering in the theater were speaking some language other than English. After a few minutes, his teammates also detected this peculiarity, but they remained quiet as they continued to observe the crowd. Everything

seemed to be going smoothly as the players eagerly anticipated hearing Fritzi Scheff's magnificent voice. When the curtain finally went up, they received the surprise of their life as a Yiddish act appeared on stage instead of Scheff.[11]

Kitty Bransfield, Honus Wagner and their teammates found out before the close of this performance that Fritzi Scheff played only six nights a week at the theater. On Sunday evening, a road show performed at the playhouse for Chicago's foreign inhabitants. Pittsburgh's players actually believed that Bransfield was fully aware that a Yiddish act was performing that night and had decided to play a joke on them. Years after Bransfield retired, he was still having difficulty convincing his old teammates that he had purchased those tickets in good faith to hear Fritzi Scheff sing.[12]

While Wagner did miss out on an opportunity to listen to the elegant Fritzi Scheff in this instance, he was referenced in 1914 during a conversation between a youngster who played for the Pirates and a high society woman in respect to Richard Wagner. Even though the German composer's last name was pronounced "Vagner," the young ballplayer did not seem to be on the same page with this sophisticated female socialite. The young Pirate was introduced to this educated, highbrow lady during a musical performance in Pittsburgh. Not wanting to come across as ignorant, the youngster attempted to muddle his way through a short conversation.[13]

> "Wonderful music, is it not?" asked the woman.
> "Yes'm. Some music, uh huh," replied the young man.
> "How magnificently matchless Wagner was!" responded the sophisticated lady, still feeling the wonder of the musical performance that evening.
> "Yes'm. Thems the words. Them words just fit him," said the ballplayer.
> "Ah, young man," said the female socialite, "I am delighted to see that you, too, show respect and reverence for the mighty dead!"
> "Huh? Dead? Aw, nix; lady, nix!" replied the young man who was now becoming agitated. "Just because old Honus hit under .300 this season ain't no sign he's a dead one. He hit in awful tough luck, and he'll come back next summer, sure!"[14]

This young Pirate had no intention of allowing this woman who was classy, refined and educated to get away with besmirching the character of a great player like Honus Wagner.

◆ ◆ ◆

This female Pittsburgh socialite who felt right at home listening to the music of Wagner probably would have been out of place attending a vaudeville performance on the stage. While players like Honus Wagner enjoyed going to the theater to watch musical performances or dramatic plays, many of his baseball brethren actually performed on the stage as part of traveling vaudeville shows. Mike Donlin and Rube Marquard of the New York Giants were two such players who turned to the stage as actors during the off-season. Donlin even retired from baseball for a few years to perform in vaudeville along with actress and wife Mabel Hite. Marquard parlayed his success as a pitcher into a decent stage career performing with Blossom Seeley, whom he eventually wed as well. Logic dictated that if two of New York's top players could be successful working in vaudeville, their famous manager was also a sure bet to be a hit on the stage.

Giants manager John McGraw participated in an extensive vaudeville tour during the off-season after his team lost to the Boston Red Sox in the 1912 World Series. When McGraw's tour reached Pittsburgh in early December, Honus Wagner drove his car from Carnegie to the Grand Opera House in downtown Pittsburgh to see if one of baseball's best managers could also act. Sitting in the second row, Wagner was easily identifiable to anyone on stage who recognized him. McGraw immediately spotted Wagner when he walked out on stage to begin his skit. "I'm going to have trouble making a hit here," began McGraw. "I see Wagner down in the second row, and it will be tough to get anything by him." Loud, thunderous laughter erupted throughout the theater. John McGraw, who had his audience from that point forward, received rave reviews for his talented acting during the show's run in Pittsburgh.[15]

For years, repeated efforts were made by theatrical syndicates to convince Honus Wagner to appear on the vaudeville stage. New York theater manager Bill Gray envisioned a three-man ensemble that consisted of baseball's greatest hitters—Wagner, Larry "Nap" Lajoie and Ty Cobb.[16] Gray's dream was fairly simple. He envisioned the three players using a machine that tested the speed of a baseball off the bat. A ball was thrown automatically to the batter, who smacked it toward a target.

Accuracy in hitting the target and the speed of the hit were shown. Gray planned on having a nightly contest at each show between these stars.[17]

Gray's dream almost became a reality during the autumn of 1910. The New York theatrical manager believed he had secured four men to participate in this contest at each show. Besides Honus Wagner, Ty Cobb and Nap Lajoie, Gray also recruited Philadelphia Athletics second baseman Eddie Collins. Gray was upbeat that this great vaudeville sensation would proceed once Wagner promised to join the troupe. This ended up being a false premise on Gray's part as Wagner backed out of the venture. Lajoie explained during an interview the following spring what had caused baseball's greatest hitters not to come together on a vaudeville stage.

Napoleon "Nap" Lajoie. For years, a debate raged over who was baseball's greatest player—the National League's Honus Wagner or Lajoie of the American League. Following the 1910 baseball season, Lajoie believed he had convinced Wagner to join him, Ty Cobb and Eddie Collins on the vaudeville stage. In the end, Wagner changed his mind, claiming that traveling made him ill (courtesy National Baseball Hall of Fame Library, Cooperstown, New York).

Gray and I went to Carnegie to line up Hans. He had promised Gray to go on the stage, but did not answer Gray's letters and telegrams. Everybody in Carnegie knew Hans, but they never saw him.

We ran across Hans' brother Al and asked him when Hans would be home. "Pretty soon," said Al. "He never stays out after dark."

Hans came—just at dusk—muddy and in old clothes, fresh from the chase. He was tickled to see us and accepted Gray's offer, which was $500 a week for him, $25 a week and traveling expenses for his brother Al, whom Hans wanted as his companion on the road. It was all fixed, Gray and I thought. A contract was left with Hans, which he was to sign and send to me.

Hans was a little shy about signing to be an actor until Gray told him all he would have to do was walk on the stage, his bat in one hand and his cap

in the other. "When the people applaud, take off your cap," said Gray. "Then take your bat and hit the ball a half dozen times."

Four days later I got a letter from Hans. It read: "Dear Larry: I'd like to take up your offer, but I can't stand traveling. It makes me ill." And he never replied to my telegrams and letters.[18]

What Bill Gray and Nap Lajoie did not understand was that Honus Wagner would never abandon the tranquil and simple life of Carnegie even if he could earn $500 a week.

◆ ◆ ◆

Honus Wagner probably would have been extremely happy if every game on the Pirates schedule were played in Pittsburgh so he would never have to leave the cozy confines of his Carnegie home. Of course, the National League's schedule makers had no intention of creating a season slate of games that were unfair and unbalanced just because its best player did not like to travel. This meant that Wagner had to spend half of the baseball season on the road, journeying to each destination by train. For a man like Wagner who loved to spend time in the outdoors hunting and fishing, long railroad trips certainly could be confining. During these excursions along America's railways, Wagner and his teammates tried to kill time by playing cards, reading, and pulling jokes and pranks on each other.

Sometimes, Pittsburgh's players even amused themselves with little games when they were waiting to depart by train. In 1911, Honus Wagner escaped ridicule as the result of one of these ruses due to an ankle injury. In the first inning at Brooklyn on August 16, Wagner turned his ankle and dropped to the ground at second base after he had singled and then motored into the keystone sack when Superbas right fielder Bob Coulson tried to gun down Max Carey at the plate.[19] The injury put him out of action for more than two weeks before he returned on September 1. Although he was not slated to play a single Sunday matinee game against the Reds on September 3, Wagner decided to make the trip to Cincinnati with his teammates.

When the Pirates assembled Saturday evening at Pittsburgh's Union Station, the early arrivals hatched a plan to come down hard on the first teammate who showed up wearing a straw hat. The scheme, which was a common practice for Pittsburgh's players, did not seem to be going so

well since each of the late arrivals appeared with a soft-thatch covering. Five minutes before the train was due to leave, Wagner came hobbling toward the gang wearing a small Panama hat. Sensing that the boys planned on having some fun at his expense, Wagner approached the gathering and shouted, "I have my fingers crossed, fellows—nix on the hat gag."[20]

This plea did not deter a few players who were getting ready to pounce verbally on the great shortstop because of the hat despite his protests.[21] Before anything moved along any further, catcher George "Hack" Gibson intervened on Wagner's behalf. Gibson was one of Pittsburgh's veteran players, having joined the Pirates in 1905. During Pittsburgh's pennant winning season in 1909, he batted .265 while appearing in 150 games. Considered one of the top defensive catchers in the National League and possessing a cannon arm, Gibson was credited with a huge assist helping Wagner out of this predicament.

"Cut it out fellows," Gibson demanded. "Wagner has only one foot to stand upon, and besides he is not of the Cincinnati party. Let that old hat stay where it is."

"Thanks, Hack, old boy," responded a grateful Wagner.

"That's all right, John," replied Gibson, "but I am going to give you a straight tip; if you show up on Monday with that same lid I will not again interfere."[22]

Bill McKechnie, a native of the Pittsburgh suburb of Wilkinsburg, was one of the players who made this trip to Cincinnati. McKechnie was a utility infielder for the Pirates from 1910 through 1912. He carved out a .227 average in 104 games in 1911 while playing in front of the home-town Pittsburgh fans. In 1910, he was almost sent back to the minors before he ever received this chance due to a misunderstanding with Barney Dreyfuss during a train ride from Chattanooga to Memphis for an exhibition game after spring training in Hot Springs, Arkansas. Dreyfuss had retired to bed early. A little poker game was going on in one of the coach cars where Honus Wagner happened to be investing a few nickels.[23]

In the berth next to Dreyfuss', Bill McKechnie and a newspaper writer were quietly discussing the events from the game that afternoon. Wagner ambled past McKechnie and the scribe to his own berth. He needed to get some more money since he had already gone broke playing

poker. He was speaking out loud to himself vowing vengeance against his card-playing opponents and vented some of his wrath toward teammates Babe Adams and Ham Hyatt, who had copped his coin. All of this commotion awakened Dreyfuss from his deep sleep. Dreyfuss sat up, peeked out between the curtains to see who was being so noisy, and spied only McKechnie.

Thinking McKechnie had wakened him, Dreyfuss cut loose with verbal vitriol that matched Wagner's. He spoke of youngsters breaking in taking the chance of being sent back to the minors and other unflattering things directed toward McKechnie. Dreyfuss finally hopped out of his sleeping berth and confronted the man he believed was keeping him from getting much-needed rest. "The fellow that woke me up goes back to the minors," yelled Dreyfuss as he glared at Bill McKechnie.

"All right; when do I go, tomorrow or tonight?" chimed in Wagner as he returned from his berth with a fresh supply of money.[24]

Once Barney Dreyfuss realized that it was Honus Wagner who had awakened him and not Bill McKechnie, talk of banishing the perpetrator to the minors ceased.

◆ ◆ ◆

Bill McKechnie was a courteous man who understood that a young player's job was to observe, ask questions and learn everything he could from the team's veterans. This approach served him well as he later became a very successful manager who led the Pittsburgh Pirates to victory in the 1925 World Series. Not every youngster who reached baseball's biggest stage exhibited humility and deference to baseball's veteran players. Once in a while, a baseball team was saddled with a recruit who believed he knew it all. According to Honus Wagner, the Pirates had a rookie catcher on their roster in 1914 who exhibited this personality trait. The young man butted in on conversations and cards games and was a general pest. Besides being a nuisance, the young catcher was one of the biggest eaters Wagner had ever seen. On one road trip, Wagner, Babe Adams and George Gibson were seated in the smoking compartment of their car when Mr. Recruit strolled in and sat down.[25]

> We were discussing some baseball topic, and you might think the busher would have been glad to listen and learn from his elders. But not him. He immediately began to tell us more about the play and the players involved

than we could have ever dreamed. Finally Gibson became peeved and decided the recruit needed a lesson.

"Say, Jay, I lost another pair of shoes night before last," he said to me. "If I weren't so tired I'd stay up tonight and watch for the thief who's been taking our shoes. It's getting to be an awful thing. Why, I'll bet our fellows have lost 20 pairs in the last month or so."

Adams and I were wise in a minute to the fact that Gibson was stringing the recruit, and Babe said: "I lost a pair the other night, too, and I want to stay up and watch tonight. I want to get my hands on that thief. But then I'm liable to have to pitch tomorrow and I need the rest."[26]

Wagner insisted that he would be the watchman since he had recently lost his best pair of "kicks" and wanted to extract some revenge by catching the thief in the act. The young recruit quickly interjected and offered to play detective. "Now you old fellows all are tired and need to be in shape to play tomorrow," he announced. "All of you go to bed and I'll stay awake and watch. I've got an upstairs berth and it will be easy for me to keep my eyes down the aisle without the thief seeing me."[27]

All three veterans agreed that the youngster should keep watch and turned in for the evening. In the middle of the night, every player in the car was awakened by the screams of someone yelling for help. Wagner stuck his head out from between the curtains of his berth and saw the recruit on the floor struggling with a black porter. The rookie seemed to be gaining the upper hand in this fight when Wagner jumped out of his berth and pried the two combatants apart. Once order was restored, Wagner, Adams and Gibson explained their joke to the young know-it-all. The youngster had remained awake, just as he had promised. When the porter came around to collect the players' shoes and shine them, the busher jumped on him, thinking he had captured the thief.

After initially being scared over this attack in the middle of the night, the porter viewed this incident in a different light later as he became "mad as a wet hen," according to Wagner. The three veteran Pirates told the busher that the porter might have him arrested for assault and battery, or some other charge. This incident cured the young baseball player of his nasty habit as he was the meekest fellow on the team from that point forward.[28]

Besides playing a joke on a misguided rookie to teach him a lesson, Wagner also enjoyed having some fun with passengers while traveling

across America by rail. During the summer of his final major league season in 1917, Wagner engaged in some humorous banter with a group of women while the Pirates traveled from Buffalo to Syracuse. As the train passed over some mountains which overlooked the beautiful Genesee Valley, Wagner walked to the rear of the observation car to view the breathtaking scenery. Seated next to him was a group of women who were fashionably dressed. They, too, were in awe of the landscape a mile above a quaint New York state village. One of the women called attention to a building resting on the hillside. The edifice resembled a sanitarium, as the roof and grounds were dotted with cots.[29]

"I wonder what building is that?" asked one of the women. When no one responded, a second lady leaned over and repeated the question to Wagner.

"Oh, that building down there?" responded Wagner. "That's a big brewery."

"A brewery!" exclaimed the astonished travelers.

"Yes," replied the diamond patriarch. "Don't you see that bunch stretched out around the place?"[30]

While it certainly seemed plausible that Honus Wagner knew this building was a brewery due to the many excursions he had taken by train in that area of New York, it was just as likely that the Dutchman recognized the lasting effects of drinking alcohol due to exposure to wayward teammates.

◆ ◆ ◆

Although most rookies did not show as much brashness as the young catcher who believed he had foiled a major shoe burglary, many youngsters reveled in the new experience of enjoying a scrumptious selection of delectable treats in the train's dining car. Some packed in as much food as they could, believing the baseball team would pick up the tab. In 1911, a lanky southpaw pitcher from Georgia named Sherrod "Sherry" Smith went to spring training with the Pirates. While Smith appeared in only four games with Pittsburgh, he eventually developed into a pretty decent pitcher with the Brooklyn Robins and the Cleveland Indians. In the spring of 1911, he also established his reputation as a top-flight eater.

Smith had come from the South Atlantic League, where athletes

did not find free meals very often. One night when the train carrying the Pirates entourage was entering St. Louis, he consumed a bumper feast. Beginning with soup and oysters, the rangy lad ate so much that his check totaled $2.85. Smith, believing the team would pick up his tab, was disappointed when the waiter told him he would have to pay the bill himself and then recoup the money from the club. In the sleeper car a short time later, Fred Clarke passed out crisp, one dollar bills to Smith and each member of the Pirates.

"What's this for?" demanded Smith.

"Supper," answered Clarke, shortly.

"Well, you're just $1.85 short," raved the young recruit.

"Say," exploded the Pirates leader, "you ought to be on the National Commission with your appetite."[31]

Smith was out the $1.85 since Clarke never did cover the young pitcher's eating too heartily that evening.[32] The work of some of these young men with a knife and fork in the dining car was nothing compared to what they sometimes accomplished eating at the team hotel. According to Honus Wagner, a ball player needed to eat more than just a roll or two to gain sustenance and remain in good playing condition. Wagner usually was reticent to discuss how much a diamond laborer should eat each day, since he did possess a fairly healthy appetite. He did remember one young busher who reached two eating extremes on many occasions due to financial reasons, eating more food when the team paid all dining expenses on what was called the American plan.[33]

When a big league club goes into a city and stops at a hotel on the European plan the players are allowed a certain sum of money for their meal. It will average about $1 a meal, I guess. But we stop at American plan hotels in some of the cities on our circuit. Now, the busher I referred to was in the dining room early and often when we were quartered at American plan hotels. And how he could eat! Why, say, he was the best ever. He kept a waiter busy bringing food to his table.

But when we were stopping at a European hotel and the secretary of the club handed out meal money, Mr. Busher didn't gormandize quite so much. He hunted up the cheapest place he could find and ate the cheapest food they had in the restaurant. Well, the gang was wise to the recruit. On the last day of one of our trips we framed up a good joke on the kid and one which cured him of the starvation life when stopping at the European hotels.[34]

Another young Pirate quickly learned a life lesson. One of Wagner's teammates called Mr. Recruit aside and explained to him that it was customary to return all of the money not spent for purchasing meals to the team secretary. After he talked to the young man, Pittsburgh's veteran walked over to the secretary and handed over a roll of bills in order to help sell his story. Upon seeing this, the busher trotted over to the secretary. "I saved more than this out of my meal money, but I'll have to owe it to you," said the recruit as he handed the secretary six dollars. "Gosh darn it, if I'd known you had to give back what you didn't spend I'd have eaten it all up, you can bet."[35]

Of course, Honus Wagner never took a back seat to anyone when the Pirates gathered to eat dinner on the road. At the Somerset Hotel in Boston in 1914, a night clerk named Mr. Stewart and the telephone girl, a Miss Spellacy, were talking about the great Honus Wagner. "Which one is Wagner?" asked Miss Spellacy.

"Watch them all in the dining room," answered the clerk. "When you see one big fellow order oysters and take all six of them on his fork, spear them clean up to the hilt and then down them all at once, well, that's Wagner."[36]

◆ ◆ ◆

The Pirates had an abundant variety of items to choose from when viewing restaurant menus from Boston to St. Louis during the baseball campaign. The same could not be said during spring training in Hot Springs, Arkansas. For a man like Honus Wagner, who played 18 seasons with the Pirates, the training session sometimes was a tedious affair. In 1912, rookie outfielder Walter Rehg found the dining experience at the Pirates' team hotel a bit monotonous. Rehg was a witty youngster who made an immediate impression on Pittsburgh's older players during his first trip to spring training with a major league club in 1912.[37]

Rehg quickly realized that the only difference in the bill of fare at Pittsburgh's team hotel restaurant each day was the manner in which the special of the day was described. One day it was "Watertown Fowl," the next, "Roast Vermont Turkey," and the third day, "Ozark Fowl." While the restaurateur was very creative, this did not change the fact that it was the same menu item each day. Tired of living on a steady diet of fowl, Rehg called the head waiter over to his table one day and made a

desperate plea as he wiped off his flippant mouth with the edge of his napkin. "Say," said Rehg in a sarcastic tone, "can't you can that bird variety and bring me just a plain old Herr's Island steak?"[38]

Spending time on the road brought both grizzled veterans and upstart rookies together. Bonding away from the diamond allowed Fred Clarke and his players to be a cohesive unit that stood up for one another during games. Players who enjoyed spending their free time together were more than willing to battle with every fiber of their being to secure victory over a baseball opponent. Life on the road consisted of trains and theaters, as well as brotherhood and camaraderie. Legends also tended to grow in the cities of National League opponents where men like Honus Wagner could only be viewed by the rooting populace on rare occasions.

While Wagner's legendary status may have received a boost when the Pirates played on the road, his sometimes mythical aura was rooted in the devotion and adulation that Pittsburgh's baseball faithful bestowed upon the game's greatest player. When a player was worshiped in such a manner, many people even believed baseless rumors when they were put forward by the press. In 1913 and 1914, there was much talk about erecting a statue of Honus Wagner in the Carnegie Institute Museum, which was close to Forbes Field in Oakland. This story was so well worked that thousands of bugs who followed baseball thought it was legitimate. "Who deserves a statue if Honus doesn't?" was one of the reasons many people put forward to justify the validity of this tale.[39]

Although no statue was built honoring Honus Wagner at the Carnegie Institute Museum, a gentleman who visited the facility expressed surprise that this supposed project had been completed so quickly. A couple from a rural western Pennsylvania town went to Oakland one day to enjoy the museum's exhibits. The husband happened to be near-sighted. When this couple came upon a case that housed a monstrous, stuffed gorilla, the husband exhibited exuberant enthusiasm. "Gee whiz," he cried in awe. "I heard tell as how they were goin' ter erect a statcher of Hans Wagner in the Instytoot, but I had no idea they'd get it done already!"[40]

For Pittsburgh hero and Carnegie native Honus Wagner, there certainly was no place like home sweet home.

5

The Game of Baseball
as Seen Through
Wagner's Eyes

There was only one medium that covered the exploits of Honus Wagner and other major league players during the great shortstop's time playing baseball. The printed word was the exclusive method, used by scribes to describe game events, offer opinions about the state of the game and chronicle interviews with those men who played baseball. Rabid fans who anxiously anticipated behind-the-scenes accounts involving their favorite players or team relied on these writers to cover the game in a straightforward and truthful manner. Since these rooters also wanted to be entertained, the actual words of a player or manager always helped bring home the point.

Writers who chronicled the great game for local newspapers or national publications used a variety of practices to bring baseball to life for readers across America. Scribes covered the teams and their games at the ballparks. They also conducted fanning bees with players and managers at league events such as the winter meetings. Some of the best information was acquired by writers who hung around at team head-quarters and discussed the game with players, managers, owners or average people who stopped by and were more than happy to join in the conversation. A fourth method was for publications to allow players to talk about the game in their own words.

Many of baseball's greatest players were either interviewed for a long series of articles or actually wrote the prose themselves. Although Honus Wagner always seemed reluctant to talk about baseball in a social setting, he eventually became more comfortable sharing his observations about the game and his time playing for Louisville and Pittsburgh. Since

he had been ordained as the greatest player in baseball, it seemed logical that devoted fans would want to read Wagner's impressions regarding the game. As his career wound down and following his retirement, he did series of articles for various publications with the help of friends, like newspaperman and politician John H. Dailey, who sometimes acted as ghostwriters. While most of Wagner's stories had a humorous slant to them, the many things he revealed about the game, his career and incidents involving himself and teammates helped to define that historical baseball era for a multitude of fans.

In many of these tales reflecting back on his baseball career, Wagner liked to talk about little known players who made an impact on him and his teammates. Infielder George Eastman was one such player. Eastman, who never appeared in a game as a major leaguer, went to spring training with the Pirates in 1913. He was a Sioux Indian whose father was a Presbyterian minister who conducted services regularly on a reservation in South Dakota. Eastman's father also owned a farm where George and his two brothers worked. Even though his father made no objection to his son playing baseball, he did not hold a very high opinion of someone earning a living in that profession.[1] Eastman received his start in baseball playing shortstop for Milbank in the South Dakota League.

Wagner understood that training camps were filled with charley horses, blistered feet, aching arms and other maladies. He also believed they were packed with plenty of fun, for it was here that veteran players had the first opportunity to baptize rookies in respect to baseball's intricacies. Eastman supplied Wagner with one of the most humorous highlights of his long career during training camp in 1913 at Hot Springs, Arkansas. Eastman was a tall, rugged youngster who immediately exhibited incredible stamina during long walks taken to help build up endurance for the upcoming season.

Each morning before breakfast, Fred Clarke and his players went on a long hike through the hills of Hot Springs. Eastman, who had grown up living on the trail, set such a blistering pace that none of the other players could keep up with him. As they puffed up one hill, he would be spurting up another a mile or so in front of them. This irritated Clarke, who was very proud of his walking ability and conditioning. According to Wagner, it was determined that a special race would be held with Clarke wagering ten dollars that he could outdistance Eastman.[2]

Early in the morning the course was outlined and the boys started out. It was not long before Eastman had taken a commanding lead, but Clarke had mapped out his strategy in advance. He took a short cut and was sure he would head off the Indian, but when he reappeared on the main road, he was amazed to see Eastman pounding along about a quarter-mile in front.

Not to be outdone, Fred hailed a rancher who was rattling along in a rickety old hack, jumped in and hid himself. He was so securely hidden that he didn't see that Eastman had hopped on the rear end himself. When they got to the hotel, the Indian jumped off and raced into the lobby. It cost Clarke the 10 dollars and also a lot of kidding from the players. Eastman never made the grade in the major leagues, but he did enliven that particular camp.[3]

Fred Clarke losing a battle of wits against a player many years his junior certainly was not something that happened often.

◆ ◆ ◆

Honus Wagner and many of his teammates certainly could relate to the plight of a rookie participating in his first spring training at the major league level. At least Wagner had played in the National League for a few months with Louisville in 1897 before he was exposed to his first training camp in 1898. When he reported for spring training, he was 30 pounds overweight. Owner Barney Dreyfuss made it a point to interview each of the recruits personally that spring in Thomasville, Georgia. When Dreyfuss approached Wagner and asked him who he was and what position he played, Wagner believed the Louisville magnate was actually joking.[4]

"Why, I'm the fellow who chased fly balls for you last season," exclaimed Wagner.

Sensing that Dreyfuss was still having a problem placing who he was, he told Louisville's owner that his name was John Wagner. After apologizing for his failure to recognize the man who had made such a wonderful impression the previous summer, Dreyfuss said: "I will see that the manager runs the fat off you so I can recognize my own men."[5]

Fred Clarke made sure that any player who showed up for spring training overweight put in enough hard work to melt away the winter pounds. While spring training was crucial for men who needed to get in shape for the upcoming season, it was also a time when players devised new tactics that could be used during the regular season, rather than try something novel when a game counted in the standings. At

times, Honus Wagner developed and tested trick plays without consulting Fred Clarke. Pittsburgh's surprised manager did not shy away from showing his disgust when these plays did not work.

One year during Pittsburgh's spring exhibition tour, Wagner and the Pirates' starting catcher concocted a simple, yet brilliant piece of strategy that they believed would work beautifully. When the opposing team had a runner on third base, Pittsburgh's third baseman was supposed to creep in like he was preparing to field a bunt. Wagner believed this would draw the runner off the bag and down the baseline toward home plate. When this happened, Wagner would bolt from his shortstop position over to third base. This was a signal for Pittsburgh's pitcher to throw a pitch-out. If everything went as planned, Wagner would take a quick throw from the catcher to retire the unsuspecting runner who naturally was watching the third baseman.

They tried this trick play during an exhibition game in Newark just before the season opened. Unfortunately, Wagner failed to reach the third base bag in time to take the catcher's throw, and the baseball bounced out to left field, where Fred Clarke was playing. When Wagner glanced out toward left field, Clarke was waving his arms in disgust over attempting such a play. That did not discourage Wagner, who felt the tactic was a good piece of baseball strategy. He and Pittsburgh's catcher decided to attempt the play once again during a tight, early season game at Brooklyn. Wagner signaled the catcher to pull the trick play, and the Pirates caught Brooklyn's runner flat-footed off third base. This play helped secure the game for Pittsburgh.[6]

While Wagner was proud that the play he had devised worked, he wondered what his manager's reaction would be. After the umpire called Brooklyn's runner out at third, Wagner looked out toward left field just as he had done during the exhibition game in Newark. This time, Fred Clarke doffed his cap to Wagner and the catcher, his signal that they had pulled off a great play.[7]

◆　◆　◆

Fred Clarke could never remain angry very long when his players took the initiative to think up strategic maneuvers to help win baseball games, even if he had initially perceived the tactic to be boneheaded. Pittsburgh's manager did have a problem when his players' eccentric

tendencies interfered with how he managed the game. Rube Waddell was the king of eccentricity whose peculiar behavior constantly kept Clarke on his toes. Honus Wagner roomed with Waddell during his first full major league season with the Colonels in 1899. Wagner always believed that Waddell was more effective that season with a tail-end Louisville club than he was with the second-place Pirates in 1900.[8] While talent and ability were not the issue with Waddell, his time playing for Clarke certainly was marred by a lack of focus and commitment that drove the manager crazy.

"Rube Waddell never took baseball seriously," said Wagner. "It was nothing more than a lark to him and he made no bones about it. I remember one time when we sent him home to Butler County for a rest. The next morning, about 4 o'clock, a fire broke out in the ballpark, and imagine everyone's surprise when the 'Rube' was on the scene ahead of the firemen instead of being 40 miles away where he should have been."[9]

Waddell's attention span deserted him on one occasion when he was locked in a magnificent pitching duel. The game remained scoreless through six innings. When the seventh inning started, Waddell could not be found anywhere. He had crawled under the back fence near the clubhouse and run over to a nearby lot to watch Buffalo Bill's Wild West Show. Rather than finish the game, Waddell elected to sit in the front row in full uniform, watching the cowboys and Indians demonstrate their shooting proficiency.[10]

Besides irritating Clarke with such immature antics, he also tortured his manager at times by performing bizarre stunts during games. On one such occasion, the Pirates had an opposing runner caught in a rundown between third base and home plate. Every fielder initially involved eventually got out of the way, leaving only Wagner and Waddell chasing the runner. Just when it looked like the runner was a dead duck, Waddell inexplicably threw the ball over Wagner's head. This boneheaded play incensed Fred Clarke. He came running in from left field and started dressing down Wagner for missing the throw. Waddell spoke up and took responsibility for the blunder.

"Don't blame Honus, Fred," Waddell said. "I threw him a curve and it was a dandy!"[11]

There was no denying that Rube Waddell was a great pitcher, even though he was a constant headache.[12] On the opposite end of that spec-

trum was a hurler who was both a great pitcher and a model citizen when he pitched for Clarke at Louisville and Pittsburgh. Charles "Deacon" Phillippe won 20 or more games in his first five major league seasons with Louisville (1899) and Pittsburgh (1900–1903). Besides being the star of Clarke's staff, Phillippe was a true gentleman who never gave his manager a moment of trouble. Phillippe's best season occurred in 1903 when Pittsburgh played the Boston Americans in the first modern World Series. He went 25–9, buttressed by a 2.43 ERA that year. Phillippe's performance against Boston in the 1903 World Series was legendary as he tossed five complete games and posted a 3–2 record. Unfortunately, Clarke had no other hurler he could rely upon as Boston claimed the World Series, five games to three.

That was only one reason why Pittsburgh was beaten by Boston after they had taken a commanding three games to one lead. During Game Four at Exposition Park on October 6, a group of devoted Boston fans known as the "Royal Rooters" started singing a popular song of the day called "Tessie" in an effort to break the concentration of Pittsburgh's players. This strategy nearly worked in the ninth inning as Boston almost rallied from a four-run deficit.[13] The Pirates lost the next four games as the "Royal Rooters" brought a band to each remaining contest and belted out different versions of "Tessie" that poked fun at Pittsburgh's players. Phillippe was particularly unnerved by this song to the point that he always became irritated when he heard it throughout the remainder of his life. Honus Wagner explained many years later in 1916 how the man his teammates affectionately referred to as "Phil" reacted whenever he heard "Tessie."

> No nervier stoic ever stepped into the box than Charles "Deacon" Phillippe, and only once did anything get his goat. That happened to be the little old song of "Tessie," and to this day the Royal Rooters of Boston have that piece played at World's Series games in commemoration of its goat-getting powers back in 1903.
>
> Phil, pitching wonderful ball, heard "Tessie" in Pittsburgh and Boston until he grew weary of her. It haunted him by night and day during the series. Despite Phil's wonderful work, we lost the series after winning three of the first four games. Phillippe has shuddered ever since of hearing "Tessie," and one day two years ago he ordered a man out of his office because he insisted on whistling "Tessie" to remind him of the Red Sox Waterloo of 1903.
>
> At the great farewell banquet given Fred Clarke in Pittsburgh last fall, the band did not play "Tessie," as has been the custom at functions given by the

Pittsburgh Stove League. The reason was that Deacon Phillippe was there, happy to greet his old retiring chief and he was so happy that even the band did not want to make him unhappy.[14]

Although the Boston Americans and "Tessie" ruined Deacon Phillippe's experience in 1903, he remained with Pittsburgh through the 1911 campaign and was a member of their championship team that defeated the Detroit Tigers in the 1909 World Series.

◆ ◆ ◆

During the 1909 World Series, Charles "Babe" Adams matched Deacon Phillippe's impressive 1903 achievement by winning three games. Adams was a rookie in 1909 who went 12–3 and posted an ERA of 1.11. He became the mainstay of Pittsburgh's pitching staff from 1910 through 1915 during the latter stages of Honus Wagner's career. Unlike Deacon Phillippe, who was scarred for life by the sounds of "Tessie" cascading from the mouths of Boston's "Royal Rooters" in 1903, Adams thrived in games when a band played musical interludes before festivities began on the diamond.

"Music never 'got the goat' of Babe Adams," claimed Wagner. "Babe is a quiet, big fellow, rather phlegmatic and not very enthusiastic over anything. But a brass band stirs his blood and his step and quickens his brain and instincts into a peppery state. He has been beaten only once with a brass band in the park and that was opening day in St. Louis in 1914."[15]

Babe Adams was not the only rookie who was an integral part of Pittsburgh's success in 1909. John "Dots" Miller took over at second base early in the campaign after starter Ed Abbaticchio faltered. Miller, a young man from Kearny, New Jersey, who certainly did not lack self-confidence, put up great numbers in 1909 as he appeared in 151 games, batted .279 and drove home 87 runs. Honus Wagner took an immediate liking to Miller and mentored him on the nuances of playing second base. Wagner was also responsible for Miller acquiring his nickname of "Dots." When a reporter asked Wagner who the new kid playing second base was, Pittsburgh's star shortstop blurted out, "That's Miller." Since Wagner said the name so fast, this writer misunderstood and wrote the rookie's first name as "Dots." This nickname stuck during Miller's five seasons in Pittsburgh, although he was sometimes referred to "Hans" and "Hans Number Two."[16]

Wagner and Miller were as close as two peas in a pod during the summer of 1909. Wagner took the speedy youngster under his wing and taught him everything that he thought would help Miller become a better player. Miller also took up residence in Carnegie so he could be near Wagner, and the two men were inseparable companions. When Pittsburgh played at home, they usually spent their evenings touring the scenery in Carnegie in Wagner's red automobile.[17] Like Wagner, Miller was of German descent and could speak the language fluently. They sometimes spoke German around second base, plotting such strategy as which man would cover the bag in case a runner on first base attempted to steal.[18]

Wagner and Miller also spoke German when giving signals to each other and used this second language to cuss when things were not going well for Pittsburgh.[19] On one occasion, with the help of mischievous Pirates catcher George "Hack" Gibson, their excessive banter in German almost caused them to be tossed from a game by umpire Hank O'Day. Wagner was also responsible for tagging Gibson with the moniker of "Hack." Although Gibson was sometimes referred to as "Moon" and "Mooney" because of his full, round face, Wagner slapped the nickname of "Hack" on him since Gibson's burly build resembled that of professional wrestler George Hackenschmidt, "The Russian Lion."[20] Gibson never passed up an opportunity to cause trouble for players on the baseball diamond, even if they were his teammates who happened to be swearing in German.

"I remember one game in which we got peeved at each other and began swearing in German," reflected Wagner. "George Gibson, our catcher, heard us, could understand what we said, and began laughing. This went on for some time."[21]

As the game progressed, Gibson decided to have some fun at Hank O'Day's expense. When this incessant chatter between Wagner and Miller in a foreign language intensified late in the game, O'Day asked Gibson what the two players were talking about. "Why, they are talking about you," Gibson told Hank. "They're discussing the rotten decision you made last inning."[22]

Although this obviously was not what Wagner and Miller were talking about, O'Day fell for the fast one. O'Day called time out and walked toward second base. "If you guys are calling me names, you'd better speak in a language I can understand or out of the game you both go."[23]

O'Day's warning seemed fairly straightforward for Honus Wagner and Jack Miller. Stop speaking German on the field or spend the rest of the afternoon sitting in the clubhouse.[24] That would have been unbearable for Miller, a bundle of energy who could not stand being away from

Second baseman John "Dots" Miller debuted for the Pittsburgh Pirates in 1909 and batted .279 that season. Miller and Honus Wagner became immediate friends and inseparable companions. Like Wagner, Miller spoke fluent German. The two players, who constantly plotted strategy on the baseball diamond speaking German, fell out of favor with umpire Hank O'Day when teammate George Gibson intimated that they were using the foreign language to talk about the arbiter (courtesy National Baseball Hall of Fame Library, Cooperstown, New York).

the field. He loved playing baseball and could not remain inactive when a contest was postponed due to bad weather.

"Few players loved the game as well as Jack Miller," said Wagner. "When a game went unplayed because of rain, Jack would get a ball and toss it against the clubhouse wall. He would keep this up for hours, and the walls of the different clubhouses around the league were pretty well marked up by his throwing against them. Rain or no rain, Jack got in his practice."[25]

◆　◆　◆

Since Honus Wagner and Dots Miller had such a strong friendship, the young player sometimes acted as the perfect foil for Pittsburgh's star shortstop when he told a story that stretched the imagination. Miller was adept at making one of those tales appear credible by striking a serious tone when he joined the discussion. In one instance, Wagner even used some subtle sarcasm on Miller's part to his advantage. During a morning fanning bee with reporters at the team hotel before a game against the Chicago Cubs at West Side Grounds on June 25, 1911, Wagner discussed a magical baseball bat he used earlier in his career which had produced some phenomenal results.[26]

> Once, over at Exposition Park I had been in a batting slump for some time. I had not been able to make a hit for a week or so, and was just about ready to ask Clarke to put me on the bench. One morning, while at home in Carnegie I went down to the cellar to see if there was any ice in the place, when I stumbled across one of the most dilapidated old bats you ever saw. It was split nearly the whole length and was badly cracked. I picked it up, took it to the game with me that afternoon, used it, and proceeded to make a safe hit every time during my next 13 tries, certainly quite a record.

"How did that bat ever get into your cellar, Jayson?" quietly asked Jack Miller, looking up from his newspaper. "Guess it must have floated in on the occasion of the last rise in that little creek that flows through Carnegie."

"Mebbe so," responded Wagner, looking out the window. "If it did float in then you had better go to Kearny and look in your own cellar to see what has drifted in; for, as I tell you, there were 13 consecutive hits in that old stick, and I used it until there were only a few splinters left."[27]

While Honus Wagner may have actually found this bat in his cellar and had great success at the plate using it, he certainly did not smack 13 consecutive clean safeties, since no player has ever accomplished this feat in major league history. Wagner always claimed there was no such thing as a perfect bat. He alleged this was impossible when the shape had to be perfectly round so foul balls could slip off the curving surface and wood tended to break when a player administered extra force smacking a home run with the sacks loaded. He believed baseball bats were strange and moody things. He also agreed with old-time outfielder Pete Browning's philosophy that bats were human and needed the proper talking-to.[28]

Wagner believed the closest he ever came to handling a perfect bat was when he played for the Louisville Colonels in 1898. The Colonels were playing an exhibition game in an Ohio River town when Wagner had the opportunity to handle this beautiful war club in his hands for one afternoon. As luck would have it, instead of Louisville's bat bag being shipped to this little town for the exhibition contest, it was sent to their next big league stop. Fred Clarke and his Colonels found themselves without any pieces of batting timber to use in a game that baseball fans from this little village had been looking forward to viewing. Honus Wagner told this story seven years after he retired.

On arriving at the local ballpark, we found some youngsters knocking flies. One of the kids was using a curious-looking bat, long, finely shaped, and of a peculiar red-brown color. I took it from him, examined it and discovered that, while it was very heavy, it balanced nicely in my hands. I slipped the boy a quarter for the loan of the bat, and we started the game, with the red stick and four others of the ordinary pattern, which had been secured by the admiring natives.

We never had to use the ordinary bats. That red one proved to be the proper medicine. Tap a fastball with the bat and it would go for two sacks, meet a curve and you could send it to the stands. With that bat a man who ordinarily hit .200 could swat over the .300 mark and I blush to think of the record I might have made with it.

All of us batted with that stick that day, rapping out about 28 hits during the game. Between innings I chatted with the youngster who owned the stick, and he explained that he had shaped it from an old table leg belonging to his grandfather. It was some strange Oriental wood, similar to mahogany, but much heavier and of firmer grain.

When the contest ended, I turned to find the boy, intending to hand him

good money for that bat, but the kid and bat were gone, apparently afraid that we intended stealing his bat. I never saw the boy again and, although I played in that town many times later on, he never came near the park. The mysterious bat, brimful of base hits, vanished the same afternoon that it appeared and its equal has never been discovered.[29]

One had to wonder if a few seasons batting over .400 and more National League batting titles could have been achieved by Honus Wagner had he secured this impeccable baseball bat made out of exotic Oriental wood.

◆ ◆ ◆

Throughout his long major league career, Honus Wagner was exposed to many greenhorn youngsters who dreamed of making the grade playing baseball. While some of these lads were very brash and self-confident about their ability, others tended to be more discreet and reserved. Two young men who were polar opposites in personality arrived on the scene one year apart for Pittsburgh in 1912 and 1913. Outfielder Walter "Wally" Rehg saw limited action for the Pirates in 1912, while fellow gardener Everett Booe appeared in 29 games in 1913. According to Honus Wagner, Rehg and Booe were as unlike as an ocean and a mill pond. Rehg was a live wire, possessing loads of the old pep and caring as little for umpires as a first-class burglar does for a policeman. Booe was a quiet chap who accepted things as they came.[30] Although the personalities of these two men were strikingly different, Rehg and Booe each angered veteran umpire Bill Klem on separate occasions.

Rehg's confrontation with Klem occurred during the morning game of the Decoration Day doubleheader at Forbes Field on May 30, 1912, which Pittsburgh lost to the St. Louis Cardinals, 8–3. The Pirates considered Rehg one of the freshest youngsters they had witnessed break into the major leagues in many years. Despite his arrogance, Rehg was loved by both veterans and youngsters alike from Pittsburgh's squad.[31] But Klem certainly was not enamored with that flippant attitude the first time he met the young Pirate when he stepped to the plate to pinch-hit for hurler Claude Hendrix.

"Who are you going to hit for?" asked Klem as Rehg approached home plate.

"I'm going to try to get one for myself, you big boob," responded Rehg.

"What is your name?" asked an irritated Klem.

"Rehg," answered the young recruit.

"How do you spell it?" queried Klem.

"You don't spell it, you simply whistle it through your nose," replied Rehg.[32]

Klem quickly became annoyed with Rehg's total lack of respect.[33] Once Klem realized that Rehg was hitting for Claude Hendrix, he announced this change to the crowd at Forbes Field.[34] After Rehg was retired, he continued to make so much noise from the bench that Klem decided to chase him. "Get off the field," bellowed Klem.

"Not a chance," answered Rehg. "This field belongs to Dreyfuss, not you. You are exceeding your authority. I refuse to leave."[35]

Rehg eventually did leave the dugout and retired to Pittsburgh's clubhouse.[36] This hostility between the Pirates and Klem carried over to the next day when they played Cincinnati at Forbes Field. Rehg was banished from the field for the second day in a row for making comments to Klem while working the coaching lines for Pittsburgh. Fred Clarke was also reprimanded for talking back to Klem. Clarke and the embattled umpire engaged in a jawing match that lasted five minutes. At one point, manager and umpire almost came to blows. Clarke's loud voice could be heard all over the ballpark, while Klem also made a lot of noise. The argument arose over Klem's claim that Pirates hurler Babe Adams was pitching illegally. Honus Wagner, who did not play in the game, was also ordered from the field after he disputed one of umpire Garnet Bush's calls.[37]

One of Wagner's closest friends and allies was visibly outraged over the decision to force him from the field. When he retreated to Pittsburgh's locker room, his dog, Jason Weatherby, who accompanied his master to Forbes Field on many occasions, wagged his tale and seemed to demand a reason for why Wagner had come into the clubhouse while the baseball game was still in progress. Wagner pointed to the umpire from the back door of the clubhouse, and within a few seconds, Forbes Field's spectators were being amused over the sight of Jason Weatherby running behind first base to register a kick. Jason voiced his opinion by growling some before he trotted out to right field. Umpire Bush thought

too much of his blue serge trousers to command the dog in any way. Even Klem, who feared no ballplayer in the National League, cringed when Wagner's dog growled. Both umpires were relieved when Jason Weatherby finally left the diamond and rejoined his master in Pittsburgh's clubhouse.[38]

One year later, Bill Klem believed he had come across another fresh youngster who was doing the bidding of Pirates teammates by exhibiting contempt for his umpiring decisions. Klem assumed he was about to have a confrontation with another young player like Walter Rehg, who had demonstrated a total lack of respect for him as an umpire. Klem did not realize that Everett Booe was a quiet man who seemed to be intimidated by his surroundings. The first time Klem met Booe during the 1913 campaign, it was under the same set of circumstances as when he had clashed with Rehg one year earlier. Booe had been selected by manager Fred Clarke to pinch-hit for one of Pittsburgh's pitchers.

"What's your name?" demanded Klem as he rushed toward Everett Booe.

"Booe," quietly answered Everett.

"Don't you boo me," said Klem, who was mad as a wet hen. "You're too fresh for a busher and in just about one second I'll ship you to the clubhouse."

"But Mister Klem," said Booe, "my name is Booe. I'm not trying to kid you."[39]

Once Bill Klem realized this youngster was telling him the truth, the veteran umpire responded by doing what he considered the only appropriate thing. Klem did something out of character for him by laughing heartily.[40]

◆　◆　◆

Young baseball players who did not know any better supplied endless entertainment and spiced things up for Honus Wagner and his teammates. In 1912 and 1913, he played the infield with two boisterous youngsters who were involved in a spirited battle for a spot on Pittsburgh's roster. Artie Butler was a utility player who could play each infield position but first base, while Jimmy Viox was mainly a second baseman. Butler and Voix joined Alex McCarthy as part of Pittsburgh's infield rotation before Butler was traded to the St. Louis Cardinals after

the 1913 campaign.[41] Wagner remembered a few instances that defined the friendly rivalry which existed between Butler and Viox.

> Before Butler was traded to the St. Louis Cardinals he played short for Pittsburgh. Arthur and Viox had a keen battle for a regular infield berth. One game Butler played short, Viox second. Artie fell chasing a Texas Leaguer. Next day he slipped on a wet field.
> "Down again," remarked Viox sarcastically.
> A few days later a ball took a bad bounce, hit Viox in the mouth, knocked two teeth out and put Jimmy on his back.
> "Who's down now, you fresh busher?" blurted Butler.
> "Yes, I'm down, but I was knocked down," replied Viox. "I didn't fall down like you."[42]

Viox had a stellar season as Pittsburgh's starting second baseman in 1913 and paced the club with a .317 average. Spitball hurler Claude Hendrix was expected to be the Pirates' staff ace that season after he had gone 24–9 with an ERA of 2.59 in 1912. Hendrix was a dreadful disappointment in 1913 as his record fell to 14–15, while his ERA rose to 2.84. When the Federal League came knocking at Hendrix's door in 1914, he abandoned Pittsburgh to play for the Chicago Chi-Feds. Although Hendrix had a rough year in 1913, he did finish strong during September. He defeated New York, Philadelphia and Chicago in succession, allowing a total of 12 hits and striking out 21 batters.[43] Even though he had handled major league competition, he did struggle against a team of minor leaguers during an exhibition game against the Louisville Colonels on September 30.

> "We stopped over at Louisville for an exhibition game," said Honus Wagner. "Barney Dreyfuss has a fondness in his heart for the old Kentucky burg, but he hates to have the Pirates beaten there. Hendrix, in the pink of condition, disposed of the Colonels in two innings and settled back to make it a nice, soft afternoon. In the third a couple of Jack Hayden's (Louisville's manager) boys rolled them off the fences.
> "Hendrix laughed, took a fresh quid of slippery elm, and sailed in again. But where the bats of major leaguers had failed the association chaps had a picnic. The harder they hit, the better it seemed that Hendrix pitched, but he got madder and redder with every ball. But that is the way it goes with pitchers, batters and clubs. A good minor league club can maul the best of twirlers, and a novice pitcher on his good day might shut out nine of the best players in the game."[44]

While Claude Hendrix was incensed over his misfortune against Louisville, he was able to joke about other embarrassing moments that

occurred during his two seasons playing for Pittsburgh. The tables were quickly turned against Hendrix in one instance during a game against the Philadelphia Phillies. He was pitching a great game, holding Philadelphia scoreless through seven innings. In the eighth frame, with two teammates on base, Phillies first baseman Fred Luderus hit a slow tapper toward the mound. Hendrix took hold of the moist side of the baseball and threw it. Unfortunately, the ball slipped from his grasp, sailed from the pitcher's box and smacked against the right field fence with a loud thud. Both of Philadelphia's runners scored as Hendrix stood on the mound, dazed and red as a beet, staring at the fence.[45]

"Fine stuff!" yelled Wagner furiously as he walked over to the mound and slammed his glove at his feet in disgust. "There goes our game."

"I know," Hendrix replied reflectively, still staring at the spot where the baseball had hit the fence, "but what did you think of that peg?"[46]

Life certainly was never dull for Honus Wagner and other members of the Pittsburgh Pirates as long as there were unique characters like Walter Rehg, Artie Butler, Jimmy Viox and Claude Hendrix around.

◆　◆　◆

Having fun on the baseball diamond and building camaraderie with teammates was only part of the equation for Honus Wagner, Fred Clarke and the Pittsburgh Pirates maintaining their excellence for more than a decade. Winning consistently against bitter rivals such as the New York Giants was the major goal that drove these men, and was even sweeter when they double-crossed a team that had stolen Pittsburgh's signals. While John McGraw once told Wagner that he was a very smart player, New York's manager had few superiors when it came to using his brain to win baseball games.[47] McGraw had no problem stealing signals from an opposing team to help New York to pull out a victory.

During one season, Honus Wagner and Pittsburgh's catchers used a specific signal to call a pitchout so the backstop could catch an opposing base runner napping at second base. In an early season game against the Giants, Wagner gave the signal for the pitchout and the throw to second base. Out of the corner of his eye, Wagner noticed that McGraw was moving around more than usual in the third base coaching box.

Pittsburgh's catcher threw the ball to second base after the pitch, but New York's base runner was nearly to third base by the time Wagner received the toss. Wagner realized that McGraw had stolen the sign and had signaled his base runner to take off for third base once the catcher started to throw the ball.

Late that season, Pittsburgh and New York were playing when this same situation arose. Wagner gave the signal to the catcher, glanced at McGraw, and saw that he was showing unusual activity in the third base coaching box. This time, Pittsburgh's catcher bluffed the throw to second base and instead gunned the baseball down to the hot corner. New York's base runner was a dead duck. They had used the same signal, but they had altered its interpretation in order to trick McGraw. McGraw, who knew he had been double-crossed, bowed to Wagner's strategic greatness and admitted that the Pirates were the smartest group of men in the league.[48]

Of course, things always seem to balance out in baseball. In 1915, Wagner fell for one of the game's oldest tricks in a loss against McGraw's Giants on July 24 at the Polo Grounds. Wagner was so mortified over his stupidity that he skipped his evening meal. He reached first base with a single. As Jimmy Viox stepped up to the plate, Wagner decided to get into scoring position by stealing second base. Not paying attention to what was going on at home plate, Wagner started running for second base as Viox's bat connected against a pitch. New York third baseman Hans Lobert raced toward shortstop as though he intended scooping up the baseball with his glove. Shortstop Art Fletcher, taking the cue from his teammate, hustled to second and began yelling to Lobert to "shoot it."[49]

Wagner figured that a ground ball had been hit and the Giants were trying to complete a double play. He turned on the jets and accelerated toward second base. It was not until he reached the keystone sack that he realized Viox had hit a pop fly to second baseman Fred Brainard. New York completed a double play when Brainard caught the baseball and flipped it to Fred Merkle at first base, doubling up Wagner.[50]

Eight years before Wagner was humiliated by the Giants, his shoddy play at shortstop had enraged Fred Clarke during a game against the Boston Doves on May 13, 1907, with the Pirates winning, 14–11. Clarke became a little worried when Boston rallied late in the game in an

While Honus Wagner was an expert batsman and the best player of his baseball era, this by no means meant that the Flying Dutchman did not make mistakes. On July 24, 1915, Wagner was duped by the Giants into dashing from first to second on a perceived ground ball although teammate Jimmy Viox had hit a popup to Giants second baseman Fred Brainard. An easy double play was the result (courtesy National Baseball Hall of Fame Library, Cooperstown, New York).

attempt to overhaul Pittsburgh's big lead.[51] His concern heightened when Wagner, who had played carelessly all afternoon, uncorked a wild throw from shortstop which soared ten feet over the first baseman's head and landed midway up the bleachers. This was too much for Clarke to bear as he came running in from left field, yelling the whole time. Wagner grinned, sauntered over to second base, and stood on his head on the bag. Evidently, Pittsburgh's star player was attempting to atone for his indiscretion through this exhibition of chastened humility.[52] This gesture also gave Wagner an opportunity to view the game of baseball he so loved from a different perspective.

6

Ham Hyatt's Slugging Prowess, a Battle with Turkey Mike and Jimmy Viox's Mad Dash

Honus Wagner interacted with many players and gained friends for life with the Louisville Colonels and Pittsburgh Pirates. Playing for more than two decades allowed him to experience many spectacular things and witness great moments on the baseball diamond. For years, baseball writers sought out Wagner's insight and perspective regarding his days as the National League's top star. While he always downplayed his accomplishments, he loved to talk about teammates who had made an impression upon him. He even had a special place in his heart for a role player whose contribution during Pittsburgh's championship season in 1909 did not go unnoticed by Dutch and his teammates.

Robert Hamilton "Ham" Hyatt debuted for the Pittsburgh Pirates in 1909. A powerful hitter who was capable of crushing the baseball, Hyatt did not see much action as a regular that season due to being a defensive liability. He played six games in the outfield and two at first base, and made 40 appearances as a pinch-hitter. He batted .299 and played most of Game Seven of the 1909 World Series against the Detroit Tigers when Bobby Byrne was forced from the contest after a collision at third base on a steal attempt in the first inning. Hyatt developed into one of baseball's most proficient pinch-hitters with the Pirates in 1909–1910 and from 1912–1914 (he played for the American Association's Kansas City squad in 1911). Honus Wagner always marveled at Hyatt's ability to perform so impeccably within this difficult role as Pittsburgh's clutch pinch-hitter.

The Pirates, at one time, had one of the best pinch hitters in the game. This fellow not only banged out singles, but had the power to pole the ball out

92

of the lot. He took great pride in his pinch-hitting ability. He was slow, however, and this prevented him from becoming a star outfielder or first baseman. He was used for only pinch-hitting and utility roles.

This pinch hitter was a Dr. Jekyll and Mr. Hyde personality. If he managed to get a hit, a walk or score a run as a pinch hitter, nothing was too good for his wife. He would bring ice cream and cake home, or even a new dress for his wife. But if he failed in the pinch, heaven help the wife. He would come home empty-handed and sometimes wouldn't even eat his dinner. The Mrs. would have to scout around for her own meal.

When he broke into the big leagues, about 1909, it wasn't long before he was known as the "Fire Engine," once he reached first base. He believed everyone should get out of his way. His sturdy physique made him fearless. On one occasion against St. Louis, Miller Huggins had the ball and was waiting for this fellow in his attempt to steal second base. He crashed into the tiny Huggins and Miller was knocked down and lost the ball. He kept on going and didn't even stop when he bowled over the third baseman. He was declared out for interference during his wild running. This utility player was Ham Hyatt.[1]

The greatest feat that Hyatt accomplished which left a lasting impression on Wagner happened to be the only home run this left-handed heavy hitter smacked at Forbes Field. Wagner was on first base when Hyatt hit a ninth-inning bomb over the right field fence against Chicago Cubs hurler Bert Humphries on May 29, 1913. The home run, which was the longest hit in Forbes Field up to that point, tied the game before Pittsburgh pushed another run across home plate to secure a 5–4 victory.[2] Wagner always claimed the baseball shot out of Forbes Field like a cannonball. For many years, old-time Pirates fans argued over whether the baseball eventually hit a building a block away from the ballpark, or the street beyond that structure. Wagner always considered Hyatt to be one of the most powerful hitters he came across during his major league career.[3]

While Ham Hyatt was an important member of the Pittsburgh Pirates for five seasons, he entered a vital profession after his baseball career ended that involved selfless public service. Following his retirement from baseball, Hyatt became a motorcycle policeman in the state of Washington.[4]

◆　◆　◆

Besides being a pinch-hitter extraordinaire, Ham Hyatt loved to play poker with Honus Wagner and other Pirates during long train rides.

Hyatt enjoyed immersing himself in a friendly five-cent ante game. He always came back for more even though he seldom won and was a hard loser. At times, it appeared to be downright dangerous for a teammate whose hand beat Hyatt's, who would rant, rave and storm to the point that the fellow who beat him usually wished he had not held the winning hand. One night during a September trip from St. Louis to Chicago in 1914, Hyatt was in a surprisingly good mood although he was losing as usual. In spite of his misfortune, Hyatt did not utter one harsh or inconsiderate comment. The other players remained confused until rookie pitcher Al Mamaux came along to view Hyatt's card-playing expertise.

"How are you doing, Ham?" Mamaux asked.

"Oh, 'bout four dollars out," Hyatt responded nonchalantly.

"Thasso?" barked Mamaux, "Well get out of that; I'll play my own money."[5]

Al Mamaux's naivety certainly had not served him well in this instance. He learned the important lesson that if he wanted to lose four dollars playing five-cent ante poker, he should play himself rather than bankrolling Ham Hyatt.

Some rookies tended to be impressionable when teammates or their manager made requests or issued orders on the baseball diamond. Honus Wagner recalled the time when a young recruit for the Boston Doves took manager Fred Lake's sarcastic instructions much too literally. Lake managed Boston for only one season in 1910 when the Doves finished in last place with a 53–100 record, 50½ games behind the pennant-winning Chicago Cubs. On May 13, Lake secured outfielder Roy "Doc" Miller's services from those Cubs in a trade involving pitcher Lew Richie.

Boston played the Pirates shortly after Doc Miller joined the Doves. In one of the games, Miller performed like a "house afire" according to Wagner and was a constant menace all afternoon. Trailing by one run late in the game against hurler Howard Camnitz, the Doves had the bases loaded with two out. It was Miller's turn to bat. Miller, standing near the dugout in front of Fred Lake swinging a couple bats, itching to get the chance to smash the ball, turned toward his manager and put forward a very candid question. "What'll I do up there now?"

"What'll I do when there are three men on base and two out?" Lake retorted sarcastically. "One run will tie the score and two will win. What'll you do? Why if I were you, I'd go up there and strike out."

"All right, sir," replied Miller.[6]

Honus Wagner had a front row seat of these proceedings from his shortstop position. Wagner later explained what happened next as Miller prepared to follow his manager's orders explicitly.

> He marched up to the plate, took three healthy swings and missed the ball each time and he then marched back to the bench. It is unnecessary for me to add that Lake was in a terrible rage and said some things that can't be printed on this page. The recruit was silent and took the "call" without a murmur. Finally, when Lake was out of breath and sulphurous language the kid said: "Well, Mister Lake, I did as you ordered—didn't I?"[7]

Embarrassing incidents were not restricted to youngsters breaking into the major leagues who did not know any better. Even a veteran player like Sam "The Goshen Schoolmaster" Leever sometimes exhibited bad judgment when he took a situation for granted. Leever played 13 seasons for the Pirates from 1898 to 1910. A four-time 20-game winner, his best year occurred during Pittsburgh's pennant-winning season in 1903 when he posted a 25–7 record and topped the National League with a 2.06 ERA. Although Leever was a mainstay of Fred Clarke's pitching staff for many years, he and battery-mate George Gibson did make an egregious mistake on one occasion that Honus Wagner reflected upon five years after Leever pitched in his last major league game.

> I am reminded of a good joke on George Gibson, a catcher with our club, and the veteran Sam Leever, who once pitched for the Pirates. These men once figured in an incident that is uncommon to ball players—that of taking it too much for granted on a rainy day in New York that it would be raining in Brooklyn. Gibby and Sam roomed together and we were at a New York hotel. A doubleheader was scheduled with the Dodgers. Leever was due to pitch and Gibson, of course, was our mainstay behind the bat.[8]

Confusion over where it was actually raining in New York ended up plaguing Leever and Gibson on this afternoon. Shortly after the two men had eaten lunch, a telephone operator rang the room and notified Pittsburgh's battery that the game was off, thinking of the one at the Polo Grounds. "Yes," remarked Leever as he looked out his hotel room window. "It's pouring down right now."[9]

Figuring that their doubleheader against Brooklyn had been postponed, Leever and Gibson contemplated how they were going to spend this unexpected leisure time. Leever decided to make the trip down to

Battery Park so he could visit some old friends, while Gibson planned on doing nothing more strenuous than relaxing in the hotel room in his underwear. An hour later, Gibson was called to the telephone once again. He was surprised when he heard the voice of Fred Clarke on the other end of the line. "For the love of Mike, are you and Sam ever coming over here to help us win this ball game?" shrieked Clarke.

"Why, Cap, it's pouring rain right now," answered Gibson. "What are you trying to do, kid me?"

"You poor lobster, if I had you here now I'd show you how much I was kidding," replied Clarke. "Will you try to remember that you are in New York and we are playing a game in Brooklyn at this moment."[10]

Gibson hung up the phone and sprang into action. He grabbed his trousers from the bottom so hurriedly that his watch and money flew out and rattled all over the room. This did not deter him from finishing the task at hand as he pulled up his trousers, threw on his coat, grabbed his hat and dashed out of the room. Gibson made it to Washington Park in record time and was able to get into the middle of that first game against Brooklyn. Poor Sam Leever was oblivious to the fact that he, too, should have been in uniform at Washington Park. Around four in the afternoon, while he walked down Park Row, he looked up at one of the bulletin boards to see what the Chicago Cubs had done that day. Leever became puzzled when he noticed the second block, which showed: Brooklyn 4, Pittsburgh 3.

"Ah shucks," exclaimed Leever to himself, "that's yesterdays' score."[11]

While Sam Leever was a dependable and diligent hurler for manager Fred Clarke and the Pirates, he certainly was not perfect. Leever and teammate George Gibson were the victims of misinformation about a rain-out at Brooklyn. Believing he had a free afternoon, Leever visited some friends in Battery Park and missed a doubleheader against the Superbas (courtesy National Baseball Hall of Fame Library, Cooperstown, New York).

This self-assurance lasted for only a few seconds until Leever peered at the bulletin board more thoroughly and noticed the lettering "First Game" next to the Pittsburgh-Brooklyn score. It finally dawned on Leever this score was from a game that afternoon. Although he felt like he wanted to jump off the Brooklyn Bridge, it was too late to do anything about this mistake now. He decided to enjoy himself the remainder of the afternoon and face the music later. Fred Clarke certainly made a big kick over Leever's stupidity once he confronted his pitcher. During the remainder of Pittsburgh's time in Gotham, Leever devoted his free time trying to find that telephone girl who had told him it was raining without specifying New York and adding that it was dry as tinder in Brooklyn.[12]

It is likely that Clarke was not willing to place any blame on this telephone girl.

◆ ◆ ◆

While Fred Clarke certainly was angry over Sam Leever's and George Gibson's error regarding rainy weather, the Pirates manager probably would have been seething if his two players had made this mistake when Pittsburgh was scheduled to play the New York Giants. Games between Pittsburgh and New York always brought out the best in every player from these two teams. While New York, Pittsburgh and the Chicago Cubs were involved in the tight 1908 pennant race, Honus Wagner and Giants outfielder Mike Donlin also found themselves embroiled in a battle for the league batting title. Wagner had already been crowned as the National League's batting champion five times. Donlin had never paced the circuit in hitting and was anxious to do so. Since Donlin had signed to appear on the vaudeville stage after the 1908 season, he reasoned that a batting title on his resume would help make him a better drawing card on the theater circuit.[13]

Donlin's chances of winning the batting title were looking pretty good until Honus Wagner and his Pirates rolled into the Polo Grounds on July 24. More concerned over the importance of this series since Pittsburgh currently was in first place, two games ahead of New York, Wagner was not worried about the batting race. His attitude changed a bit after Donlin started riding Pittsburgh's pitchers, telling them how he planned on doing heavy damage at the plate. This infuriated the Pirates hurlers, who told Wagner to keep on hitting. They vowed to bear down

and take care of the boastful Donlin in easy fashion. The interest of baseball fans in New York and Pittsburgh was profound since scribes had written about how the two leading players in the batting championship would be going head to head.[14]

When this series began, Donlin was batting .336, while Wagner checked in with a mark of .324. The tables quickly turned in Wagner's favor as he went on a rampage, going 9–for–12 in the first three games and raising his average to .340. Donlin, on the other hand, faltered horribly, with an anemic 1–for–11 showing that dropped his average to .328. The second game of this series on July 25, which Pittsburgh won over New York, 7–2, was the critical turning point for Wagner, who rapped out five hits that afternoon. Baseball statistics guru Al Munro Elias was in attendance at the Polo Grounds as Wagner put a psychological stranglehold on the batting race. The man who was responsible for compiling all of the hitting, pitching and fielding statistics for major league baseball explained how Wagner broke Donlin's spirit that fateful day in New York.[15]

> I'll always remember the day the Pirates came to New York when Wagner and Donlin were only separated by a point or so. The first time Honus came to bat he laced out a two-base hit, and as he pulled up at second he looked out to Donlin and held up one finger, Mike just looked back and scowled.
> Wagner's next trip to the plate resulted in another scorching hit and this time he waved two fingers at Mike. Then came a third wallop and a fourth and a fifth, each accompanied by the pantomime, as Honus rubbed it into his rival.
> By this time Donlin was so mad he was purple in the face and it didn't help him any when he was able to make only one hit in four or five times at bat. The upshot of it was that Wagner left New York sporting a big lead, which he never relinquished.[16]

Honus Wagner never looked back as he won his sixth batting title with a .354 batting average. Mike Donlin finished second in the Senior Circuit with a mark of .334. Donlin was so upset over his inability to match Wagner during the crucial July series at the Polo Grounds that he was involved in a confrontation with an unhappy Giants fan during one of the games. Someone in the overflow crowd jeered him about Wagner's superior batting dominance. Donlin became so enraged that he finally dove into the crowd to gain his revenge against the insolent spectator.[17] Wagner believed that Donlin, who later became his teammate

in 1912, was one of the hardest losers he ever met during his time in baseball. Whether it was performing on the baseball diamond or playing a friendly game of cards, Donlin could not tolerate anything short of total victory.

> Mike Donlin was another hard loser. Mike wanted to win in everything all the time and it mattered not what the stakes were. At pool, billiards, baseball, cards or anything else, even down to an argument, Mike was a hard loser. To win was glory for him. He would sit in a friendly card game where the stakes were next to nothing and he would fight the cards and his friends and then take them out to dinner.
>
> One night in Boston in the year Mike was with us the boys played fan-tan for 10 cents a corner. A man could not win or lose a dollar on that basis in 24 hours. Mike could not stand for a bonehead play on the diamond or in the card room, and when one chap passed a seven-spot and forfeited Mike's play so that he lost a 40-cent pot he was furious. It wasn't the 40 cents that riled him so much as the loss of the game and the way he lost it. After berating everybody, he cooled down and asked the boys out for a lunch that cost more than Mike could have won or lost playing fan-tan for a month.[18]

According to Wagner, misfortune sometimes followed Donlin on the diamond even on days when he excelled at his craft. Wagner always liked to hearken back to the game at the Polo Grounds on June 15, 1912, to hammer home this point. Although Donlin cranked out four hits against his former team and drove in four runs as Pittsburgh prevailed, 5–4, he was thrown out trying to take an extra base on each hit. Wagner claimed that Donlin was thrown out twice trying to stretch singles into doubles, was gunned down at third after he decided not to settle for a double, and then came up just a bit short at home plate when he tried to stretch a triple into an inside-the-park home run. Wagner also stated that Fred Snodgrass was responsible for retiring Donlin on three of these occasions when he should have been making a play to catch the lead runner.[19]

While recalling this game, Honus Wagner was right about one thing and incorrect about a few others. Donlin was retired four times in the game, but Snodgrass had no hand in any play. Left fielder Josh Devore was responsible for throwing Donlin out at third and home, while he was also tagged out at third base in the seventh inning trying to advance on Wagner's ground ball to Buck Herzog. Since he went 4-for-5 in the game, New York pitcher Doc Crandall was able to retire him on one

occasion.[20] Over 20,000 New York fans cheered wildly throughout the rainy afternoon for their former favorite son, who was making his first appearance at the Polo Grounds that season. Always the grand showman, Donlin profoundly bowed to the crowd after smacking each of his four hits.[21]

◆　◆　◆

Winning was always the foremost thing on the minds of players like Honus Wagner and Mike Donlin, who helped define what the game of baseball was all about during the first two decades of the twentieth century. While conditions were very primitive for those who competed during Wagner's era, players continued to strive toward excellence despite many hardships because they had a genuine love for the game of baseball. When Wagner was asked in 1915 to comment on how the game had changed in the past ten years, he intimated that legions of players had always persevered since baseball was more than just a game to them. It was a way of life.

> What do I think about baseball conditions today, so far as the playing end is concerned, compared with those of 10 years ago? Well, let me go back in my mind 10 years and try to show you what a change there has been.
>
> I remember as if it were this minute the first time the team I was a member of was ordered South in the spring to get into physical condition. Some of the players got on the railroad train with their baggage wrapped in newspapers, and they carried their uniforms, shoes, gloves, etc., in what is known as a uniform roll.
>
> We had no trainers in those days, and there was no hot shower, for the players after practice, unless it was a rubber hose attached to a water plug. Instead of tile or concrete floors we stood in a wooden tub—a regular old-fashioned washtub—and splashed ourselves with water, often cold, as best we could. After finishing our "shower" we were compelled to use a "family towel," for seldom were there more than two or three bath towels for the entire team of 25 or more men.
>
> Oil lamps were used in clubhouses and frequently in the hotels, although occasionally we did strike an inn where they had gas. Sometimes we had to travel all night, or the greater part of a night in a day coach, for Pullmans were a luxury then. But the players did not growl when they had to carry their own baggage a mile or more from the station to the hotel after sitting up all night in a day coach. It did not matter if we had to play three games of ball in a day, we were out there playing and doing our best to win, for we liked baseball.[22]

Wagner's longevity was due to a strong work ethic, his fondness for nature and his roving disposition. According to Pittsburgh baseball writer James Jerpe, Wagner's philosophy of eating what he wanted to and enjoying the outdoors provided the perfect recipe for a long, successful career. "When a man of his natural physique can eat what he wants," said Jerpe, "drink what he wants and do what he pleases in the open air all the year around, it isn't any real wonder that he prolongs his athletic career and stands off the slowness and staleness that come to the best of them as the years go by."[23]

Wagner certainly fit into the category of being a meat-and-potatoes type of guy. He preferred the simplest kind of fare and plenty of it when mealtime rolled around. If the Pirates were staying at the Waldorf-Astoria in New York, he would ignore such delicacies as lobster a la Newburgh, pate de fois gras and crab ravigote to feast on ham accompanied by an appropriate side dish depending on whether he was eating breakfast, lunch or dinner.[24] Wagner explained how his unregimented training method, which was similar to that of friend and teammate Fred Clarke, served him well throughout his major league career.

I have no regular method of training. I do not deprive myself of anything I want. I eat when I'm hungry and go to bed when I am sleepy.

What may be one man's meat may be another man's poison, so I would not attempt to tell what I eat and how much I eat. Some young fellow might arrange his bill of fare after my model and "eat him out of baseball." But I have found that plain, wholesome food, as much as I want of it and whenever I want it, has agreed with me thoroughly. So far as the sleeping goes, I seldom am out very late at night and get up plenty early in the morning. I have been getting up early for many years, and am used to it and enjoy it.

When the baseball season closes I do not go out of training; that is, I do not sit around and get fat and lazy. I spend a great deal of time climbing over the hills. I walk quite a distance each day. My favorite pastimes are hunting and fishing and in enjoying them I get plenty of walking. A fellow who can enjoy hunting as I do will walk 20 miles, carrying a gun, and not once think he's tired.

Then, when the weather becomes too severe for outdoor exercise and sports, I play basketball, and let me tell you there is no exercise better calculated to make a man physically alert at all times, and if you have any surplus weight on you basketball will take it off in a hurry. You must be in good condition to play basketball. The man who hasn't the wind who gets leg-weary won't last five minutes in the cage.

When the time for reporting at the training camp comes round in the

spring, I am in condition. I take part in all the work outlined by the manager, and do just what the recruits and regulars do. But I am not bothered with aching arms and legs. I rather like the workouts in the South. They are mild to me after my strenuous life during the winter months.[25]

While Honus Wagner's off-season activities were similar to those of blue collar workers who labored in factories throughout western Pennsylvania, he pointed out the key difference between a steel worker and a baseball player. "The former only has to please his boss," said Wagner. "The latter may satisfy his manager, but he has to do his work each day before thousands of critics, who are quick to pick slight flaws in the work and blame it on his age and condition."[26]

◆　◆　◆

While many baseball careers were ruined due to individuals not putting in the necessary work through training or good personal habits, some players never reached their full potential due to a love of the night life and bouts of excessive drinking. One man who contradicted this theory was Rube Waddell, a teammate of Honus Wagner's for one full baseball campaign and parts of three other seasons in Louisville and Pittsburgh. Wagner believed that Waddell was a curious sort. Although he thought Waddell was a pest at times, Wagner claimed one could not help liking this eccentric fellow who furnished so many laughs during his illustrious career. Wagner marveled at Waddell's ability to endure in the game despite his penchant for drinking even though the prevailing wisdom was that southpaws did not last very long.[27]

Players who were classified as lushes usually did not continue in the baseball business for any great length of time. Wagner reasoned that being both left-handed and intoxicated, Waddell's career should have been very brief. Wagner also believed that Waddell's most interesting characteristic was his artistic sense of executing "the touch." Waddell was never known to pay for anything, anywhere, under any set of circumstances. For years, it was a mystery regarding what he actually did with the money he earned playing baseball. Waddell would touch up someone, asking for money, within ten minutes of being introduced to that person, and he was so artistic at executing the touch that he usually got away with it. Since Waddell never repaid his debts, Wagner was smart enough to leave his money at home when he visited the southpaw

hurler on one occasion many years after Fred Clarke had sent him packing.[28]

> One winter, not so long ago, I had nothing to do and took a notion that I would run up to Butler, Pa., where the Rube lives, and which is not very far from Pittsburgh. The Rube, when not engaged in elevating the stage or tending bar, and during intervals of his frequent marriages and divorces, lives near Butler, and lives with, also off, his father—a fine old farmer, rich and pretty shrewd.
>
> Mr. Waddell was dead glad to see me and suggested that we go out and paint up the town of Butler. I couldn't see it, mainly because I had thoughtfully forgotten to bring any money and had bought a round-trip railroad ticket when I started. I knew that if I had any coin the Rube would borrow it and how could I refuse a gentleman who was offering me the hospitality of his home?
>
> When I explained to the Rube that I had forgotten my wallet, he was stuck for a few minutes and then began to figure out ways and means of touching his father. At last a great thought dawned upon him, and, dragging me along, he marched into the sitting room, where the old gentleman was reading the weekly paper.
>
> "Father," said Mr. Waddell, Jr., very respectfully, "I have some very important business to transact over in Butler, and Mr. Wagner will go over there with me. Let me have $20—I will need about that amount before I get home."
>
> Mr. Waddell, Sr., looked upon his son with a doubtful eye. "See here, George Edward," spoke the old gentleman. "I gave you $10 only last night. Where has that money gone to already?"
>
> "Father," answered the Rube most earnestly, "you remember that pair of pants I had out in the barn—to do the stable work in? Well, I thought I could use those pants for a bank to put my nest-egg in. So I put the $10 in the pants. Last night, father, you, in the kindness of your heart, told a tramp he could sleep in the barn. Father, that wicked tramp stole those pants and my nest-egg with them!"
>
> The old gentleman, shaking his head, coughed up the $20—and then Rube had $30 with which to paint the town.[29]

Southpaw hurlers kept life interesting for Honus Wagner and his Pirates teammates. Rookie left-hander Sherrod "Sherry" Smith, the youngster who in 1911 had eaten much more at one meal than the allotted one dollar Fred Clarke doled out to each player, did not understand the nuances of traveling by train as the Pirates journeyed to their spring training site. Smith was a raw prospect who believed he could work his way out of trouble on the mound by blazing away even faster when opposing batters hit him hard. This prevented the lad from ever making

103

his mark with the Pirates. Smith was also a bit unrefined in respect to proper protocol while enjoying the amenities of railroad travel. He had never been in a sleeping car. Traveling to Hot Springs to begin the 1911 spring training session, Smith blockaded the aisle of the team's car with bats, bags and all kinds of luggage.[30]

"Get out of the way, you Alabama busher," yelled a teammate.

"Yep, I'll get out of the way," replied Smith defiantly, "when someone tells me where I can find Down Berth 6."[31]

If Rube Waddell were a member of the 1911 Pittsburgh Pirates, he would have been more than happy to show Smith the way to Down Berth 6 if the rookie was willing to lend him some money.

◆ ◆ ◆

Spring training could become tedious as players anxiously awaited the start of another baseball campaign. Practice and exhibition games may have sharpened each man's skills leading up to the season, but these contests did not produce the same kind of excitement and anticipation as a mid-summer tilt against a bitter rival. During Honus Wagner's time as a player, the regular season was also loaded with exhibition contests against minor league and independent teams, college squads and local baseball aggregations. While players usually took a casual approach in these exhibitions, the games were beneficial from a public relations standpoint because fans in various towns and cities were exposed to major league baseball.

Since most major leaguers had a laid-back attitude in exhibition games, baseball rooters sometimes were treated to humorous displays. These major leaguers were more than willing to teach a disrespectful youngster from the other team a lesson. Such an incident occurred in 1912 when the Pirates played an exhibition game on August 11 against an independent team called the Long Branch Cubans. The New Jersey team featured numerous Cuban players, including pitcher Dolf Luque (who was referred to as Lugui in that day's box score) and catcher Mike Gonzalez, both of whom eventually had successful major league careers.[32] Long Branch's left fielder did not waste any time criticizing the Pirates and enraged Bobby Byrne and Jimmy Viox by constantly quarreling with them.[33] Honus Wagner explained how the Pirates eventually gained revenge against this bad-mannered adversary.

The Cuban player in left field was fresh in the way he talked to some of us and he made Viox particularly sore. The time came in the game when Viox had a chance to show him up and he did. Jimmy hit a long home run into the bushes in left field and this Cuban was so busy trying to find the ball he couldn't see what was going on.

Viox went around the bases once and then while this Cuban was still scratching in the weeds Jimmy started around the second time. The Cuban came up out of the bushes just about the time Jimmy got past second base on his second time around. He threw the ball on a line to home plate and then tore madly in toward the diamond. The Cuban catcher was in on the joke and he took the ball and pinned it on Jimmy ten feet from the plate.

Then the umpire helped out by calling Jimmy safe. The way that Cuban left fielder did rant and explode Spanish cuss words at us big leaguers and the umpire for the rest of the game was funny, for no one put him wise and just let him go on making a fool of himself.[34]

Mike Gonzalez was the catcher who gladly participated in this little joke at the expense of the Long Branch outfielder.[35] Following a solid season for the Cubans in 1913 when he batted .333, Gonzalez joined the Cincinnati Reds one year later. Pitcher Dolf Luque also made the jump to the National League in 1914 after he went 22–5 in 1913.

As the 1913 baseball campaign was winding down, Pittsburgh was thwarted during an October exhibition game by a hurler who had a brief stint with the Chicago Cubs in 1911. Cyril "Cy" Slapnicka was brilliant for the American Association's Milwaukee Brewers in 1913, appearing in 47 games and going 25–14 for the pennant winners. Slapnicka was equally dazzling against the Pirates on October 3 as he struck out six and defeated Pittsburgh, 5–4.[36]

This trip to Milwaukee was an interesting experience for Honus Wagner. He had not been in the city 15 minutes before he was invited to inspect all of the area breweries. Since the Pirates were locked into temperance clauses within their contracts that year, Wagner declined the invitations, saying, "beer vats might have proved tempting for a cold plunge that hot day."[37] Devoted baseball rooters throughout Milwaukee were excited over the opportunity to watch baseball's greatest player for the first time. Of the 7,296 fans in attendance at Athletic Park, about 7,000 of them were Germans who cheered for Wagner. They shouted at him from the stands in German, and once or twice he provoked laughter and wild applause by answering in that language.[38]

During his long career, Wagner always professed that experience

and a cool head would prevent a batter from being flustered by anything that he heard in the crowd. On this afternoon, he did fall victim to the funniest German rooter he had ever heard in his life.

> On my second trip up the bases were full with two out and the crowd was frantic. They did not know whether to pull for me to hit or for Slapnicka to strike me out. One fat German who had evidently worried over the thing finally struck a happy compromise between me, himself and Milwaukee's chances, and he cried out:
> "Hey, Honus, don't sthrike oudt, but make for us a long oudt."
> A long fly was his way of sparing me from disgrace. I laughed so hard the more I thought of it that Slapnicka had no trouble striking me out.[39]

Rather than manage the Pirates from the dugout, Fred Clarke watched this game along with his wife from a field box near the bench since it was his 41st birthday. While Pittsburgh newspapers reported that Mrs. Clarke was the first person to offer her husband many happy returns of the day, these publications did not mention whether Honus Wagner and John "Dots" Miller had plotted strategy or cursed while speaking German.[40]

◆ ◆ ◆

Honus Wagner was always more comfortable talking about baseball in a quiet, one-on-one setting, rather than speaking in front of a group of people. Unfortunately, his status as baseball's top player meant that he was constantly considered a hot property on the banquet circuit. While he was very deft at dodging public speaking functions, he was corralled at times to give speeches at such events. On one occasion when Pittsburgh was playing an exhibition game in St. Joseph, Missouri, he was coerced into saying a few words at a banquet given by the town's chamber of commerce honoring the Pirates. Wagner, who had made up his mind that he would make the best of this situation, carefully rehearsed what he was going to say at this banquet.[41]

> I was going over my speech in my mind all through the meal, and thought I had it down pat when I heard the toastmaster introducing me. I got to my feet and then for the life of me I couldn't think of a word I had intended to speak. I was standing there like a ship without a steering wheel, and finally realized that I'd have to put something across. I began something like: "I don't know what to talk about, but—"
> "Then sit down!" Chick Fraser shouted loud enough for every person in the banquet hall to hear.
> I didn't say another word, but sat right down.[42]

Although Honus Wagner was reluctant to discuss baseball and his career within certain venues, he felt inclined to talk about the game in enough instances so that newspapers were able to chronicle personal insights as told from his perspective. In most instances, Wagner made a concerted effort to avoid boasting about his great accomplishments. Of course, this did not mean that the words of other players were not used to offer proof that he was baseball's pre-eminent player. As Wagner's career was winding down, former Chicago Cub and current Boston Braves player Johnny Evers made an interesting revelation in a letter offering birthday salutations. Evers told Wagner he had copied and learned a lot from him during his career. Evers' only regret seemed to be that he had not adhered to Wagner's principles of good sportsmanship and fair play on the ball field.[43]

"I am sorry I didn't pattern after you in that respect," wrote Evers.[44]

In Johnny Evers' defense, most baseball players did fall short in that regard.

7

Tommy Leach, Truck Eagan, Bill McKechnie and Other Teammates

A great debate raged throughout the first decade of the twentieth century regarding who was baseball's greatest player. For years, people supported either Honus Wagner or Cleveland's Napoleon "Nap" Lajoie. This discussion became more complicated when Ty Cobb broke in with the Detroit Tigers in 1905 and won his first American League batting title two years later. Wagner, Lajoie and Cobb each possessed sterling credentials that substantiated any endorsement which crowned these three men as the game's greatest player. However, there was never any argument over Honus Wagner being the National League's top performer.

Having this title thrust upon him never altered Wagner's belief that baseball was a team game where success was achieved due to all nine players working together. While he was one of the greatest who ever played baseball, Pittsburgh's success from 1900–1909 was not solely rooted in the accomplishments of one player. The Pirates certainly would not have captured National League pennants in 1901, 1902, 1903 and 1909 without solid performers who complemented Wagner on the diamond, men like Jack Chesbro, Deacon Phillippe, Sam Leever, Claude Ritchey, Vic Willis and Ginger Beaumont.

From 1901 to 1911, Honus Wagner, Fred Clarke and Tommy Leach were considered the top trio in baseball. Leach was Wagner's teammate from the time he debuted for the Louisville Colonels in 1898 until he was traded to the Chicago Cubs on May 30, 1912. He was a consistent performer who played both third base and the outfield. Adept at legging out doubles and triples due to his blazing speed, Leach also led the

National League in home runs in 1902 with six. While Wagner and Clarke both burst on the baseball scene in a blaze of glory, Leach had to experience some growing pains before achieving his status as an elite player.

When Leach broke into the major leagues, young players who dreamed of making a name for themselves faced overwhelming obstacles. He was a diminutive player who stood five feet, six-and-one-half inches tall, and weighed around 135 pounds. Breaking in as a rookie was difficult enough without small stature being a possible hindrance as well. "When I broke into the National League it was a case of fight your way in—and I mean fight," said Leach. "We had to furnish our own bats, as well as gloves and shoes, and the only batting practice a rookie could get was to squeeze it in somewhere between morning practice and the afternoon game. And then you almost had to bribe somebody to pitch to you."[1]

After appearing in three late-season games for Louisville in 1898, Leach was finally given an opportunity by Fred Clarke in 1899 to start at third base. Leach, who was excited about his big chance, banged out two hits with the same bat he had used for the New York State League's Auburn Maroons one year earlier. Believing he would take batting practice with the regulars, Leach arrived at the ballpark early the following morning but found that his bat had been sawed into three pieces which were lying at the bottom of his locker. He never found out who the prankster was. While such problems were eradicated once Leach became an established star, he did continue to have difficulty gaining admittance into various National League ballparks. It seemed that gate attendants at baseball grounds throughout the country did not believe he was really a player.[2]

> When I first came into the league, we still dressed in our hotels and made the trip to the ballpark in a bus. New York was the exception; they already had a dressing room for the visiting players, and when we played the Giants we used to get into uniform right up there at the Polo Grounds.
> As most players were fairly good-sized fellows, I used to wait for some of the older Pirates and go into the park with them. However, one day the other men got in ahead of me, and I boldly approached the player's gate with my uniform roll tucked under my arm. The man stopped me and asked: "Whose uniform are you carrying?"
> I told him it was my own. That annoyed him and he said: "Just for being

From 1901 to 1911, Fred Clarke, Tommy Leach and Honus Wagner (left to right) were considered the top trio in baseball. While Clarke and Wagner were immediate successes when they broke into the major leagues, Leach's path to greatness was a little rockier. Early in his career, some gate attendants at National League parks mistook him for a little runt who was trying to sneak into the ballpark (courtesy National Baseball Hall of Fame Library, Cooperstown, New York).

a fresh kid, I won't let you in, and you can stay there until the owner of the uniform comes out for it."

I tried to get him to send someone to the clubhouse to identify me, but he merely laughed. He still thought I was trying some trick to get in without paying. I must have been out there nearly an hour, when one of the New York players who came along late, passed through the gate. I told him my troubles, and the gateman finally let me in, though he still wouldn't believe I was a ballplayer.

When I finally got into the park, Fred Clarke asked: "Where the devil have you been? I ought to fine you for being late." I'll tell you I never tried to go through that New York gate alone after that.[3]

Since he was known as "Wee" Tommy Leach throughout his career, it's not surprising that some people mistook him during his early baseball days for a brazen little runt who was trying to sneak into the ballpark.

◆　◆　◆

Tommy Leach became Pittsburgh's starting third baseman in 1901 when Jimmy Williams, who had handled duties at the hot corner the previous year, jumped to the American League's Baltimore Orioles. As a utility infielder for the Pirates in 1900, Leach had appeared in 51 games and batted .213. Becoming a starter in 1901 certainly did wonders for him as he posted an average of .305. Rookie Charles "Truck" Eagan received an opportunity to be the team's utility infielder. Eagan, who had played for the Sacramento Gilt Edges of the California League in 1900, was released on May 5, 1901. When Eagan's name came up during a fanning bee at team headquarters in 1904, Barney Dreyfuss offered a simple explanation for why Eagan never made it with Pittsburgh: "The trouble when with us was that he had too strong an arm."[4]

One old-time baseball fan claimed that Eagan was one of the best men in scooping up a ground ball that he had seen in many years. During his short time playing for the Pirates, Eagan was a well-liked guy who became friends with every member of the team. Honus Wagner took a fancy to this youngster from San Francisco and decided to pull a standard joke on Eagan that he played on many rookies. While the team was in St. Louis for an April series, Wagner wrote perfumed notes to Eagan, pretending to be an adoring young lady named "Miss Sadie." One note asked Eagan to meet her in the ladies' parlor at Pittsburgh's hotel at noon.

A fairly intelligent man, Eagan caught on that his teammates were

playing a prank on him. He went to the ladies' parlor at noon and sat down, pretending to wait for "Miss Sadie" to appear. He was seen reading the notes and smiling as Wagner and his teammates quietly approached the room. When the conspirators moved to a closer vantage point to peep into the parlor and have a good laugh at his expense, the youngster from San Francisco was no longer sitting in the chair. He was eyeing the players from a better position behind some curtains. Wagner liked to pull this gag as each young player was manipulated by clever little love-letters, mostly from an adoring female fan, recalling some great achievement on the field and requesting a meeting.[5] In this instance, the joke ended up being on Wagner and his teammates.

If Eagan had felt compelled to upgrade his wardrobe to make this whole con appear more credible, he could have enlisted the services of the master of haberdashery, teammate Rube Waddell. Pittsburgh's eccentric southpaw always strived to look dapper, sporting a snazzy suit while traversing about town. Over time, Waddell acquired the habit of borrowing around $30 from team secretary Harry Pulliam to purchase a new suit. Half of that money usually went toward fresh duds, while the remaining amount suited Waddell's other pressing needs.[6] Honus Wagner recalled one time when razor-wielding catcher Tacks Latimer benefitted from Waddell's decision to purchase a new suit.

> Well, Waddell bought a suit and went to his room. Taking off the old one, frightfully bagged at the knees and yet as gaudy-looking as ever, Waddell donned the new raiment. He started to toss the old one out the window when Tacks Latimer, his catcher and roommate, yelled: "Here, don't throw those clothes away, Rube. Give 'em to me."
>
> Rube tossed the old suit into Latimer's lap and went out, picking the price tags off the vest. Two nights later his eyes rolled with envy as he saw Latimer strutting around the hotel lobby in his old suit. The more Rube saw of Latimer, the more he figured that the old suit was all right.

"Here, come upstairs and make a change," ordered Rube, taking Tacks by the arm. "I like that suit best." And the pair disrobed, Latimer getting a suit only three days out of the store.[7]

It seems quite plausible that Rube Waddell probably would have been more than happy to show up for the meeting with "Miss Sadie" looking suave and debonair sporting new attire, if Truck Eagan had declined the invitation.

◆　◆　◆

The Pittsburgh Pirates aggregation that claimed three consecutive National League pennants from 1901 to 1903 was a close-knit group of players.[8] Joining Tommy Leach and Honus Wagner in Pittsburgh's infield was second baseman Claude Ritchey, a native of Emlenton, Pennsylvania. Ritchey was Wagner's teammate in Louisville and Pittsburgh from 1898, until he was shipped to the Boston Doves on December 11, 1906. He was an earnest, steady player, both at the plate and in the field, for Fred Clarke's Pirates. One of baseball's top clutch hitters during the early 1900s, Ritchey put up solid averages of .296 (1901), .277 (1902) and .287 (1903) during Pittsburgh's three pennant-winning seasons. Wagner adored Ritchey while the two men were teammates. They were sometimes referred to as the "Cheese Sandwich Brothers" due to their affection for that food.[9]

While Ritchey generally enjoyed eating cheese sandwiches, he wasn't fond of all cheeses. Usually unflappable, Ritchey lost his head on one occasion in the Northside clubhouse at Exposition Park during an encounter with limburger cheese. Catcher Heinie Peitz, Ritchey's teammate with the Pirates in 1905 and 1906, accidentally or purposely dropped a piece of limburger cheese on the clubhouse's hot stove. Ritchey swore he would not get dressed for the game until the clubhouse and locker room had been cleansed and fumigated. Honus Wagner thought it odd that his teammate would become so flustered over a little piece of toasted cheese.[10] Fellow Pirate Harry Smith took a much different approach once he realized that Ritchey had a deep aversion toward limburger cheese.

Smith, born in Yorkshire, England, in 1874, was a little-used catcher who played for Pittsburgh from 1902–1907 as an emergency catcher. After appearing in 61 games and batting .175 in 1903, Smith did not see action in that many contests over his next three seasons with Pittsburgh. Nevertheless, he was appreciated by his teammates and was the life of the Buccaneers crew during those years. While numerous Pirates liked to play little pranks on their teammates, Smith was the king of practical jokers who pulled gags that at times irritated the other players. When the team traveled by train, he kept teammates awake in their sleepers all night using horns, cowbells and ratchets.[11] His career was winding down when fellow backstop George Gibson joined the team in 1905.

"He was Peck's bad boy for sure," shuddered Gibson while he discussed Smith's antics. "He would torment me with everything from throwing paper wads and shooting peas at us from upper windows of hotels to green-appling our clothes or sousing us with armfuls of water-soaked paper towels while we slept in our berths."[12]

Remembering how Claude Ritchey reacted to a small piece of limburger cheese toasting on the hot stove, Smith decided to pull a prank at the second baseman's expense. He walked into the clubhouse at Exposition Park and rubbed toasted limburger cheese on the jerseys of every player. As the players arrived that afternoon, the strong smell in the clubhouse drove them frantic. As each player took his uniform from his locker, the smell became stronger and more unbearable. Ritchey finally discovered the trick when his fingers happened to become smeared with something under the collar of his shirt—ripe, toasted limburger cheese. Everybody on the team was extremely angry and Ritchey wanted to shoot Smith. It took a lot of coaxing on Fred Clarke's part to convince Ritchey to put on his uniform that afternoon.[13]

A third-string catcher who saw limited duty for the Pittsburgh Pirates, Harry Smith was the team's resident practical joker. Constantly awakening teammates with horns, cowbells and ratchets when the Pirates traveled by train, Smith also caused the usually calm Claude Ritchey to lose his cool when he smeared limburger cheese on every uniform in Exposition Park's locker room (courtesy National Baseball Hall of Fame Library, Cooperstown, New York).

Smith breathed a sigh of relief that Ritchey did not have a gun, the only thing he seemed to fear. Fred Clarke, who did carry a weapon when Pittsburgh was on the road, knew this. Clarke pleaded, threatened and fought with Smith to stop his nonsense, but nothing seemed to sink in. The Kansan finally had enough during a train trip

when horns and rattlers awakened the sleeping Pirates entourage. Clarke quietly arose from his berth, grabbed his gun and made his way to Smith's berth. He pulled open the curtains and shoved the revolver in Smith's face. Smith implored Clarke to put the gun away because it might go off.

"Yes, if might go off!" roared Clarke. "And it will go off if you don't cut this stuff out."[14]

Smith promised to behave. This incident kept Harry in line for a while until Clarke had to pull out the gun on another occasion during a spring training at Hot Springs.[15] While Clarke had endured Smith's practical jokes for some time before he finally responded, he never showed any patience when it came to players shirking their responsibilities getting into shape for the upcoming baseball season. Many Pittsburgh players did not appreciate Clarke's strict regulations regarding long mountain hikes. He kept a watchful eye out for those who attempted to evade the heavy work. He suspected that Smith was up to something when pitchers and catchers were sent out on a seven-mile hike over rough, mountainous terrain in Hot Springs.[16]

Smith had assured the battery men that he would lead them through all of the shortcuts and over level mountain paths that could be more easily slogged. Clarke followed at a good distance in order to keep an eye on his charges. He knew the roads along the hiking route as well as Smith. He was aware of one narrow path running along the mountain cliffs that Smith was likely to use as a shortcut. Clarke hid behind a rock across a ravine and waited. He was just within revolver range of a high embankment above the little roadway. After waiting for quite some time, Clarke saw Smith leading George Gibson, Sam Leever and others toward this forbidden path. Just as Smith reached the turn in the road under the high embankment, Clarke aimed about ten feet above the catcher's head and emptied his revolver into the mountain's side.

Panic set in as Smith stood paralyzed for a moment, wondering if he had run into an ambush. When the third or fourth shot rang from Clarke's revolver, a portion of the embankment gave way, causing a small landslide that swept Smith off his feet and almost buried him under the earth. Clarke became alarmed for a moment. His fears were assuaged when he saw the other players make a scrambling retreat and Smith started to dig himself out of the loose soil. Once he regained his faculties,

Smith ran screaming down the mountain path with his head hunched in his shoulders, as though he anticipated another volley. This experience cured Smith of his habit of leading teammates over the shortcuts during long hikes.[17]

Although Harry Smith may have been the Pirates' prime practical joker, there was no doubt it was best not to trifle with Fred Clarke's training workout regimen.

◆ ◆ ◆

Honus Wagner, Fred Clarke, Tommy Leach, Deacon Phillippe and Sam Leever were the only men who played for all four Pittsburgh National League pennant winners from 1901 through 1909. By 1909, players such as Claude Ritchey and Harry Smith were a distant memory to fans. The 1909 squad that defeated the Detroit Tigers in the World Series was loaded with a group of youngsters that included Howard Camnitz, Charles "Babe" Adams, Albert "Lefty" Leifield, Owen "Chief" Wilson and John "Dots" Miller. Outfielder Owen Wilson, from Austin, Texas, debuted for the Pirates in 1908. Even though he had a tough rookie campaign in which he batted .227 with only 18 extra-base hits, Fred Clarke stuck with the youngster despite complaints from fans. Wilson rewarded Clarke for having faith in him by hitting .272 during Pittsburgh's pennant-winning season in 1909.

Wilson achieved stardom in 1911 when he batted .300, smacked 12 home runs and drove in 107 runs. One year later, he established the major league record for triples in a single season when he blasted 36 three-baggers. Wilson was dubbed "Chief" by Honus Wagner during his rookie season. Wagner and Wilson were at a Wild West Show in Chicago when Wagner realized that the sun-burned Texan resembled one of the Indian chiefs from the act.[18] Besides being a solid outfielder during his six-year career with Pittsburgh, Wilson was an honest man who faithfully adhered to the precepts of good sportsmanship on a baseball diamond. He was forthcoming in regard to disagreements with umpires, even if his input brought about a negative decision for the Pirates.[19]

One time with the bases loaded, a Phillies player smacked a ball down the right field line that appeared foul according to the Pirates. The umpire insisted that the ball was fair. Pittsburgh's players howled in

protest. "Well, I'll leave it to your right fielder if the ball wasn't fair," said the umpire in the spirit of compromise.

"You're on," yelled the Pirates.[20]

The Pirates believed the ball was fair and were not trying to pull a fast one.

> "We were confident that it was fair," said Wagner, "and anyhow, we thought Wilson, who was playing in the right garden for us, would see it that way— not dishonestly you know, but a player almost sees a thing the way he wants to see it and convinces himself he is right, too.
>
> "The ump walked out to Wilson and asked his honest opinion about the hit. 'Fair,' said our fielder without any hesitation. And we all went back to our knitting and didn't question another decision during that game."[21]

Two and a half years before Chief Wilson joined the Pirates, southpaw Albert "Lefty" Leifield made his major league debut for Pittsburgh on September 3, 1905. Leifield was stellar for the Pirates in 1906 (18–13, 1.87 ERA), 1907 (20–16, 2.33 ERA) and 1909 (19–8, 2.37 ERA). Leifield was usually Fred Clarke's choice to oppose Cubs ace Mordecai "Three Finger" Brown. The two men were involved in many epic battles as Pittsburgh and Chicago fought to claim National League supremacy from 1906–1909. Barney Dreyfuss hated to lose to John McGraw's Giants and became extremely agitated when Leifield failed to close the deal in a game against New York.

Honus Wagner and his teammates recognized that Dreyfuss had a burning desire to win and loved to beat the Giants. One afternoon at the Polo Grounds, Leifield pitched a masterful game and kept New York at bay through eight innings. In the ninth frame, a hit, an error and a walk loaded the bases for the Giants with two outs. Leifield coolly forked over two strikes on New York third baseman Art Devlin. Extra innings appeared to be a certainty until Leifield's next pitch bounced off Devlin's shoulder and forced in the winning run.

In their locker room, the Pirates could see Dreyfuss through the clubhouse window, fighting and elbowing his way through the crowd on the field. Dreyfuss headed straight for the clubhouse and hammered violently on the door with his fist. Someone opened the door for Pittsburgh's owner. Once inside the clubhouse, Dreyfuss singled out Leifield from the perspiring Buccaneers, shook his fist angrily, and cried: "Hey, Lefty, next time you want to hit anybody with the ball with three on in the ninth, hit me."[22]

There is no evidence that Leifield ever took Dreyfuss' advice and plunked him in the shoulder before the southpaw pitcher was traded to the Chicago Cubs in 1912. Although Dreyfuss was a sore loser, he did understand that games sometimes were lost due to a hurler's wildness or the unshakable honesty of his right fielder.

◆ ◆ ◆

Chief Wilson was Pittsburgh's right fielder until December 12, 1913, when he was packaged in a deal along with first baseman Dots Miller, infielders Artie Butler and Cozy Dolan, and pitcher Hank Robinson that garnered first baseman Ed Konetchy, third baseman Mike Mowrey and pitcher Bob Harmon from the St. Louis Cardinals. Wilson's work ethic and sportsmanship led the soft-spoken outfielder to be admired by his teammates. Infielder Bill McKechnie and Wilson were best friends in Pittsburgh. Wilson was one of McKechnie's ushers when he married Miss Beryl Bien in his hometown of Wilkinsburg, Pennsylvania, on the evening of June 15, 1911. McKechnie's teammates exhibited characteristic generosity when one of their own became a benedict by presenting the bride with an exquisite chest of silver as a wedding present.[23]

The day before, Pittsburgh's players also held a little ceremony of their own in the locker room at Forbes Field. When McKechnie arrived, all of the single men on the team conducted a parade procession in honor of the groom's upcoming nuptials. He was compelled to stand in the center of a group of hilarious young men who sang the popular refrain "No Wedding Bells for Me." This collection of bachelors, who called themselves the Insurrectos, consisted of Honus Wagner, Max Carey, Bobby Byrne, Alex McCarthy, Dots Miller, Chief Wilson, Claude Hendrix and a few others. The Insurrectos carried banners with appropriate inscriptions. When order was finally restored, McKechnie was forced to stand up on a chair and make a short speech.[24]

After he finished speaking, the married members of Pittsburgh's team warmly welcomed McKechnie into their ranks and made him feel right at home. They also told him to ignore the taunts that came from these jealous youngsters. Every member of the Pirates had a grand time celebrating McKechnie's upcoming wedding, no one more than McKechnie himself, a member of one of the tightest-knit, good-natured

band of ballers that ever gathered in a locker room.[25] While the parade and McKechnie's wedding were both joyous events, some members of the Insurrectos started to ponder switching to the married side when they learned that Fred Clarke had given the groom a week's vacation to enjoy his honeymoon. An interesting exchange occurred in Pittsburgh's clubhouse the afternoon following the wedding ceremony.

"I do not know what is in the air," remarked Fred Clarke when he met up with his hired hands beneath Forbes Field. "Seems to me that all you youngsters want to get married."

"That's all right, Captain," replied Claude Hendrix, spokesman for the untangled Pirates. "Now, Cap, here's a proposition. Give us young fellows a chance and we will hike right into the ranks of the settle-downers."

"What are you trying to work me for—a week's vacation?" responded Clarke. "I guess if I granted every fellow a week off for a honeymoon trip all you young fellows would be sending me invitations to your nuptial events. Now, I am going to tell that, while I have given McKechnie a brief leave of absence, if any of the rest of you think you can gain a week's vacation by getting married you are badly mistaken. This wedding business has got to be cut out, and you hear me."[26]

There was glum silence in the room for a few minutes. The gloomiest member of the party was Honus Wagner. Clarke finally broke this silence. "Now, I will take back part of what I have said," remarked Clarke as he turned his gaze toward the Carnegie bachelor. "I am willing to make an exception. If Wagner will promise me to get married I certainly will give him one week free from work on the diamond."

"You are on, Cap," shouted Wagner. "Give me one week's vacation and I promise you that I will present you to Mrs. Wagner."

"It's a go, John," said Clarke.[27]

Wagner quickly realized he had made a huge mistake blurting out this response to Clarke in front of the whole Pirate team. The locker room buzzed with activity as Clarke and his players began laying bets that Wagner would not carry out his end of the agreement. Wagner remained silent for some time before Pirates trainer Edward LaForce rapped for order. LaForce tried to help the great player out of this predicament. "Boys, this is rather rough on the grand old man," said LaForce. "I really do not think he has any idea of 'hooking up' else he

would have accepted all the bets you have fired at him." He turned toward Wagner and asked: "What have you got to say, John?"[28]

Every eye turned toward Wagner, who was sitting in the corner of the room. After a few minutes, he mustered the courage to rise from his seat. "Cap, that was all a bluff," said Wagner. "I know you would give me a week off to get married. You have always been kind to me, but if I am to be forced to face Hymen's altar in order to get a brief respite from duty, please tell theses newspaper fellows that your old friend and fellow worker for the good of the Pirates is going to continue to prance in single harness for a long time to come."[29]

Jim Orris, Wagner's good friend from Carnegie, always claimed that the Flying Dutchman was dedicated to remaining single until he quit playing baseball.[30] Wagner kept this promise until he married Miss Bessie Smith on December 30, 1916, at St. John's Lutheran Church in Carnegie.[31]

◆　◆　◆

Honus Wagner was able to reflect on old times with a friend from Carnegie when the Boston Rustlers played Pittsburgh on the day of Bill McKechnie's wedding in 1911. Patrick "Patsy" Flaherty, Wagner's pal since they were kids, was playing in the Rustlers outfield after performing as a pitcher throughout his major league career. Flaherty was also a teammate of Wagner for parts of four seasons, with Louisville (1899), Pittsburgh (1900), and once again with the Pirates in 1904–1905. He was brilliant in 1904 with a 19–9 record and a 2.05 ERA. While Flaherty thoroughly enjoyed playing with his friend for those few seasons, he absolutely relished their barnstorming tour through Pennsylvania and Ohio following the 1905 baseball campaign.

> I tell you that there are more readable incidents on an exhibition tour than in the whole championship season. I have laughed so heartily that I have grown fat. Umpires? Well, there is where we start in on. I shall never forget the flaying John Wagner and myself gave to the fellow who handled the game at Zanesville. We began with a request that he show us his dark lantern. He did not catch on at first, and shot back something about not having such a thing on his person. Then Wagner took a shy in this style: "Why, you live up an alley." I noticed that the fellow got red at this and was distressed for a few seconds. Later on we found out that he actually lived up one of those four by five thoroughfares. He ran a wet goods store on an alley.

The best thing we struck was when we demanded that a balk be called on a certain pitcher. "Isn't that a balk?" I shouted. "Balk," came the reply, "why, my dear sir, I would not know a balk if I seen one." At West Newton, the man behind the plate was supposed to be an off-the-chain, rough-and-tumble mixer, a regular country town bad man. We were worried not to twist his tail. The boys got him going good and strong and waited for the fireworks, but he was so good natured that he reminded me of the time Arthur Irwin umpired in the league.[32]

Honus Wagner loved to commiserate with dear friends like Patsy Flaherty. As the top player in the National League, Wagner also forged close relationships with young Pirates who tended to idolize the big Teuton. "Dashing Dan" Costello was a utility outfielder for the Pirates from 1914–1916, with his best season being 1914 when he appeared in 21 games and batted .297. One year later, during a game against Philadelphia at Forbes Field on September 11, Costello came to Wagner's aid when Phillies hurler Erskine Mayer pulled a stunt that peeved the young Pirate. While Wagner was batting with one teammate on and two out in the sixth inning, he stopped to argue with umpire Al Orth over a strike decision.[33] As was his right, Mayer delivered the ball in an attempt to surprise Wagner while he was arguing with Orth and sneak over a third strike. This aroused the ire of Costello, who was coaching from the box at third base.[34]

"I'm off of you for life," Costello yelled to Mayer. "You might have hit Wagner. I'm going to ride you from now on."

"Well, as you don't get in more than ten games in a year you had better do your riding on a hobby horse," replied Mayer.[35]

When the inning ended, Wagner was ejected from the game by Orth for making disparaging remarks. Wally Gerber was his replacement at shortstop.[36] Although Wagner's day was done, Dan Costello was only getting started riding Mayer. "I'm on you," yelled Costello when Pittsburgh batted one inning later. "I used to be for you, but I'm sure on you now."

"You are?" scoffed Mayer. "And who are you. I don't see you in the lineup. Who are you anyway?"[37]

Mayer's comeback rattled Costello somewhat. He was fuming so much that he babbled something to Mayer about showing him who he was if the opportunity arose to face the Philadelphia pitcher at the plate before this series ended. Whether it was fate which intervened, or Fred

Clarke was curious to see how Costello handled himself, he selected Costello as a pinch-hitter for Gerber to lead off the ninth inning. As the youngster stepped to the plate, Mayer started laughing at him.

"So you're the fellow who's going to show me, are you?" Mayer asked. "Now you tell me what you can hit, and I'll put it in there for you. Here comes one straight over the middle!"

Mayer's first pitch was a fast one that came whizzing by around the youngster's chin. Costello swung wildly and missed the offering by a foot. "Well, well," said Mayer defiantly. "If you can't hit that I don't know what to give you."

Following more insulting banter by Mayer, he slipped a second strike past Costello. Mayer decided Costello was just about angry enough to start going after bad balls. He fed the left-handed batter a low ball on the outside of the plate. Costello went after the pitch just as Mayer had surmised and lifted a weak pop foul that third baseman Milt Stock secured for the inning's first out.[38] After all of his loud talk, Dan Costello was meekly subdued in the end. Pittsburgh lost this game to the first-place Phillies, 3–2.

◆　◆　◆

Pittsburgh's roster was loaded with impressionable youngsters like Dan Costello during the 1914 and 1915 baseball campaigns. With the Pirates' glory days now far away in the rear view mirror, Barney Dreyfuss and Fred Clarke gave many young players trials as Pittsburgh placed seventh in 1914 and fifth in 1915. While many of these baseball neophytes never made the grade, a local recruit from the Pittsburgh suburb of Dormont named Albert Leon "Al" Mamaux achieved stardom in 1915. A Duquesne University graduate, Mamaux was eased into the major league environment by Clarke during his rookie season in 1914. This proved to be a prudent strategy as Mamaux took the National League by storm in 1915 by going 21–8 and posting an ERA of 2.04.

Although Mamaux had become a major league star at the age of 21, the novice hurler did experience some growing pains in 1914. He learned a bitter lesson during a late-season game against the Chicago Cubs at West Side Grounds on September 14—not to acquiesce to every wish put forward by a baseball icon. After being summoned to pinch-hit for George McQuillan in the fourth inning, he did a decent job of keeping

Chicago in check until everything came crashing down in the eighth frame. With two runs in, Frank Schulte at second base and Bob Fisher occupying first, Mamaux made a critical mistake when he allowed Roger Bresnahan to break his concentration.[39]

> I'll never forget one of the first big league games I pitched. It was in Chicago, and I obligingly tossed a ball to Roger Bresnahan, of the Cubs, and darned near lost the ballgame then and there.
>
> There were two men out and Chicago players on first and second bases. Roger was coaching at third base. He was talking to me—not trying to kid me or get me up in the air, but chatting in a friendly sort of way. Finally, there was some sort of an argument at the plate. The ball had been returned to me by our catcher and I was standing near the pitching mound trying to steady myself and looking at the ball.
>
> "Say, Al, toss that ball here so I can take a look at it," Bresnahan yelled to me.
>
> I didn't give the thing a second thought. I just tossed it to him, and darned if he didn't step to one side and yell to the runners to "Come on." They came, all right. Each advanced a base, and they could have gone farther if Jimmy Viox hadn't run like an Indian and retrieved the ball in a hurry.
>
> Well, maybe our gang didn't ride me. I heard nothing else for a month or more. But it cured me. I wouldn't toss a baseball to an opposing coacher now if the umpire told me to do it. I'd hand the onion to the ump and let him do what he wanted with it.[40]

Honus Wagner believed such mistakes were tolerable since veteran pitchers could also lose their composure and do puzzling things on the mound.[41] Due to problems away from the diamond, Al Mamaux was a member of the Pittsburgh Pirates for only four full seasons. During that time, he played for four different managers. After Fred Clarke retired following the 1915 campaign, Jimmy Callahan managed the Pirates until he was fired in 1917 and replaced by team scout Hugo Bezdek. Wagner was actually the team's pilot for five games before Bezdek was hired on July 4. Having made his mark as a college football coach at Arkansas and Oregon, Bezdek stipulated that he would agree to take over the reins running Pittsburgh only if the team's older players were willing to lend a helping hand. Years later, in 1925, when Bezdek coached Penn State's football team, he explained how this arrangement worked out during a game against the New York Giants in 1917.[42]

> I told Honus Wagner, who was temporarily in charge, that I would do so on the condition I get help from the old heads.

"We'll tell you everything we know Hughey," Wagner said. "Just call on us at any time."

One day we were playing the Giants in New York, the score was 1 to 0, our favor, with the Giants at bat in the ninth, two on base and two out. Heinie Zimmerman came up to the plate, waving his big bat. A bad man was Heinie. The pitcher threw one that was called a ball. He threw another, and Heinie swung hard and missed. The pitcher, however, didn't look good to me.

"Hans," I said, turning to Wagner on the bench with me, "shall I pull that pitcher, and call a fellow in from the bullpen?"

Hans scratched his head, and said: "Hughey, this is a ticklish situation."

Well, the pitcher threw another ball and then another. I said to Hans again: "Shall I yank that pitcher, Hans?"

Hans gave a deep thought and then said: "Hughey, use your own judgement!"[43]

Managing never seemed to agree with Honus Wagner when he was pressed into duty on occasion for the absent Fred Clarke. It came as no surprise that Wagner's attitude had not changed much in 1917. First and foremost, he always put forth his best effort on the baseball diamond and just wanted to be treated like one of the boys.

8

Adversaries from the Cubs, Giants and Fellow National League Clubs

Following the National League baseball campaign in 1900 when the Brooklyn Superbas claimed the coveted bunting, three teams dominated the Senior Circuit for the next 13 seasons. Baseball fans in Pittsburgh, New York and Chicago rejoiced on numerous occasions as the beloved team they rooted for claimed every National League pennant from 1901–1913. The Pittsburgh Pirates finished in the top spot four times, winning titles in 1901, 1902, 1903 and 1909. John McGraw's New York Giants were the pace-setters on five occasions, claiming titles in 1904, 1905, 1911, 1912 and 1913. The Chicago Cubs won four flags, turning the trick in 1906, 1907, 1908 and 1910. All three franchises could make a strong argument for being a dynasty during this 13-year span since each team won three consecutive championships.

When the Pirates, Giants and Cubs faced each, the games resembled wars that sometimes included bare-knuckle mêlées. These bitter adversaries were willing to do anything to be crowned as champions at season's end. While fights did break out at times between these opponents, teammates would also swing at each other when mistakes were made or times got tough. This was not surprising when talented players with a deep thirst for winning collided and fought for every inch of diamond real estate each day.

Second baseman Johnny Evers and shortstop Joe Tinker of the Chicago Cubs were two scrappy players who exhibited true fighting spirit on the diamond. Along with Frank Chance, Evers and Tinker were immortalized when Franklin Pierce Adams wrote a poem about this great double play combination in 1910 called "Baseball's Sad Lexicon."

Things were not always rosy between Evers and Tinker from 1902 to 1912. Sometimes referred to as the "brawl team," Cubs players constantly fought with opponents, umpires, fans and themselves. During an exhibition game in Bedford, Indiana, on September 13, 1905, Evers and Tinker began fighting near second base. Tinker was angry with Evers over a slight regarding a ride to the ballpark. After Chicago's players had dressed in their team hotel for the game, Evers hailed a horse-drawn taxi and drove off by himself, leaving Tinker and other players standing on the sidewalk.[1]

After this incident, the two players did not speak to each other except to communicate on the baseball diamond.[2] Opponents like Honus Wagner, who marveled at their ability on the field, realized both men were powder kegs waiting to go off. Evers and Tinker were smart and aggressive and demanded team play. Although Frank Chance was the Cubs manager, Evers and Tinker were quick to remind him of any bad plays. They took great pride in their defensive play around short and second, and if either man was slow in completing a play, the other was ready to chew him out.[3] Wagner reflected upon a specific incident when Pittsburgh made a one-day trip to Chicago for a Sunday game and Evers expressed his displeasure toward Tinker in the clubhouse after the contest.

> I remember one instance in a game in which I played for the Pirates against the Cubs. I was on first base, with a runner on third, and one out. The ball was hit to Tinker with the hit and run on. As Tinker played the ball to Evers, I took Evers out by stopping him from completing the double play. Tinker was so mad that he immediately hopped on Evers and told him plenty.
>
> After the game, I happened to be using Tinker's locker. I was dressing when Evers walked over and hit Tinker on the nose. Blood spurted out and all over my clean shirt, the only one I had with me for we were only playing there one day. Evers offered to loan me a shirt, and apologized to me, but not to Joe. But with all their fussing, they played great ball.[4]

Chicago's roster was loaded with many cocky characters besides Johnny Evers and Joe Tinker. Outfielder Frank "Wildfire" Schulte was known for his sharp, biting sense of humor. One of the National League's top power hitters from 1910–1912, Schulte smacked 21 home runs and drove home 107 teammates in 1911. On August 26, 1910, he blasted two home runs as Chicago secured a 3–1 victory over the Giants. After the game, he went up near the press box at West Side Grounds and remarked: "I wonder if Tinker-to-Evers-to-Chance won this ball game."[5]

◆　◆　◆

Joe Tinker and Johnny Evers never missed an opportunity to harass or chastise somebody. They questioned every close decision that went against them and kept umpires on their toes at all times.[6] Tinker, Evers and their teammates also had the utmost respect for Honus Wagner. When Evers made his major league debut on September 1, 1902, Tinker had already established himself as the Cubs' shortstop. Another youngster, Larry Schlafly, debuted for Chicago on September 18. The pennant race had long been decided. Pittsburgh established a record for victories in a season with a 103–36 record.

Three days after Schlafly played his first game for Chicago, the Cubs hosted the Pirates in a doubleheader at West Side Grounds. Pittsburgh pulled off a sweep, winning both games, 4–1. Schlafly, who played right field in the first game, anchored the hot corner spot next to Joe Tinker during the second tilt. Wagner was in one of those hitting grooves for Pittsburgh where he was driving them a "mile-a-minute." Opposing players were at risk since it was comparable to getting in front of a rifle ball trying to stop one of Wagner's drives.[7] Many years later, Tinker reminisced about how he had a little fun with this wide-eyed rookie when he faced Wagner for the first time in the infield during this second contest.

Joe Tinker played shortstop for the Chicago Cubs from 1902–1912. He and second baseman Johnny Evers fought with each other on the baseball diamond during games on many occasions. On September 21, 1902, Tinker had some fun at the expense of fellow rookie Larry Schlafly the first time he played third base against Honus Wagner and the Pittsburgh Pirates (courtesy National Baseball Hall of Fame Library, Cooperstown, New York).

I play deep at short, but I always played very deep for Wagner. I looked around in the third inning of this particular game and there I saw Schlafly as far back as I was.

"Get in there, Larry," I said. "This fellow will bunt on you."

Larry moved in toward third base. Just then Wagner caught hold of an outcurve and hooked the ball down to Schlafly. It was going like a bullet. Larry stuck out his right hand, the ball hit his fingers and bounced into the bleachers. The ball almost smashed Schlafly's hand. It began to swell and it was a sore looking mitt when we walked toward the bench.

"Call that a bunt?" asked Larry as we left the field. I said nothing. I knew how his hand pained him.

In the sixth inning Wagner was at bat again. I looked around for Larry and he was playing deeper than myself. "Come on there, Larry, play in close to the bag. This fellow will outguess you this time and bunt."

"Is he going to bunt again?" asked Larry.

"Sure, he'll bunt," I replied.

"Me for the fence," shouted Larry.[8]

Self-preservation was the mantra of most National League infielders when the great Honus Wagner stepped to the plate, swinging his deadly war club. While many players admired and idolized Wagner, they also feared the physical damage he could inflict when connecting against a juicy offering. Ten years after Larry Schlafly was almost decapitated by a blistering drive off Wagner's bat, Cubs third baseman Henry "Heinie" Zimmerman had a season for the ages as he led the National League in hitting (.372), hits (207), doubles (41), home runs (14), RBIs (104) and slugging percentage (.571) in 1912. Known as "The Great Zim," he never acted modest or humble. Despite his overinflated ego, he demonstrated common sense when it involved survival on the baseball diamond.

Zimmerman possessed the proper level of sagacity when playing against Honus Wagner and never wanted to be on the losing end of one of Wagner's robust drives. He once coached a rookie pitcher to insure that the third baseman would not be exposed to bodily harm with Wagner at the plate. In the seventh inning, Chicago's starting pitcher ran into trouble and allowed the Pirates to load the bases. The novice hurler was summoned from the Cubs bullpen to extinguish the fire. Zimmerman stood close by the mound as the rookie chucked a few warm-up tosses to his catcher. Standing near home plate, swinging a couple of bats and waiting to take his cuts was the bowlegged, lantern-jawed Honus Wagner.[9]

"Who's the hitter?" the boy asked Zimmerman.

"Wagner," Zimmerman replied glumly.

"How do you pitch to him?" the youngster queried.

"Whatever you do," Zimmerman said, "don't pitch him tight. Keep the ball outside."[10]

Zimmerman returned to his position at third base, Wagner stepped up to the dish, and the young hurler gazed toward home plate. The youngster obeyed orders to the letter and threw an outside pitch which Wagner promptly belted down the right-field line for a double that drove home all three runners. "I thought you said he couldn't hit an outside pitch," the lad snapped at Zimmerman after the dust had settled.

"I didn't say he couldn't hit it," Zimmerman calmly replied. "All I said was don't pitch him inside."

Zimmerman explained that he did not need to have Honus Wagner drilling dangerous line drives toward him down at the hot corner since he had a wife and a daughter at home.[11]

◆ ◆ ◆

Heinie Zimmerman did not hold the minority opinion regarding a prudent baseball strategy of hoping for the best when Honus Wagner stepped up to the plate. This intimidation factor existed even for a man like John McGraw, who feared nobody and tended to do the bullying. McGraw understood he could not stop the strongest cog in the wheel of his main National League nemesis. New York's manager believed the proper course of action was to limit the damage Wagner did. Once, an impetuous young pitcher who had just joined the Giants was brought in during the late innings. With Wagner due to hit, the youngster asked McGraw for some input.[12]

"What shall I pitch to him?" asked the youngster.

"Just pitch—and then duck," advised McGraw.[13]

McGraw had a host of superb hurlers at his disposal from 1904 to 1909. Joe "Iron Man" McGinnity, Christy Mathewson, Luther "Dummy" Taylor, Leon "Red" Ames and George "Hooks" Wiltse prevented Pittsburgh's hitters from flexing their baseball muscles on many occasions. On July 1, 1908, McGraw added another twirler with loads of potential and a solid pedigree. The Giants purchased southpaw Richard "Rube" Marquard from the American Association's Indianapolis Indians for

$11,000. New York's investment initially seemed misguided since Marquard was a colossal bust during his first two seasons with the Giants.

In the end, McGraw looked like a genius when everything came together for Marquard in 1911 as the southpaw went 24–7 and posted an ERA of 2.50. He was even better in 1912, topping the National League in victories by going 26–11, supported by a 2.57 ERA, a major improvement over his first full season in 1909 when he could not muster anything better than a 5–13 record. Marquard also reeled off 19 straight victories from the start of the 1912 campaign until he was beaten by the Chicago Cubs on July 8. New York used special signals because pitcher Dummy Taylor was deaf and this signaling system confused Marquard the first time he faced Wagner in 1909.

> The Giants have signals of their own, and not a team has ever even come close near to getting onto them. We tell what's coming off in so many words, too. The old style of lifting caps, tugging at belts, standing on one foot, and then the other, and gripping the bat is obsolete with us. We use the mute language which Dummy Taylor taught us when he was with the team.
>
> Manager McGraw has shortened the sign talk to letters for quick work. When he wants the hit-and-run played he flashes "H-R" from the coaching line. "D" means delayed steal, and so on. The other teams know what we use, but the Giants are so speedy no other players can catch on.
>
> I was up against it the first time I faced Hans Wagner. I looked at McGraw on the bench. He flashed back "A." Hans hit a high fly, which I thought was lucky for me, because I didn't know what ball bothered him. I asked McGraw what "A" stood for.
>
> "Anything," replied McGraw. "That Dutchman has hit every kind of ball a mile. Just give him anything and trust to luck and the fielders."[14]

No man from New York's pitching staff had more significant battles against Honus Wagner than the immortal Christy "Big Six" Mathewson. Wagner had a simple philosophy regarding Mathewson. "It was give and take between Big Six and me for 14 years, but he was probably the greatest of them all."[15] This certainly was not an understatement since Mathewson was the undisputed top pitcher in the National League. Mathewson had particularly scintillating seasons in 1903 (30–13, 2.26 ERA), 1904 (33–12, 2.03 ERA), 1905 (31–9, 1.28 ERA), 1908 (37–11, 1.43 ERA), 1909 (25–6, 1.14 ERA) and 1910 (27–9, 1.89 ERA).

Although Wagner did experience a good degree of success against Mathewson, a tale started making the rounds that Mathewson had finally figured out a way to subdue the Dutchman by watching his feet in the

batter's box. A great deal of amusement grew out of this tale. Various newspapers carried cartoons of Wagner in many humorous batting postures. They had his huge feet concealed in wash boilers, buckets, paper bags and burlap sacks. As Wagner walked up to the plate at the Polo Grounds, the crowd yelled: "Matty, watch his feet!"[16]

On one occasion, Wagner summoned the showman inside of him and had a little fun. When he stepped into the batter's box, he started wiggling his left heel very vigorously. The crowd of 15,000 fans at the Polo Grounds roared with laughter. Mathewson was confident he would prevail since he had gotten Wagner into a hole. Wagner connected squarely with his next pitch. The baseball shot like a cannonball and smacked a sign in deep left field, three feet from the top of the fence. The ball just missed going out onto Eighth Avenue, which would have been a Polo Grounds first.[17]

The careers of these two baseball warhorses were winding down in 1917 when Wagner and Mathewson went head-to-head against each other as managers. Mathewson had been the Cincinnati Reds skipper since being traded by New York on July 20, 1916, while Wagner acted as Pittsburgh's temporary manager from June 30 through July 3 after Jimmy Callahan was fired.[18] The Pirates went 1–4 during Wagner's managerial tenure in 1917 and played three of those games against Mathewson's Reds. Mathewson remembered with fondness how Wagner handled being the boss in one of these contests.

> Honus went out on the first base coaching line and stood there thinking, as the game went on. Someone sent the batboy out from the Pirates' bench to ask the manager who he wanted down in the bullpen to warm up.
> Honus looked at the boy a minute, hitched up his belt, and said: "Oh, I don't know; just tell 'em to send out anybody they like."[19]

Once the batboy ran back into the dugout and related the manager's instructions, Wagner resumed his occupation of observing what kind of stuff Cincinnati's hurler possessed. Wagner did not feel the need to worry since the game was still young.[20] Although managing never seemed to suit his fancy, he put up a good front during fielding practice prior to the game against Cincinnati on June 30. "I'm the manager for a couple of days; show me some speed," said Wagner as he frolicked around first base like a schoolboy.[21]

◆ ◆ ◆

Before Christy Mathewson's final full season with the New York Giants in 1915, a young hurler named William "Pol" Perritt joined the team in February through a trade with the St. Louis Cardinals. Perritt had two solid seasons in 1916 (18–11, 2.62 ERA) and 1917 (17–7, 1.88 ERA) for the Giants. He was also one of many National League twirlers who almost fell victim to a vicious drive off Honus Wagner's bat. Although Wagner belted only 101 home runs in 21 seasons, he certainly could inject velocity into the mushy baseball that was used during the Deadball Era when he got his 200-pound frame behind a swing.[22] Luck was on Perritt's side when he was subjected to such punishment on a Wagner home run.

"I threw Wagner a fastball and was still in my follow-through," said Perritt, "with my arm extended in front of me, when the ball came back at me like a rifle bullet. I couldn't have ducked if I tried, but fortunately the ball sailed under my arm and then began to rise, and cleared the center-field fence."[23]

While Pol Perritt was not obliterated by the scorching pellet off Wagner's bat, things were not as fortuitous for his former Cardinals teammate Dan "Kid" Griner. Griner, who broke into the major leagues for St. Louis along with Perritt in 1912, went 10–22 with a 5.08 ERA during his first full season in 1913. St. Louis finished last that year during second baseman Miller Huggins' first season piloting the squad. Griner had an odd pitching motion when he joined the Cardinals in 1912. He tended to follow through too aggressively. On September 6, 1912, at Robison Field, the Pirates savagely attacked Griner on their way to an 8–0 victory.[24] Prior to the start of spring training in 1913, Huggins reminisced about what happened when Griner opposed Wagner in the third inning of that game.

> Griner had a great trick of delivering the ball, and then charging forward almost up to the catcher. He'd run a mile in a game. He claimed he made his dash because it terrified the batter.
>
> One day Griner was pitching to a Pittsburgh ball player named Hans Wagner—yes, the justly revered Hans. He threw a fast one and then began his dash. He got two steps when the ball, on the return, caught him in the diner. They didn't serve any meals in that diner the rest of the week.[25]

Honus Wagner ended up with a single, while Kid Griner's day was done as he hobbled off the field in pain and was replaced by Jacob "Rube"

Geyer.[26] Kid Griner, Pol Perritt and other pitchers should have adhered to Brooklyn Superbas hurler George "Nap" Rucker's philosophy regarding Wagner. Rucker, a star pitcher and innings-eater for Brooklyn, lasted ten years in the National League from 1907 to 1916, with his best season in 1911 when he posted a 22–18 record along with an ERA of 2.71. While being interviewed by a reporter the following summer, Rucker did not hesitate when asked which player in the National League gave him the most trouble.[27]

"Hans Wagner," responded Rucker. "What that big Dutchman has done to my stuff is a shame. I know he doesn't play any favorites among the pitchers, but it seems as if he couldn't wait until I came along. It doesn't matter where I put it—around his neck, across his shoestrings or behind his back—he just beats it to a pulp."

Asked if he had ever fooled Wagner, the Superbas hurler responded in a calm and concise manner. "Only once," said Nap. "I ducked Pittsburgh on a trip a few years ago. That's the only way to fool Hans. Don't go into the box. I have got so now that I put them right over the plate for him and then watch him touch all the bases."[28]

While Rucker's comments could be construed as sage advice, Wagner was not triumphant on every occasion. On July 17, 1914, Pittsburgh's Babe Adams and New York's Rube Marquard were locked up in one of the most epic pitching duels in major league history. The game at Forbes Field lasted 21 innings as New York prevailed, 3–1. Both hurlers went the distance and Adams did not allow a walk. Pittsburgh protested the game due to an adverse decision by umpire William "Lord" Byron in the sixth inning. After Wagner singled he believed he had legally come around to score on Jimmy Viox's single to center field.[29] Giants third baseman Milt Stock explained years later why Lord Byron ruled against the Pirates.

> Wagner was on first base, with two men out. The next batter hit a single to Snodgrass [it was actually Bob Bescher], in center field, on which Wagner set sail for third. The ball was thrown perfectly and it was a question who would get there first. Just as Wagner slid into third base, throwing up a duststorm, the ball hit him in the back. I immediately started for the ball and couldn't find it. The shortstop, second baseman and pitcher joined me to look for it.
>
> By this time we were frantic, for Wagner kept taking a bigger lead toward the home plate every moment. I even looked under the third base bag. No

ball! Suddenly Wagner started for home and at the same time a great light dawned on me. I started full speed after him. He touched the plate and nothing happened. But just as he was about to sit down in the dugout the ball dropped to the ground.

Of course the umpire was right behind me and called him out for interference. It seems wise old Hans had caught the ball under his armpit and was just kidding us with his short dashes off third, though he says to this day he didn't know the ball was there; that it had caught in his pocket.[30]

Whether Honus Wagner's intentions were malicious or not was of no consequence to the Giants. In the thick of the 1914 National League pennant race, winning the argument and claiming a victory mattered most.

◆　◆　◆

In the end, New York did not prevail in their quest to capture a fourth consecutive pennant in 1914 as a team other than the Giants, Pirates or Cubs won the title for the first time since 1900. George Stallings' "Miracle" Boston Braves claimed the pennant after they had occupied the National League basement on Independence Day. The Braves topped off this amazing accomplishment by sweeping Connie Mack's vaunted Philadelphia Athletics in the 1914 World Series. This was the first time that veteran manager George Stallings had tasted the sweet nectar of a pennant victory. He had failed in previous stints running the Philadelphia Phillies, Detroit Tigers and New York Highlanders.

During his rookie campaign as a major league manager with Philadelphia in 1897, Stallings made a colossal mistake that both haunted him for years and caused him almost to weep at times. He had fixed up a deal whereby he was permitted to select any player he wanted from the Atlantic League's Paterson Silk Weavers roster and sign him once the season concluded. Early that summer, he made the trip to New Jersey to look over Paterson's players. He decided that a lithe and limber athlete named Emmet Heidrick, who later was a decent player for both the St. Louis Cardinals and St. Louis Browns, was his man.[31]

"I don't want to dictate your choice," said Paterson manager Charles McKee, "but if I were in your place, I'd take the fellow Wagner. He's a diamond in the rough."

Stallings took one look at the clumsy, awkward person named Wagner and giggled. "Say, that guy is too clumsy to even mind the bats,"

replied Stallings. "He might do in the minors, but he'll never be any good in the majors. He's too slow and too clumsy."

"All right, Mr. Stallings," responded McKee. "Just suit yourself. Only I think that someday you'll regret that you didn't take this Wagner fellow."[32]

While securing Wagner may have helped lengthen Stallings' managerial career in the National League, at least he was either running American League teams or in the minors during the height of the Flying Dutchman's great career. After being replaced by Bill Shettsline as Philadelphia's manager on June 18, 1898, Stallings did not oppose Wagner again until he took over the reins as skipper of the Boston Braves in 1913. Although Stallings achieved baseball glory in 1914, his first season at the helm managing the Braves was no picnic as Boston went 69–82 and placed fifth. Things did not always run smoothly when incidents like the one involving outfielder Jay Kirke severely tested Stallings' sanity.

Early in 1913, before Stallings sold Kirke to the Cleveland Naps on May 14, the left fielder caused his new manager much grief. When the opposing team's best hitter stepped up to the plate for the first time, Kirke played back near the left field fence. The hitter promptly dumped a safety over the infield. Believing he had caught on to this player's strategy, Kirke moved in for him the next time he batted. The opposing hitter took a mighty swing and sent the ball soaring over his head for a triple. Impervious to this chain of events, Kirke moved back to the fence when this man batted for the third time. He was so close to the barricade that he could reach out and touch its palings. The batter took a soft swing at the baseball and lifted it over the infield once again for his third hit of the game.[33]

When Kirke returned to the bench, Stallings was seething. After moaning and groaning, holding his head and sliding up and down his seat on the bench, Stallings finally busted loose with an angry diatribe. "What you doin' out there, what you doin' out there—first you go out and then you come in and then you go out—if you'd had a gun out there I'd a swore you was drilling!"[34]

One reason why Stallings turned things around so quickly in 1914 was that he acquired brilliant second baseman Johnny Evers through a trade with the Chicago Cubs on February 11. Evers was a sparkplug for

the Braves that year, appearing in 139 games and batting .279 in his final season as a full-time major league player. In 1915, Boston once again was in last place in July. While they did come roaring back for the second consecutive year, the Braves ended up in second place behind Philadelphia. As Boston tried to remain vital in the race during a late–August series against Pittsburgh at Braves Field, Evers witnessed what he believed was the funniest moment he had ever seen involving Honus Wagner.

> The funniest stunt I ever saw Honus Wagner pull off happened in Boston last season. Honus was on third, with one out. The batter flied to the outfield, and Honus started for home the moment the ball was caught. The drive was comparatively short, and the ball beat Honus to the bag by about six feet. However, in a desperate attempt to score, Wagner made a great slide to the plate.
>
> "Yer out," yelled umpire Lord Byron.
>
> That "out" retired the side. The Pirates started onto the field, and the Braves came in, but Honus Wagner remained on the ground near home plate, in the original position in which he finished his slide, except that he had propped up his head on his hand.
>
> "Hey, you, get up," ordered Byron. "You're delaying the game."
>
> Honus didn't answer by word of mouth or movement of speech.
>
> "Get up, I say," again commanded Byron.
>
> "Say, lookit here," answered Wagner, slowly. "I'm an old man, ain't I? And old men get tired, don't they? Well, gimme a chance to rest up after that sprint."
>
> It was nearly a minute later before Wagner arose, and it was two minutes before he got into position to play. Wagner had delayed that game almost five minutes through his action in "resting up"—and no one cared. It looked so funny to see Wagner taking things easy that the crowd, when it became "wised up" to what was going on, broke into cheers for the grand old Dutchman.[35]

There certainly was no harm in allowing the grand old man of baseball who had thrilled millions of fans for years to rest and catch his breath for a few minutes.

◆ ◆ ◆

Johnny Evers was not the whole story for Boston in 1914–1915. Hurlers Dick Rudolph and Lefty Tyler anchored George Stallings' staff, while outfielder Joe Connolly and first baseman Butch Schmidt supplied a spark with the bat. Young shortstop Walter "Rabbit" Maranville was

also critical to Boston's success in both 1914 and 1915. A man who definitely marched to the beat of his own drum, Maranville was a feisty character whose crazy antics became legendary. He eventually took control of the hallowed swath of ground where Honus Wagner had roamed at Forbes Field for so many years when he was traded to Pittsburgh on January 23, 1921.

Maranville enjoyed interacting with Wagner during games between Boston and Pittsburgh. In 1915, Maranville offered some insight into what was discussed between players from opposing teams during a game. Months after the Braves had played Pittsburgh at Forbes Field on June 9, Maranville explained how he and Boston rookie second baseman Ed Fitzpatrick tried to distract Wagner, who went 3–for–4 that day, while he was standing on second base after blasting a double to left field.[36] Fitzpatrick and Maranville engaged Wagner in some friendly chitchat involving his hobby of raising chickens on a farm where he could be found doting over the birds day and night during hatching season.[37]

> "Well here you are again, old top," remarked Fitzpatrick.
> "Yep, here I am again," replied Wagner, ducking, dodging and getting back to the keystone sack as the two infielders almost ran around him in a circle in order to hold him at second.
> "How many chickens have you got on your farm?" asked Maranville after he received a pickoff throw from Boston's pitcher but missed the Dutchman.
> "Not many," responded a panting and perspiring Honus.
> "Well, about how many?" insisted Fitzpatrick.
> "Oh, about 15,000," answered Wagner as a lusty hit rang off the bat of Jimmy Viox. "But I must go now. I'll see you fellows again."

All Fitzpatrick and Maranville could do was watch as Wagner's old legs chugged into third base, rounded the bag, and headed home. As Maranville finished relating this story to *Pittsburgh Gazette Times* baseball writer James Jerpe after a doubleheader between Boston and Pittsburgh at Forbes Field on August 2 had been postponed due to rain, a broad smile came across his face. "I am glad I broke into the game early enough to see a few years of that great old boy."[38]

The game of baseball certainly had evolved since Wagner broke in with Louisville in 1897. This subtle method of catching a player off-guard by engaging him in casual conversation, which was more in vogue as his career was winding down, had been used before. It had not been a prominent strategy when rough-and-tumble players preferred a more

direct approach. William "Kid" Gleason was one such player who gave no quarter to anyone during his playing career, which lasted from 1888–1912. Gleason, who spent most of his career playing second base for the Philadelphia Phillies and New York Giants, was one of the scrappiest players that ever pushed a runner off a base.[39] Following his retirement as a player, he became a coach, and then manager of the Chicago White Sox.

While coaching the White Sox in 1916, Gleason was asked by a baseball writer to compare the current game to when he played. With a disgusting shrug of his shoulders, a resolute Gleason vented his frustration over the fact that baseball no longer carried the aggression prevalent during the 1890s. "There's too much candy in the game now," stated Gleason. A few months after making this statement, Gleason harkened back to those bygone baseball days when he visited old friend and current Pirates manager Jimmy Callahan in a Philadelphia hotel on a hot summer night while the Pirates were in town.

Honus Wagner was talking with Callahan when Gleason arrived. After the three gentlemen discussed current events for a few hours, Wagner turned to Gleason and said: "Say, Kid, you remember the day Clarke and the boys cut your shoes off in Philadelphia?" Gleason's eyes took on a retrospective gaze as his mind drifted back to a game about a dozen years earlier. He made no reply to Wagner's remark. No response was necessary since it was obvious from the look on Gleason's face that he recalled the incident.[40] A few minutes after Gleason bid Callahan a fond farewell, Wagner explained what had happened in that game.

> We started a series here, and Fred and some of the rest of the speedsters had the Kid almost barefooted before the fifth inning arrived, but every one of us who reached second during the remainder of the series carried a Gleason-brand trademark.
>
> After the Kid's second shoe started to unravel from the spike wounds he got real sore. Clarke was on first and a grounder was hit to short. A force play was started, but Gleason deliberately took his foot off the bag and sank the ball in between two of Clarke's ribs. They had to call time while the ball was yanked from Fred's hide. The Pittsburgh team was glad when that series was finished.[41]

Honus Wagner also seemed to be in agreement with Kid Gleason about the state of baseball affairs in 1916. Wagner conceded that players were now eating candy instead of plug tobacco.[42]

◆ ◆ ◆

A strong, interstate rivalry has always existed between the Pittsburgh Pirates and Philadelphia Phillies. Bill Shettsline held the position of manager, team president or business manager for the Phillies throughout Wagner's career.[43] While Shettsline was able to witness many great Wagner baseball feats, one play in particular from later in the Flying Dutchman's career stood out in his mind. There was one man out in the inning and the Phillies trailed Pittsburgh by one run. With Philadelphia's Sherwood "Sherry" Magee occupying third base, Wagner was playing in to cut off the run. The Phillies' John "Hans" Lobert stepped to the plate and smacked a pop fly about 20 feet behind second base.[44]

Wagner scampered back, never turning, as the baseball arched itself in front of him. Honus ran with the ball that he could not see. The phenomenal baseball instinct that had directed Wagner's every move on the diamond guided him to the correct spot before he stuck out his hand. The baseball fell into his grasp and he turned a complete somersault, holding onto the sphere. Magee was 20 feet down the line, but he scooted back to the bag since, as baseball writer James Jerpe once said, Wagner's throw was "as true as a die." The ball traveled on a line straight into catcher George Gibson's mitt. Wagner had make a spectacular play by blindly catching the baseball and throwing a perfect strike to home plate from a sitting position.[45]

Both baseball players and devoted fans from Philadelphia were constantly tortured during Honus Wagner's 21-year major league career. In one game during catcher Red Dooin's managerial tenure with the Phillies, which lasted from 1910–1914, things looked good for rooters at Fogel Field since staff ace Earl Moore was on the hill. A group of actors had turned out to cheer for their beloved Phillies. The youngest thespian later recalled using a truly Shakespearean tone, how comedy and tragedy collided as the day's climactic scene played out when Honus Wagner stepped to the plate.[46]

Pittsburgh was playing the Phillies, and it was near the end of the game with the score a run or two in favor of Dooin's Darlings, when the Pittsburghers came in for their half of the closing stanza. By some means or other Byrne, Clarke and Leach got on and filled the three sacks to overflowing. A bunch of actors, including Tony Grady, Joe Mitchell, Lou Anger, Leo Donnelly and myself, sat in the upper pavilion alongside of the press box, all of us dyed-in-the-wool home team Phillie rooters.

As Moore went to his place in the box and glanced at the three bases filled with race horses, Joe Mitchell turned to me, and pointing to Honus Wagner picking out his bludgeon, said: "Kid, the stage is set." I sighed and replied: "Joey, you've emitted a mouthful."

Wagner found a club that looked like a foremast on a warship and started toward the plate. Things were so quiet that one could hear the umpire's indicator tick. Just then Tony Grady leaped to his feet and in a voice loud enough to be heard in Wilmington yelled: "Wagner, you're wanted on the phone!"

Eight thousand people laughed uproariously—including Wagner himself. That was comedy—but what happened a few moments later was tragedy. He cleaned up.[47]

Whether he was clearing the bases with a big hit or making an unbelievable play at shortstop, Honus Wagner always made life difficult for opponents, adversaries and mere baseball mortals. His propensity for performing amazing exploits on the diamond came as naturally to him as breathing did to any ordinary person.

9

Baseball's Greatest Player Enjoying Life's Simple Pleasures

Honus Wagner truly loved playing the game of baseball. Each day that he suited up and represented the Pittsburgh Pirates as the National League's top star, he had one goal in mind. He wanted to perform to the best of his ability to help his team win games. While his zeal in respect to playing baseball was genuine and unassailable, Wagner gravitated toward other passions that gave him equal enjoyment and fulfillment. He was uncomfortable being thrust into the limelight and desired the quiet life in his hometown of Carnegie. Rather than being placed on a pedestal as baseball's premier player, he preferred to play the role of an average Carnegie citizen who enjoyed life's simple pleasures.

Like many other residents from this municipality that was located about six miles from downtown Pittsburgh, Wagner loved to spend pleasurable hours going fishing and hunting. The big Teuton was also an automobile enthusiast who enjoyed taking long rides around Carnegie and neighboring municipalities. He also loved to play another sport that involved more physical contact than the game that helped him earn a living. Due to his competitive nature and the desire to remain in shape in the off-season, he gravitated toward basketball as an athletic alternative during Pittsburgh's winter months. While hunting, fishing and playing basketball presented an opportunity for Wagner to engage in hours of enjoyment and pleasure, these pursuits served a secondary purpose. All three interests allowed him to remain in shape for the upcoming baseball campaign.

Wagner made his basketball debut in February of 1902, playing for the Carnegie fireman's team. He traveled throughout western Pennsyl-

vania and the surrounding area with his team of All-Professionals that included brother Al Wagner and friend Patsy Flaherty.[1] Barney Dreyfuss preferred his star player participating only in hunting and fishing for entertainment and conditioning. Dreyfuss took exception to Wagner playing basketball during the winter, fearing that he might suffer a serious injury that would prevent him from executing his baseball duties in the summer. In an effort to help alleviate some of Dreyfuss' concerns, Pittsburgh's owner and manager Fred Clarke came out to watch Wagner play. Basketball games then were played in a wire cage. On this night, when Dreyfuss and Clarke saw Wagner's team, the contest was particularly rough.[2]

The Wagner five were playing a tough team that resorted to physical domination as they spilled Wagner and his teammates all over the floor in an effort to claim victory. On several occasions, Wagner was scratched when he was knocked and body-checked into the wire netting. Both of his arms, his face and body were bleeding. When Dreyfuss came into the dressing room to see Wagner after the game, his star player looked like he had been carved up with a knife. "It's too rough, Honus," said Dreyfuss with deep concern. "Why, look how you are bleeding."

"Oh, that's nothing," replied Wagner. "You'd be surprised to know that the doctor tells me the blood sometimes comes thru my skin when it isn't bumped or cut at all."[3]

Although it was evident that Dreyfuss did not believe Wagner's tall tale, he walked out of the locker room without another word. While Fred Clarke did not so strenuously object to Wagner playing basketball during the off-season, he believed that participating in the sport was not beneficial for his star player. Clarke ignored his own objections and permitted Wagner to play because the Dutchman loved the game. Dreyfuss finally consented as well after Clarke persuaded him to allow Wagner to continue playing basketball for that same reason.[4] Dreyfuss' concerns certainly were legitimate since opposing squads seemed to rise to the occasion when they played against Wagner's basketball team.

Many opposing players, possibly feeling that Wagner should stick to playing the game he was great at instead of dabbling in their sport, never hesitated being physically abusive toward the star Pirate. On February 27, 1903, Wagner's team made a trip to one of his favorite towns for a Friday night game in Butler County, the stomping grounds of for-

mer teammate Rube Waddell. While Waddell was not in attendance, some of his relatives were in the audience. Although Wagner was eager to make a good showing, the Butler squad planned on making life miserable for him. Every Butler player intended to exhibit how basketball should be classified as a contact sport.[5] A fan who attended the game offered his impressions regarding the evening's events at the gymnasium.

> Well, we heard that Honus was no ping pong player, so he had to take his medicine. Say, but he did dive in and round that floor with the Butler push right on his trail. Biff bang they came against him, just as he would attempt a shot for the basket and away would sail the giant ball tosser into a mess. "Get into the game, Honus," shouted his pals. He did, but what he did cannot be found in the score book for he never ran up a goal. The nearest he came was a shot which lodged just outside of the basket. Hans was husky, that was all. Such is the penalty of fame. Had he been a slob ordinary player the Butler boys would have let him alone.[6]

It seemed that fame and notoriety on the baseball diamond did not allow Honus Wagner to receive positive, special treatment when he stepped into the wire cage to play against an opposing basketball team. If anything, that celebrity status led opposing players to deal with him in a ruthless manner.

◆　◆　◆

Honus Wagner was not the only major league baseball player from his basketball team who was subjected to such abuse. Other friends of the Carnegie native who joined him on the hardwood found the going quite tough at times. Hans Lobert, who made his major league debut with Pittsburgh on September 21, 1903, and later played with the Chicago Cubs, Cincinnati Reds, Philadelphia Phillies and New York Giants, was a member of Wagner's traveling team for a number of years. When Lobert was in town for a series at Forbes Field in August of 1915, the two German players reminisced with writer James Jerpe about one moment of basketball glory.

"Do you remember that night in Irwin?" Lobert asked Wagner.

"Will I ever forget it," exploded Wagner. "I can feel that bump yet."[7]

Wagner and Lobert had received the same type of reception in Irwin, Pennsylvania, that the Dutchman experienced during many other

encounters against dogged basketball opponents. Both men, who were playing forward that night, learned that the entire Irwin team had planned to "get them." The German stalwarts fought through this adversity and repelled their opponents quite nicely until Lobert set himself to chuck a shot at the basket, flanked by Wagner. Just as Lobert tossed the ball toward the basket, the whole Irwin battering ram that seemed more suited for a football game smashed into him. Lobert crashed into Wagner and the two men went through an inch board partition, tearing down the structure and landing in a pile of garbage in an adjacent room.

"But we made the basket, didn't we?" laughed Lobert.[8]

An opponent wishing to cause Honus Wagner bodily harm was only one of the drawbacks to staying in shape over the winter by playing basketball. Poor facilities added uncertainty any time Wagner stepped onto a court. He estimated that his team, which usually entertained crowds six nights a week, played as many as 100 games a season. Wagner reasoned that such a heavy workload kept his legs in shape, helped with wind and endurance, and prevented him from getting flabby during the winter months. He remembered one contest when he luckily did not suffer a serious injury in a town near Pittsburgh called Braddock.[9] The combination of clumsiness and a slick floor created a moment that ended up being embarrassing rather than catastrophic.

As Wagner was running down the floor chasing the basketball, he slipped, fell and skidded along the court on his back. There was a piping-hot radiator at the end of the basketball court. His leg slipped under it before he unknowingly turned up his foot, which caused his leg to lock up underneath the radiator. Attempts on Wagner's part to free his leg, which was pinned beneath the radiator, were futile. The game had to be delayed for 20 minutes while a plumber disconnected the piping so Wagner could free his leg.[10] While Barney Dreyfuss probably would have been outraged to see his best player sidelined due to losing a battle with a radiator, Wagner being disabled with pneumonia certainly was another unacceptable, disturbing scenario.

In one instance, Wagner's basketball team played a game in Jeannette, Pennsylvania, while the area was experiencing sub-zero weather. After the game concluded, the players barely had enough time to leave the gymnasium to catch a train back to Pittsburgh. Wagner and his teammates put overcoats over their basketball togs because they did not have

enough time to dress. Since the players were perspiring profusely as they walked to the train depot, they were letting off steam in the cold air like a puffing locomotive. The men changed clothes in the baggage car, shivering and freezing the entire time.[11]

Such temperatures seemed to be of no consequence for Honus Wagner when he was doing something he enjoyed. During the winter of 1915–1916, Wagner arrived at the office of Barney Dreyfuss as zero degree weather gripped Pittsburgh. Once inside the office, Wagner doffed his overcoat and hat. Moments later, he opened his coat, revealing the absence of a vest. Walking over to the radiator, Wagner ran his hand over it and said: "Gee, they've got the steam heat turned on." He conversed with new Pirates manager Jimmy Callahan for about 15 minutes, fixing his eyes on the skyline outside the entire time. Suddenly, the grand old man of baseball could not stand it any longer.[12]

"Well, boys, I'm going out," exclaimed Wagner as he grabbed his hat and topcoat. "I can't stand it to be cooped up on a day like this. Me for the sunshine and air. Gee, I've a big notion to go fishing."

"What kind of fish do you catch at this time of year?" someone asked.

"Well, fish ain't so plentiful just now," replied Wagner, "but I could go swimming all right. Many a time I've had a dip when the temperature was lower. I like to be outdoors. It's the only place for a man to be, anyway. Good bye."[13]

Given the choice of attending an important social function or going fishing or swimming, it was a sure bet that Honus Wagner would select being at one with nature in the great outdoors each and every time.

◆ ◆ ◆

Throughout Rube Waddell's baseball career, the press constantly reported on the fishing peculiarities of the eccentric pitcher. Although Waddell received more press notices regarding this particular inclination, he certainly did not fish more often than Honus Wagner. One major difference was that while Waddell would leave in the middle of a game to go fishing, Wagner took his diamond responsibilities seriously. Wagner avoided only outside social functions related to the game such as banquets and speaking engagements when the opportunity to take his reel and tackle box to a favorite fishing hole presented itself. He would

not miss a game, but hated society and parlor spectacle. Waddell, not always concerned about a diamond contest, never missed a social affair when he had the opportunity to attend a function.[14]

Due to Wagner's love for fishing and the outdoors, being named as a Pennsylvania Fish Commissioner in the spring of 1914 seemed like a logical progression. Wagner was responsible for hiking through the rugged parks in Allegheny County with a tub of bass sprouts and planting them in straight rows in an abandoned rock quarry filled by rainwater. He also owned more fish ponds of his own than a king and always seemed to know where the best places were for an angler to produce a decent haul. Wagner frequently enjoyed fishing when the Pittsburgh Pirates were playing at home. With a reel and bucket of live bait in tow, he boarded a train in Carnegie most mornings at daybreak and headed for the hills. When the locomotive reached one of the planted rock fishing quarries, the conductor slowed the train down so Wagner could hop off.[15]

In conforming with the nature of the streams that Wagner frequented, he believed the proper bait should always include wire nails. Around noon, he emerged from the woods with a string of bass, flagged down an incoming freight train, and made it back to Carnegie in time to eat lunch. That afternoon, he was on the diamond at Forbes Field, "busting the pill on the nose, plucking grounders out of the dust and putting the bee on base stealers," as Charles Dryden wrote in 1914. While none of the other players knew Wagner had been fishing, the Dutchman made many folks happy when he charitably offered them a fat bass. Such a generous gesture went a long way toward cutting down the high cost of living for these Carnegie denizens. An honest man, Wagner never had any time for bragging about fish he did not catch as some did while imbibing at a local establishment.[16]

Wagner loved the peace and tranquility that was a part of spending endless hours fishing. When Pittsburgh played on the road, he usually asked the desk clerk at the team hotel to direct him to the nearest fishing hole. Unfortunately, his quiet time was interrupted on numerous occasions during one of the Pirates' trips to Hot Springs, Arkansas, for spring training. As usual, Wagner was invited to various functions at the Arkansas resort which did not interest or appeal to him. He desperately tried to avoid these social gaieties by sequestering himself in a quiet

fishing spot, but each time he was found, rounded up and brought back to the hotel. He acquiesced to his Hot Springs friends since he was a good-hearted gentleman who did not like to hurt anybody's feelings.[17]

Wagner could not figure out how he was being discovered day after day, hiding out at his various favorite fishing holes, wanting to be left alone to his own devices involving hooks and lines. He eventually discovered that a kindred spirit was responsible for revealing his whereabouts. Among his many fans in that town was a veteran fisherman. This man had learned of Wagner's fondness for fishing. The local fisherman, reasoning that one angler would know the habits of another, traveled straight to spots that he would have selected and found the Pirates' star shortstop's hiding place nine times out of ten.[18]

While this veteran fisherman from Hot Springs could achieve inner harmony and serenity by spending time in the outdoors, such tranquility was not always realized by Honus Wagner. His status as a diamond legend precluded him from enjoying such pleasures since baseball lovers across the country constantly wanted to interact with the game's greatest player.

◆ ◆ ◆

The big Teuton took great pride in his vast collection of fishing tackle. Some of the plainest, least expensive-looking gear actually carried the heftiest price tags.[19] Honus Wagner was a devoted, dedicated artisan when it came to fishing. Besides utilizing the sport as a means to spend some quiet time alone, he loved to go fishing with teammates as a bonding mechanism. While camaraderie certainly grew from these excursions where men could fish and talk about life, humorous incidents were inevitable when the trip involved Wagner, who was a master at this craft, and a novice angler. Wagner recalled one fishing expedition involving Claude Hendrix. Besides being an exceptional pitcher, Hendrix was the freestyle eating champion of the National League.[20] Early one morning on a jaunt through the East, Wagner and Hendrix went fishing near New York. Before they left, Hendrix complained because he had missed breakfast.[21]

> Claude and I one day decided on a deep water fishing trip. He hired the large motor boat while I got busy and obtained the fishing tackle and bait. I questioned some old fishermen around the boat dock and they told me to use clams for bait.

I bought about five dozen clams, put them in a sack and gave them to Claude. I started the motor and we chugged out. We moved around for about an hour before we found a place to cast anchor. I got the tackle ready, gave him a pole and line and asked him to pass the bait.

"What do you mean bait?" he asked.

"The clams," I said.

"Oh, was that bait?" Hendrix replied. "I was hungry so I ate 'em."[22]

Wagner looked into the bait sack and noticed that Hendrix had missed one clam. He took it, threw it and hit Hendrix in the left eye. Hendrix yelled bloody murder as he rubbed his optic while Wagner pulled up the anchor and started for shore.[23]

Although this fishing trip ending up being a major disappointment, an encounter with another Pirates hurler in 1914 did cause Wagner to chuckle over the boastful nature of this youngster. Erving "Erv" Kantlehner was a southpaw from San Jose, California, who debuted for the Pirates on April 17, 1914. After being used mostly as a relief pitcher by Fred Clarke in 1914, Kantlehner was a hard-luck swingman in 1915 who posted a record of 5–12 despite a respectable 2.26 ERA.

Kantlehner was an ambitious and eager young man. When not pitching ball for the Pirates in the summer, he was a stenographer and church organist back in San Jose.[24] Throughout the early months of 1914, Kantlehner constantly bragged to Honus Wagner that he was the finest bass fisherman in California. Skeptical about the young hurler's claim, Wagner arranged a fishing trip while Pittsburgh was on the road. As these two men traveled to the lake where they planned on fishing, Kantlehner informed Wagner several times that a bass had to weigh two pounds before he would keep him.[25]

We set our boat out in the weeds, and it wasn't long until Kantlehner got a real bite. He hooked the fish and began to reel him in. I could tell by his every action that he had never fished before, but he somehow managed to get the fish into the boat.

It was a bullhead, but without letting on, I told him the proper way to unhook a bass was with his right hand. He used his right hand, and the fish horned him. Kantlehner let out a yell. I told him again to use his right hand, for he was a southpaw, was scheduled to pitch the next day and couldn't afford to hurt his salary hand.

That brought an end to the fishing trip. But Kantlehner showed the fish to everyone around the hotel as the bass he had caught. After getting the Bronx cheers a few times, he gave that up—and fishing too.[26]

The details surrounding Kantlehner's prowess as a bass fisherman did not remain within the confines of Pittsburgh's locker room as humorous fodder for Wagner and his teammates. Newspapers somehow caught wind of this funny tale and printed accounts in publications across the country. This ended up spelling bad news for Kantlehner when his father read about it. Just as Kantlehner had boasted to Wagner that he was a superior fisherman, the young hurler had bragged to his father that he would be doing great things for Pittsburgh. During his rookie season, Kantlehner received a letter from his father that was not very flattering in respect to both of these points.

"See, here, son, I want you to get in there and show me something," wrote Kantlehner's father. "You told me when you left to get the Pittsburgh papers and read about you. Jehosophats! I have spent all my loose change on the blamed sheets and they cost 10 cents out here, and I haven't seen the good old California name of Kantlehner in but one of them yet, and that was about you fishing with that old guy Wagner and cracking a joke about it. Now cut out the fishing and give me some pitching or come home and chop wood."[27]

Honus Wagner and Erv Kantlehner's father certainly agreed in one area. They both believed that Kantlehner should definitely abandon all thoughts of being a fisherman. Concentrating on his pitching would keep everyone happy.

◆　◆　◆

Pinning down Honus Wagner to talk about baseball when thoughts of hunting and fishing danced in his head was a difficult task. On one occasion in December of 1915, Wagner preferred to chat about rabbits rather than participate in a "hot stove" forum with some Pittsburgh baseball scribes. Although he had just completed a glorious hunt involving the festive rabbit, writers wanted to probe him about baseball.[28] This large gathering of scribes was keeping a vigil at Barney Dreyfuss' office, waiting for Pittsburgh's owner to name a successor to manager Fred Clarke, who had retired at the conclusion of the season.

"Will you manage the Pirates next year?" was the first question fired at Pittsburgh's shortstop like a hot ground ball.

"Me manage the Pirates? Huh!" responded Wagner. "I want to kill some more game before it's too late. Say, hunting is great this year, only it is tougher because there is no snow."

"Well, Jay, you still lead 'em all in fielding, notice it?" another writer asked.

"Yes, the rabbits are pretty plentiful and I have bagged my share," beamed Wagner with pride. "Say, I like this hunting stuff more every day."

"You're looking in great shape; guess you'll be hopping around that short position like a two-year-old next year?" queried a third scribe.

"It's all doped out, going to be some fishing parties on the spring training trip next year," replied Wagner.[29]

Scribes were always at a disadvantage when attempting to coerce Honus Wagner to talk about baseball in the wintertime.[30] Only hunting and fishing supplied Wagner with winter pleasure. Hunting was even enjoyable for him when he accidentally shot a pig on a dear friend's property. Walking miles through the woods during one of these excursions also acted as the perfect off-season training regimen for a player like Wagner, who wanted to be in prime physical condition once the baseball campaign opened.

Pirates hurler Charles "Deacon" Phillippe was a frequent companion of Wagner's on off-season hunting expeditions. Wagner and Phillippe had planned to try their hunting luck a month after the devastating disappointment of losing the 1903 World Series to the Boston Americans. Days before the two men were supposed to embark, Phillippe received word that Wagner was ill. Phillippe immediately hustled over to Carnegie to check on his sick friend. Wagner had a bad cold and headache. His doctor claimed he was suffering from the grip (flu). Phillippe rode the trolley to Carnegie seven consecutive days until Wagner's illness had passed and he was feeling better once again. The two players rescheduled their hunting trip through Crawford County for the week before Thanksgiving.[31]

Shortly before Phillippe and Wagner embarked on that trip, Pittsburgh's star hurler reminisced during a fanning bee at Pirates headquarters.

Farmers are all right. The great trouble is that some men with guns go roughshod over the fields, let down fences and often shoot stock. That's not fair, and you know it. Whenever Honus and myself get in a locality when the land owner is sore on hunters we always obey his orders to get off. Now and then we try the salve plan.

Two weeks ago we were in Washington County and one farmer walked along the edge of his farm for two hours to see that we did not get on his line. By gosh, do you know that we had it on him, for on one of his hikes he flushed a covey of quail, which flew right over onto the free soil where Dutch and myself were working. Did we get them? Well, can a dog eat meat?[32]

While these hunting trips with Wagner also acted as a means for his teammates to melt away the winter pounds, anomalies did occur. It usually was not a good idea to spend a few days relaxing at the Wagner homestead, feasting on huge meals put forward by the accommodating hosts, before a hunting trip. This was the case for second baseman Claude Ritchey in 1904. The plan to put some fat on Ritchey's scrawny body was Wagner's idea since the second baseman's weight had dropped precipitously by season's end. On December 16, Honus and his father Peter Wagner stopped off at Pirates headquarters since they had to come into the city for some horse medicine.[33] Wagner regaled those who were in the office with some tales about Ritchey.

"My sleigh is ready for any of you fellows who want to borrow it," stated Wagner in anticipation of the upcoming Christmas holiday. "Great times on the road nowadays. By the way, how is the baseball world going? I have been away so much recently that when Claude Ritchey asked me if they rapped the 'spitball' I had to say: 'Search me, Ritch.' By the way, Ritchey is getting fat. I was with him ten days, and the day he walked fifteen miles from the hunting camp, saying that if he got home so stout Mrs. Ritchey would not know him. At the close of the season he did not have as much meat on him as a hoe handle."[34]

Whether he was fattening up Claude Ritchey prior to hiking miles searching for game or shooting quail with Deacon Phillippe, Honus Wagner cherished every moment he spent during the winter months hunting throughout the hills of Pennsylvania. Wagner simply could not stand to be cooped up indoors.

◆ ◆ ◆

Spending time in the outdoors became problematic at times when nature and technology clashed. Covering ground on foot in the snow while hunting was not an issue if the party looking for game possessed the necessary equipment for survival in the wilderness. Problems sometimes arose when hunters relied on something other than their feet to help them reach a country destination. Complications were magnified

when these hardy men did not have an accurate understanding of a new, novel mode of transportation called the automobile. A little over a week before Christmas in 1910, Honus Wagner experienced some rough hours in the cold and snow one night due to his failure to grasp the premise that an automobile did not move without gasoline.

Wagner's car stalled in the snow ten miles from the nearest gas station, with his automobile absolutely empty of fuel. Wagner and his two hunting partners, Eddie Dennis and Matt Mowrey of Carnegie, passed several hours stuck in the snow, hoping to be rescued, until Wagner rescued the party by hiking ten miles through the hills near Imperial, Penn-

Honus Wagner was one of the first baseball players to be classified as an automobile aficionado. Wagner and auto magnate Henry Ford became close friends after the two were introduced to each other in New York. Wagner went on test rides with Ford through Central Park when the automobile was a relatively new invention. In this photograph, Wagner looks quite content sitting in one of the automobiles that he owned (courtesy National Baseball Hall of Fame Library, Cooperstown, New York).

sylvania, carrying a big gasoline tank on his shoulders. With snow a foot deep and not a stretch of level road for 500 feet, he tramped over steep hills until he found a road keeper who sold gasoline. Wagner then made the return trip to where his friends were stranded carrying a tank full of fuel. The hunting party finally was moving after Wagner's automobile was revived by the precious fuel. They reached Carnegie at midnight, with Eddie Dennis the only casualty of this ordeal, suffering from minor frostbite of the foot.[35]

While Wagner absolutely loved hunting and fishing, he had a deep appreciation for automobiles and treasured any opportunity to drive. One of the first baseball players ever classified as an automobile aficionado, Wagner enjoyed the thrill that could be achieved through speeding along a road in an automobile. Auto magnate Henry Ford was one of his many friends. Wagner was introduced to Ford in New York when both of their great careers were just getting started. The industrialist often took baseball's legendary player riding in Central Park in the automobile when it was a relatively new invention.[36] Wagner also assisted Ford so the auto magnate could make modifications during these test runs.

"Henry was always thinking," Wagner often recalled. "He had me steer his car while he stood on the running board and adjusted various points. We used to leave a trail of smoke 100 yards long as we 'raced' through the park."

Due to his love for cars, Wagner later was the proprietor of one of the first garages in suburban Carnegie. Wagner, one of the first Carnegie residents to own an automobile, sold the Cutting, the Regal and the Oldsmobile.

> I had a good repair man and a good paint shop, but people were afraid of the 'horseless carriages' in those days. If I sold 20 gallons of gas in a week, I was doing big business. And usually, I took about ten gallons myself, for my own car. My garage didn't do too much business, but it was a convenient place for the boys to loaf and talk baseball on cold winter evenings.[37]

Since Wagner was so devoted to driving automobiles, it was a bit surprising that he was involved in a second harrowing experience because he had not filled the car with gasoline before embarking on a trip. In this instance, a posse of citizens from a small town near Pittsburgh who mistook him for a highwayman wanted to toss him in jail.

This incident occurred in the spring of 1921, four years after he had retired as a major leaguer. Wagner was journeying to this small town with the Carnegie Tech squad that he coached to play a game. After the contest, Wagner and three of his players started back for Pittsburgh in Wagner's car. They had traveled only a few miles when the automobile quit cold. Wagner's car was out of gas.[38]

Wagner and one of his players walked down the road in search of an establishment that sold gasoline. Wagner waved his arms for an approaching car to stop and offer assistance. The driver of the vehicle accelerated to full speed and nearly ran Wagner down. Unable to find any help, Wagner and his companion returned to their car. When they reached the automobile, they found the other two members of Carnegie Tech's team shackled and being guarded by a motley gang of farmers armed with guns and revolvers.

"Here comes the other two that was in the gang," cried an angry voice from the posse as Wagner and his companion were also seized and bound.

"We got them all now—off to jail with them," commanded the group's leader.[39]

The posse, Wagner and his three players walked for five miles to the local jail. Wagner finally found someone who recognized him. Apologies and explanations were offered as Wagner and his players were released. It seemed a gang of men had been stopping cars along the road and robbing the occupants. Wagner and his companion matched the description of these thieves. Wagner's attempt to stop a car had been reported by the frightened motorist who had sped by, almost striking the Carnegie Tech coach. Following this incident, the whole countryside was pressed into service to make the raid in an effort to capture the culprits.[40]

Hopefully this was a well-learned lesson for Honus Wagner about filling the tank of his automobile with gasoline before voyaging to areas unknown. Prudence would eliminate the possibility that the vehicle could run out of gas, with its occupants being characterized as the western Pennsylvania version of Butch Cassidy and the Sundance Kid.

◆ ◆ ◆

When the time came to purchase a new automobile, Honus Wagner resembled a young kid who had just received a new baseball bat or glove

as a present. He was filled with glee and could never resist the temptation to take a look at a brand new model once it rolled off the production line. During the era when Wagner played, some people purchased automobiles after years of careful deliberation, while others recognized a good thing when they saw it and quickly procured the vehicle. Wagner definitely fell into the latter class when it came to buying a new car. He was an exceptional judge of an automobile's quality who usually decided within a few minutes if the vehicle was good enough to be added to the Wagner collection.[41]

Wagner at one time was connected to an automobile concern in Pittsburgh that handled the Maxwell car. In October of 1913, he made a Wednesday afternoon visit to the salesroom of the Forbes Motor Car Company, Maxwell dealers in Pittsburgh. Wagner stated that he had heard great things about the "Maxwell 25" and wanted to see one. Within five minutes, he was convinced that the "Maxwell 25" could climb with its automobile counterparts and was so pleased that he purchased the vehicle and drove it back to Carnegie.[42] While he was always very excited when he looked into buying a car, that enthusiasm left him in the rare instance when someone attempted to purchase a vehicle from him. He was identified as a salesman with a dealership basically in name only due to his enormous popularity in Pittsburgh.[43]

On one occasion, however, a local physician who wanted to purchase a car made an appointment to meet Wagner. Intending to buy a Maxwell, this doctor believed he was doing Wagner a favor by giving the great ball player the chance to earn a commission on the sale. Wagner neglected to keep the appointment. The physician, not discouraged in the least, rescheduled this appointment several times, but Wagner meticulously avoided each meeting. Disgusted at last with this course of events, the doctor purchased an automobile from a competitor. Wagner had missed each engagement with this physician because he was out in the woods hunting. "I couldn't attend to business," said Wagner. "I was too busy." Not even several hundred dollars in commission could convince Wagner to leave the outdoor life behind for just one day.[44]

Wagner enjoyed being around automobiles so much that he even entertained an occupation that involved these riding machines when he retired. While becoming a race car driver was not in his future, Wagner pondered the possibility of earning a living while sitting behind the

wheel of an automobile. Future employment aspirations were discussed by various Pirates during a long home stand in June of 1913.[45]

"When I'm through I'm going to work in a bank," said Claude Hendrix.

"Farming for mine," chirped in Babe Adams.

"I'm going to run a string of cabaret shows," said first baseman Jack Miller.

"Well, fellows, when I'm through I'll try to land a job with some rich guy who will treat me decent as his chauffeur," interjected Wagner. "I like automobiles, and as I will not have to work hard after I quit baseball, a nice job in a garage will be interesting enough for me."

There was silence in the room for a few minutes before one of Wagner's teammates piped in and said: "By the time Wagner quits baseball he'll have enough money to play around his own garage and drive his own cars."[46]

This claim sounded like a fairly logical premise.[47] Wagner thrived so well financially that he occasionally refused to accept money as payment for services rendered. One Pittsburgh business concern that was obsessed with creating a calendar which displayed Wagner in many of his characteristic baseball poses approached the star player about the idea. The owners believed such a calendar would be a valuable advertising feature since the poses would fit into certain schemes they had entertained. These photos had so much value in this company's eyes that they were willing to pay out big money to Wagner.[48]

Wagner must have been in a good mood when the representative of this concern approached him. Wagner heartily endorsed the project and agreed to participate in the photo shoot. He posed for the pictures and in due time received a check in the mail for $300. A few days later, he appeared at the Pirates team office and struck up a conversation with a secretary.

"That man sent me a check for three hundred dollars," said Wagner. "What shall I do with it?"

"Why," responded the secretary. "Don't you want the money?"

"No," responded Honus.

"Well, in that case," said the secretary, "I suppose you had better send it back to him."

"I'll do it," replied Wagner.[49]

Wagner remained true to his word as he sent this check back to the businessman.[50] He could not justify receiving such a large sum of money for doing very little work. He was a principled man who believed satisfaction should be achieved only through hard work. For Wagner, who preferred to be recognized as just an average Carnegie citizen, enjoying time hunting, fishing and driving around in automobiles was his proper reward for giving maximum effort and achieving supreme results on the baseball diamond. Whether he was hunting with teammates such as Deacon Phillippe, going through a stringent initiation process in 1903 to gain acceptance into the B.P.O. Elks, or entertaining friends at his residence, Wagner truly loved life's simple pleasures.[51] During the winter

Honus Wagner heartily enjoyed going hunting and fishing, and he loved his dogs. While he is sitting in this photograph with two of his best friends, Wagner resembled his dogs in that he loved to roam in the great outdoors and was most at peace with nature (courtesy National Baseball Hall of Fame Library, Cooperstown, New York).

prior to the 1902 baseball campaign, Wagner arose from a chair in his home while teammate Fred Clarke was visiting.[52]

"It's time," declared Wagner.

"Time for what?" asked Clarke.

"Why to give the dogs a run," dryly answered Dutch.

Within a few minutes, nine beagles were dashing up to their master, eager for a little chase over the valleys and knolls. The beagles startled a couple of bunnies as Wagner and Clarke gave them a 30-minute run. The merry, ringing barks of these happy dogs resounded over the hills.[53] There was nothing like the freedom of being able to roam around in the great outdoors, whether it involved beagles, an average Carnegie resident or the greatest shortstop in baseball history.

Encounters with the American Worker, an Angry Rabbit and Austrian Royalty

Honus Wagner's popularity was not based solely on his many celebrated diamond achievements. Possessing sound character traits, unrelenting determination and a resilient desire to achieve success were also key facets of Wagner's personality that people throughout America admired and respected. Exhibiting the proper temperament as a man was every bit as important as collecting hits and winning baseball games for the Pittsburgh Pirates. Wagner excelled at maintaining the appropriate balance between humility and confidence throughout his life.

Becoming a diamond icon did not come easily for all players. Wagner achieved this status without any debate due in large part to his gracious generosity. He was always willing to help both rookies and veterans. The great shortstop never rejected a request for guidance, encouraged them, and gave them tough love when it was needed. Wagner also motivated some of the visionaries and builders most responsible for helping America become such a great country.

Since Honus Wagner was a dedicated automobile enthusiast, he became a favorite of the factory men who built these machines. In 1913, the Pirates were scheduled to play an exhibition game against the Buffalo Bisons on August 28. Although it had been raining for hours, a large crowd was at the ballpark when the game was cancelled around 3:00 p.m.[1] While many of these rooters were disappointed they did not receive an opportunity to watch Wagner play that afternoon, a group of Buffalo

workers had been more fortunate a few hours earlier. Wagner, Fred Clarke and three other Pirates paid a visit to a large automobile factory in Buffalo. The company employed 2,500 men, who always ate lunch in the factory. Clarke explained what occurred when the Pirates walked through a full dining room that seated 1,700 hard-working men sitting down to enjoy a hearty meal.[2]

> You never saw such an ovation in your life. Every man in that room stood up and yelled at the top of his voice for Wagner. They took their knives and forks and beat a tat-too of praise upon their plates, until the noise was deafening. Honus walked the length of that room, and it took a lot of nerve to do it. But if this reception didn't warm his old heart, he's not human.
>
> After lunch we were taken through the entire factory. After we came out I told John he owed the company money. "How's that?" he queried. "Why," I told him, "there are 2,500 employees there, and every one of them neglected his work for at least 30 seconds to look at you. Figure it out for yourself, and see how much of the company's time you robbed them of." Honus laughed, and said he guessed he'd have to buy one of their machines to even up.[3]

Men such as these automobile factory laborers, who worked hard to earn a living, loved Honus Wagner due to the blue collar approach he displayed on the baseball diamond. Another man who was a designer rather than a builder found true inspiration in Wagner's majesty during a game. Outfielder Max Carey, a teammate of Wagner's from 1911 through 1917, recalled how Wagner was linked to an invention that was eventually valued at $30 million. Walter Victor Turner, manager of engineering at the Westinghouse Airbrake Company near Pittsburgh, was considered to be one of the leading pneumatic engineers in the world. Born in Epping Forest in Essex County, England, on April 3, 1866, Turner was responsible for developing more than 400 patented inventions used on various railroads and industrial plants.[4]

According to Carey, Turner was experiencing some difficulties improving an airbrake called the "K" Triple Valve. Although everything looked to be perfect in respect to design, the airbrake did not work. Despite this inventor's diligent efforts, one valve refused to work, and Turner was unable to unearth the reason for this mystery. Hoping to take his mind off the job, Turner went to Forbes Field to watch the Pirates play. He had never attended a game and did not seem very interested at first. His brain was consumed with thoughts of the puzzling problem involving that stubborn "K" Triple Valve. His attention even-

tually was directed to the field for a moment as Honus Wagner was danc-ing around second base, looking for an opening to steal third.

Finally, Wagner broke for third base. As he neared the hot corner, the Flying Dutchman came into the bag using a fall-away slide. The third baseman attempted to tag Wagner, but the big fellow seemed to fade away from the tag. Turner rose from his feet and shouted out loud to himself: "That's it, the fall away! Just the thing for my valve!" He immediately left the ballpark and hurried back to his laboratory. Inspired by Wagner's fall-away slide, Turner figured out the problem and was able to make the proper adjustments. His "K" Triple Valve brought in $30 million within three months of its inception.[5]

It seemed appropriate that the many men who were the very fabric of this hard-working nation received inspiration from the great Honus Wagner since he had adopted a similar blue-collar philosophy on the diamond.

◆　◆　◆

While Honus Wagner was a hero to many, Pittsburgh's star player remained grounded in respect to what was required of him during the long baseball campaign. He was always accommodating to young players who were looking for help or guidance. Throughout the latter stages of his career, Wagner habitually roomed with one of the Pirates' younger players rather than a veteran while the team was on the road. One reason was his habit of rising at 4:00 a.m. to go fishing. He would experience less trouble with a rookie than a veteran over this idiosyncrasy. Of course, the main purpose was his generous disposition as he tutored novice players so they could succeed at the major league level.[6]

In 1914, rookie outfielder Joe Kelly was one such player that Wagner offered to help become a bonafide major league player.[7] Kelly had done fine work for the Western League's St. Joseph Drummers in 1913 with a .318 batting average. Wagner ended up having his hands full on the road in 1914. Kelly appeared in 141 games and batted .222. He was also fanned by pitchers on 59 occasions, many times never taking the bat off his shoulder as he looked at called third strikes. Kelly's average actually dipped down to .151 on May 21. On one occasion while Kelly was immersed in a horrible slump, he batted with the bases loaded. After much mental trauma and physical exertion, he struck out. As he reached

the bench muttering gruffly to himself, Wagner attempted to console the youngster in his rough, sympathetic manner.[8]

"Do you know, I went to the plate with the bases full once," Wagner said to Kelly, "and it was in the World's Series, too. A little hit of mine would have scored the winning run, and do you know, I struck out."[9]

Wagner's little tale helped to cheer up the crestfallen Kelly. He was willing to tell a lie that focused on his failure so that Kelly might feel better about his situation. In reality, Wagner never struck out with the bases loaded in 15 World Series games. As for fanning when the game was on the line, this was a lark as well (although Wagner did strike out on three occasions with a teammate on base during the early stages of games in World Series play). Wagner's clutch hit actually iced Game Seven of the 1909 World Series against the Detroit Tigers on October 16 at Bennett Park. In the sixth inning, with Tommy Leach at second and Fred Clarke on first, Wagner blasted a triple to left field off George Mullin that drove in his two teammates. He also came around score on left fielder Davy Jones' throwing error as Pittsburgh took a 7–0 lead. The Pirates claimed the deciding game, 8–0. Rather than brag about his success in this situation when talking to Joe Kelly in 1914, Wagner discreetly preferred to inform the youngster that he had struck out.[10]

Wagner did not restrict his insight or assistance just to teammates. He also went out of his way to give young players from opposing squads a morale boost. As Wagner's career was winding down, writer William A. Phelon noted his propensity for striking out when facing young hurlers in certain situations. Phelon surmised that Wagner deliberately struck out to flatter the youngster on the slab. When the Pirates were leading by a safe margin and a young hurler was on the mound, Wagner struck out more frequently out of the goodness of his heart, with a wild, terrific swing at the final pitch.[11] The crowd hollered in sheer delight, and the kid pitcher welled up with pride over fanning the great Honus Wagner. This young man now had a tale to tell of how he struck out Wagner and made him miss the big pitch by a mile. To Phelon, these strikeouts could be accidental, with Wagner actually bearing down, but he dismissed this premise. Why did Wagner fail more often under these circumstances, while he thrived the majority of the time against a star hurler in a tight game, with teammates on base?[12]

Phelon came to the conclusion that Honus Wagner failed on pur-

pose during certain encounters against young pitchers due to his overwhelming generosity.

◆　◆　◆

Wagner's most famous player protégé was Pirates second baseman John "Dots" Miller. After receiving a tryout and impressing Fred Clarke in 1908, Miller was farmed out to the McKeesport Tubers of the Ohio-Pennsylvania League for more seasoning. A year later, Miller replaced veteran Ed Abbaticchio as Pittsburgh's starting second baseman. He hit .279 and drove home 87 runs as Pittsburgh claimed the National League pennant and defeated Detroit in the World Series. His strong rookie campaign in 1909 placed him in that elite class of National League players where Wagner had resided for a decade. Miller and Wagner became great friends both on and off the field as Pittsburgh's star shortstop took the gregarious rookie under his wing and taught him how to become a better player.

Pittsburgh fans were well aware of the strong friendship between Wagner and Miller during their five years together with the Pirates. What many people did not know was that Wagner's influence had started years earlier before the youngster played for McKeesport, when he was growing up in Kearny, New Jersey.[13] When asked in 1910 how he became a winner in such a relatively short period of time, Miller explained that he owed all of his success as a player to Honus Wagner.

> I win by watching Wagner. When asked to tell how I won I was going to refuse because it does sound "swelled" for a young fellow to tell such things or claim to win, until I remembered how it was.
>
> I win because Honus Wagner taught me the game, showed me how to play it something after his own style, so in telling how I win I am only praising the teacher and the man I think is the greatest ball player of them all.
>
> Wagner had me under him for years. He began to show me the game when I was a kid, and took an interest in me from the first. He showed me how to make plays, told me what a fellow ought to do and what he ought not, and coached me all the time. Still I wasn't a winning player until he got me to Pittsburgh where I could play alongside of him every day and watch him. I learned more about the game just watching Wagner than I ever thought there was in it. The first time they tried me I was not ready, and they sent me back. Wagner still had faith in me and kept coaching me along, and the second time I managed to stick. Whether I would have been a good ball player or a bad one but for him I cannot tell.

I watch Wagner closely all during a game, and move so as to be in the play with him. We talk back and forth and exchange signals once in a while, but I think he does this more to help me and make certain I will not make mistakes than for anything else. I know that watching him keeps me from watching batters and runners as closely as I ought and that if he was out of it I would have to change the system, but I can tell more now by watching Honus than by watching the others. No one knows what a great player John Wagner is until he has played alongside of him.

I play a deep field, and it was Wagner who showed me what angles to take on different balls and how to shift runners. He showed me how to hit without changing my natural batting position at all. In fact he seemed to know more about me than I knew of myself.[14]

Months after Dots Miller wrote this glowing tribute to Wagner, another young player, Alex McCarthy, arrived in Pittsburgh during the 1911 season. A utility infielder throughout most of the campaign, McCarthy did not get a chance to show what he could do until Wagner injured his ankle on August 16.[15] McCarthy jumped in at short and played fine baseball. He seemed to have a great future ahead of him due to his determination and ability. Wagner's big German heart warmed up to this youngster from the moment he joined the Pirates in spring training. One day on the bench, they watched a renowned shortstop on the opposing team perform his craft.[16]

"Watch that fellow, Mac," said Wagner, "and play them like he does."

McCarthy looked at the Flying Dutchman with a surprised expression. "Sure," McCarthy replied, "I don't need to watch him. I've got my pattern alongside of me."[17]

From that day forward, McCarthy watched Wagner's every move on the baseball diamond. He studied the great shortstop, talked to him and thought about how he performed every waking moment of the day. "Honus" was his ideal, and McCarthy had no better friend or stronger supporter than the baseball icon from Carnegie. When Wagner suffered his ankle injury in the game against Brooklyn at Washington Park, his teammates were downcast and devastated. He reassured them, pointing out that his latest student was more than capable of handling the shortstop duties while he was sidelined.

"Don't worry boys," said Wagner. "McCarthy is a better shortstop right now than I've been for ten years."[18]

Alex McCarthy showed that he had learned his lessons well during

his rookie campaign when Honus Wagner acted as his teacher. McCarthy took over as Pittsburgh's starting second baseman in 1912, appeared in 111 games and batted .277. Dots Miller shifted over to first base that year to fill a long-standing hole in the Pirates infield. Miller responded by having his best season since his 1909 rookie campaign as he batted .275 and drove home 86 runs.

◆ ◆ ◆

The year before Dots Miller made his highly successful major league debut, Honus Wagner and his Pittsburgh Pirates were involved in one of the tightest pennant races in National League history. When the 1908 baseball campaign concluded, the Chicago Cubs sat on top of the National League, with Pittsburgh and New York one game behind. Things would have been different if New York's Fred Merkle had not failed to touch second base as the winning run scored and then was called out against Chicago at the Polo Grounds on September 23.[19] The contest was declared a tie by National League president Harry Pulliam and replayed on October 8 as Chicago defeated New York, 4–2, to clinch the pennant.

If the Pirates had defeated the Cubs during their final regular season game on October 4, Chicago's victory over New York in the season finale actually would have allowed Pittsburgh to be crowned National League champions. With the pennant hanging in the balance as 30,247 crammed into West Side Grounds, Chicago eliminated Pittsburgh from contention, winning 5–2.[20] For veteran players like Honus Wagner, Fred Clarke, Tommy Leach, Deacon Phillippe and Sam Leever, their disappointment in 1908 was surpassed only by losing to the Boston Americans in the 1903 World Series. Wagner considered that final game against Chicago in 1908 one of the most significant battles he was involved in during his career.

"One of the most important games I ever played," said Wagner, "because we lost it and several hundred dollars of World Series money, was the last of the season with the Chicago Cubs in 1908, when they had the famous Tinker-Evers-Chance combination."[21]

Chicago ace Mordecai "Three Finger" Brown was too much for the Pirates. He kept Pittsburgh off the board for five innings as Chicago built a 2–0 lead against Vic Willis. Pittsburgh tied the game in the sixth

inning before the Cubs added single tallies in the sixth and seventh against Willis, and another run off Howard Camnitz in the eighth frame. Down to their final three outs, Honus Wagner started off the Pirates' ninth by cracking a single to center field. Wagner had not experienced a grand day thus far as his two errors had led to two Chicago runs. *The Pittsburgh Gazette Times* claimed that Honus "played the field all afternoon much like a cheese sandwich without mustard."[22] With Wagner on first and nobody out in the ninth inning, second baseman Ed Abbaticchio stepped up to the plate, hoping to keep the rally going.

Fred Clarke pulled Abbaticchio aside and instructed him to crack the first one through that looked good. Abbaticchio faithfully followed his manager's instructions as he blasted a drive over first base that fell a few feet fair into the overflow crowd in right field. Wagner stopped at third base as Abbaticchio pulled into second with a ground rule double. As first baseman Alan Storke stepped to the plate, umpire Hank O'Day's loud voice calling the hit a foul ball bellowed above the cheering of Chicago's frenzied crowd.[23] Clarke and the Pirates protested O'Day's decision, but the arbiter could not be swayed by their arguments. Wagner was forced to return to first base, while Abbaticchio resumed his position in the batter's box. Brown grooved a fastball that he took for a called third strike. Pittsburgh's season officially ended when Joe Tinker executed two force plays at second base.[24]

Two years later, some Pirates claimed that Hank O'Day had misgivings about this critical decision. O'Day apologized to Fred Clarke, asserting that calling Abbaticchio's two-bagger a foul ball was his only mistake as an umpire.[25] For Honus Wagner, the disappointment surrounding this game lingered for quite some time. While he believed the outfield crowds behind ropes did their work well that day to assist the Cubs, he was not enough of a sore loser to admit this was the deciding factor. The Pirates had hoped to land the pennant for Clarke as a 36th birthday present.[26] Wagner became very introspective when he eloquently described the sadness and heartache following Pittsburgh's game that fateful day.

But I remember how we sat dazed in the clubhouse after the game. We had come up from behind wonderfully that year and to lose it all in an afternoon was a grief that was hard for the most stoical to bear. The wild joy in the Chicago clubhouse contrasted pitifully with the gloom in ours. I remember

seeing one or two tear drops in the eyes of some of our younger fellows, but can you blame them?

Before the game a certain man bought two railroad tickets. One called for Kansas and the farm; the other for Pittsburgh and the World's Series. Two hours after the game a sun-tanned Kansan plunked himself in the cushions of a Pullman chair and gazed sorrowfully out of the window. The man was Fred Clarke, one of the hardest losers that ever looked at a ball game. He had lost it all in two hours, but the other passengers did not know that he was anything other than what he looked—a prosperous Kansas farmer without a care or worry.[27]

While it was his great feats on the baseball diamond that had elevated Honus Wagner to the status of elite player, it was his virtuous nature that separated him from the many men who played the game. There was also no doubt that Wagner was Fred Clarke's equal as one of the hardest losers that ever played the game.

◆ ◆ ◆

Redemption came quickly for Honus Wagner and his Pittsburgh Pirates following this stinging defeat by the arch-rival Chicago Cubs. Pittsburgh closed out the first decade of the twentieth century by claiming their fourth National League pennant in the past nine years. Although Chicago increased their victory total from 99 in 1908 to 104 in 1909, Pittsburgh claimed the pennant with a record of 110–42. The 1909 World Series was the first that pitted the two league batting champions against each other. Honus Wagner won the 1909 National League batting crown with a .339 average, while Ty Cobb of the Detroit Tigers was tops in the American League with a mark of .377. The 1909 Fall Classic was also the first time in baseball history that the World Series went the distance, as Pittsburgh prevailed over Detroit four games to three.

One of the most famous stories about Honus Wagner was the legendary battle between Pittsburgh's veteran shortstop and Detroit's young outfielder in the 1909 World Series. While this tale has been part of baseball folklore for many decades, the story involving a confrontation between Wagner and Cobb at second base is more of a yarn than undisputable truth. As the years went by, Wagner embraced this tale as his own and related it to anyone who asked him about the 1909 World Series. The incident in question supposedly happened in Game One at Forbes Field on October 8.

According to Wagner, bench jockeying was particularly brutal from the outset of Game One. Detroit's players let the Pirates have it with a verbal barrage, while Wagner and his teammates dished it back to them with interest. Hostile taunts were exchanged between the two benches with practically every pitch.[28] Detroit grabbed a 1–0 lead in the first inning against Babe Adams before Fred Clarke tied the game in the fourth with a home run off George Mullin. After left fielder Davy Jones led off the fifth inning for Detroit with a single to right field, he was forced at second base on Donie Bush's ground ball to Wagner. Bush was erased in the same manner when Cobb smacked a grounder to shortstop. The following is how Wagner frequently related the famous tale of what happened next when Cobb came at him on a steal attempt with his spikes up.

> "Hey Krauthead, I'm coming down on the next pitch," Cobb hollered, and I told him to come ahead and by golly he did.
> Catcher George Gibson laid the ball right in my glove and I stuck it on Ty. I guess it wasn't too easy either, because Cobb needed a couple of stitches to sew up his lip. That's the type of Series it was from start to finish.[29]

While Wagner's assessment regarding that World Series being a rough battle was accurate, his description of this encounter with Ty Cobb is not substantiated by eyewitness testimony. Accounts from that time painted a much different picture. One newspaper described this incident as nothing more than an ordinary play. As Cobb broke for second base in this steal attempt, George Gibson was forced to pull down a high pitch from Babe Adams. Gibson's throw toward second base was in the dirt. Wagner made a wonderful, one-handed grab of the ball on the first bounce and slapped a tag on Cobb's body as he slid into the bag. Although it looked as if Wagner had applied the tag before Cobb reached second base, umpire Silk O'Loughlin called the runner safe. After Wagner and Fred Clarke kicked for a few minutes over the call, play resumed and Sam Crawford made the inning's final out on a foul popup to Gibson.[30]

The fact that both of these star players had a deep admiration and respect for each other indicated that such an incident likely was an embellished tale that did not happen. Prior to Game One, while Cobb was standing near the plate playing catch with a teammate, Wagner had spied Cobb, walked over to Detroit's great player and grabbed him by

the hand. The greeting was cordial as Cobb also shook Wagner's hand. The two players talked for a few minutes as the fans cheered their approval. Cobb had been interviewed by reporters two hours after he arrived in the Smoky City. One scribe asked the young outfielder if he thought he would record more hits than Wagner in the World Series.[31]

"Oh you mustn't compare us," replied Cobb. "He is a baseball veteran, and I am only a youngster. He has had years of experience, and is up in all the tricks of the trade. I have never seen him play, but from what I have heard of him, he must be a wonder. I don't know if I will make a single hit in the series, but I don't care if Wagner hits .400 and I only bat .100, if the Tigers win out."[32]

Ty Cobb exhibited a humble spirit during this interview. Cobb, who became an immediate favorite of Pittsburgh fans, was accompanied by his wife and mother at all times while in Pittsburgh when Detroit was not practicing or playing.[33] Honus Wagner admired Cobb and his overwhelming baseball talent. Weeks after the 1909 World Series concluded, Wagner showered Cobb with effusive praise.

One of the most famous incidents about Honus Wagner was an alleged encounter with Detroit's Ty Cobb during Game One of the 1909 World Series at Forbes Field on October 8. Cobb supposedly yelled to Wagner: "Hey, Krauthead, I'm coming down on the next pitch," before he attempted to steal second base in the fifth inning of that game (courtesy National Baseball Hall of Fame Library, Cooperstown, New York).

Cobb is the fastest man I have ever seen. I never thought he could have that much speed. I heard a lot about Cobb, and how fast he was, but he surprised me by the speed he showed on bases in the World's Series. I wouldn't say that he is the fastest man that ever played ball, because I have not seen all of them, but he has as much speed and

a lot more than any man I ever played against. Cobb is what I call a perfect player. He lacks nothing. There is not a thing that a ball player should have that Cobb hasn't got, and he's got a bunch of things that no other ball player has. He is perfect in every respect. I can't find any weakness, and I see nothing that he could improve on.[34]

Considering the level of respect that Honus Wagner and Ty Cobb had for each other, it seems highly unlikely that the young Tigers outfielder would have taunted a man whom he revered by yelling "Hey, Krauthead." While baseball folklore may dictate otherwise, any rough confrontation in the 1909 World Series between players from Pittsburgh and Detroit's squads may have been due to nothing more than two teams fighting and battling to claim baseball's greatest prize.

◆ ◆ ◆

The people of Pittsburgh celebrated and partied like they had never done before on the evening of October 18, 1909, when the conquering champions were honored for defeating Detroit in the World Series. The festivities began at 8:30 p.m. with Pittsburgh's players weaving throughout the downtown area in a procession of automobiles along with city officials and the mayor. This pageant scene moved through Oakland to Forbes Field for a special ceremony. Once inside Barney Dreyfuss' new baseball palace, a large crowd of hollering fans paid tribute to the World Champion Pittsburgh Pirates. Megaphones were used so dignitaries and players could make stirring speeches to the raucous crowd. Congressman James F. Burke and Mayor William A. Magee presided over this grand celebration.[35]

Each Pirate received a rousing ovation when introduced to the crowd assembled at Forbes Field. There was a tremendous commotion when Congressman Burke and Mayor Magee grabbed hold of a big, husky-looking man who was making efforts to avoid his turn in the spotlight. Fred Clarke joined the two politicians to help drag Honus Wagner up to the podium. Pittsburgh's most famous player was blushing like a girl and acting much like a bashful schoolboy. Every man, woman and child in the grandstand jumped to their feet, shouting in mighty chorus, waving pennants, blowing horns, shaking rattlers and making any noise they could. Every band on the field began playing at the same time. It was doubtful if any other person had ever received such an ovation in Pittsburgh, as 20,000 denizens applauded their hero in unison.[36]

Honus Wagner constantly did his best to avoid the limelight, though it was very difficult given his status as the National League's best player. He had a particularly hard time avoiding the masses in Cincinnati on Sunday, July 31, 1910. Outside the Palace of the Fans, a youngster caught sight of Wagner as he was leaving the ballpark. "Chee! Fellers! Here's Hans Wagner!" shouted the young lad. Like bees swarming from a hive, neighborhood youngsters came running from all directions toward Pittsburgh's great player.[37] He looked for an escape route, but within a minute was surrounded by a ragged group of urchins from the slums of the city. He smiled and opened his arms wide as a welcoming gesture. After Wagner talked to the youngsters for a few minutes, he reached into his pocket and scattered several pennies onto the street. While his young fans scrambled to pick up the coins, he hopped onto a passing car and waved farewell as the vehicle disappeared down the road.

When Wagner reached the Pirates' quarters at the Havlin Hotel, a stylishly dressed man walked up to him and made a request. "I want you to meet some people who want to talk to the world's greatest ball player," said the man.

"Wait a minute," replied Wagner. Leaving the well-dressed gentleman standing there, he bolted for the telephone booth and hid in a little storage room behind the booth. "Tell me when they're gone, will you?" he said to the telephone operator. She kept watch as Wagner had to remain in hiding for 15 minutes before the coast was clear and he could go to his room.[38]

Had this Cincinnati gentleman wanted to talk about guns, dogs, hunting, automobiles or basketball rather than wishing to parade him in front of a bunch of high-brow socialites as "the world's greatest baseball player," Wagner probably would have obliged. He loved to converse about these subjects.[39] Receiving excessive adulation from people while Pittsburgh played on the road was a huge problem for him. He explained this to a writer while the Pirates were speeding on a train from Indianapolis to Cincinnati prior to the opening game of the 1909 season on April 14.[40]

> I'm kind of sorry the season is opening. I like to play, but I hate traveling, the crowds, the hotels, and all this fuss and noise. I wish the Pirates could play all their games at home so that I could spend every night at Carnegie, where the people have seen enough of me to know that I am just like other

humans, and have become well enough acquainted with me to pass me on the street without stopping and gazing at me as if I were a nine days' wonder.[41]

Due to his modest nature, Wagner never understood why people fussed over him so much since he believed he was no more important than a doctor, policeman, laborer or any other Carnegie resident.

◆ ◆ ◆

Offering help to teammates, opposing players, friends and business associates was something that came naturally to Honus Wagner even after he had become an established star in the National League. In 1913, he assisted a young shortstop named Walter "Rabbit" Maranville who was a rookie with the Boston Braves. Maranville, a future Hall of Famer who had a few solid seasons with Wagner's Pirates from 1921 to 1924, received critical tutelage about tagging opposing runners attempting to steal.

This lesson occurred after Maranville believed he had tagged Wagner out at Forbes Field and argued with the umpire to no avail. After the game, Wagner called on Maranville at Boston's team hotel and offered to teach the youngster the nuances of playing around second base. The following morning, Wagner, Maranville and a batboy went out to the ballpark very early. The batboy smacked ground balls to the two infielders so Wagner could show Maranville how a shortstop should make plays around the keystone sack.[42]

"Kid, you had me out by feet yesterday afternoon," explained Wagner, "but you didn't make the umpire believe it. I don't touch nine out of ten men who come sliding into me at the sack, but the umpires believe I do because I make it appear natural. I go about my business, and they can't call the play but one way, the way it looks to them."[43]

Wagner taught Maranville how to tag a runner so that there was no chance of being spiked while making the umpire believe he actually had made a proper tag.[44] However, Wagner may have pulled off the most important assist of his life months earlier during the Pirates' exhibition tour prior to the opening game in Cincinnati on April 12, involving European royalty.

Shortly after the Pirates broke training at Hot Springs in 1913, the squad traveled by train to play an exhibition game in Tulsa. On the

Honus Wagner was always willing to lend a helping hand, tutoring both teammates and players from opposing teams. He also showed his chivalric side when he came to the aid of Princess Stephania Kaunitz of Austria on April 3, 1913. After the two met while the Pirates' train had a stopover in Claremore, Oklahoma, Wagner and his teammates helped push Princess Stephania's car out of the mud when the wheels became stuck (courtesy National Baseball Hall of Fame Library, Cooperstown, New York).

morning of April 3, the train made a scheduled stop in Claremore, Oklahoma, for three hours. The players decided to take an automobile trip into Claremore to go sight-seeing. Barney Dreyfuss was considering the area as a potential, future training site because the town was famous for its radium bathhouses. Following his inspection of the town, Dreyfuss intimated that Pittsburgh might come to Claremore in March of 1914 for spring training.[45]

The Pirates' entourage was not the only celebrity entity in Claremore that day. Princess Stephania Kaunitz of Austria was also visiting Claremore to use the radium baths since she suffered from eczema. Informed that the great Honus Wagner was also in town, Princess Stephania expressed a desire to meet him. Arrangements were made and the Austrian princess was whisked away to the Pirates' private Pullman car that was sitting idly on the railroad tracks. When Princess Stephania was introduced to Wagner, she said: "I am delighted to meet you. Have read and heard so much of you, but never dreamed I would have this great pleasure."[46]

Honus Wagner was embarrassed and blushed like a school girl as he took the princess' hand. Upon invitation from Princess Stephania, Wagner climbed into the automobile and posed for a picture. He drove around in a circle before he finally mustered enough courage to say something to this member of Austria's royal family. "This is a great honor," said Wagner.[47]

Princess Stephania smiled, thanked him and assured him that she was delighted and would always keep this special photo. The princess assured Wagner that she would remember him forever and always treasure this meeting. As the car transporting the princess pulled away once the meeting concluded, it stalled in the mud. Wagner and his teammates quickly jumped to the rescue, put their shoulders to the wheel, and pulled the car out. Princess Stephania thanked Wagner and the other Pirates, waving her hand as the car sped away.[48] Chivalry certainly was alive and well in 1913 thanks to Honus Wagner's gallant personality. Besides being the consummate teammate and an ideal baseball player, Wagner was a true gentleman in every respect whose politeness and graciousness was beyond reproach.

"First in the Hearts of Baseball Fans"

Honus Wagner reached the zenith of his spectacular baseball career when the Pittsburgh Pirates claimed their first world championship in franchise history by defeating the Detroit Tigers in the 1909 World Series. In late May that year, Cleveland baseball scribe Tip Wright made the trip to Pittsburgh to watch Wagner in person at Exposition Park. Wright marveled over Wagner's ability during a game against the Chicago Cubs on May 29. He was particularly impressed when Wagner gobbled up Art "Solly" Hofman's sharp ground ball over second base that seemed destined to reach the outfield for a hit and turned a lightning double play with two Cubs aboard in the first inning.[1] President William Howard Taft was also in attendance on this afternoon as the contest was delayed until he reached Exposition Park at 4:00 p.m.[2] Although Pittsburgh lost in 11 innings, 8–3, Wright could not contain his enthusiasm about the world's greatest baseball player.

> Wagner has the largest hands in baseball, and once he grasps a ball it is lost in his palm. He is a marvel of muscular strength and activity. About five feet 10 inches tall, he carries his 200 odd pounds as lightly as a featherweight. His bowlegs give him an awkward appearance, yet he turns the most startling plays with astonishing ease.
>
> When fielding, or running the bases, he runs close to the earth, and he runs as fast in this position as a sprinter. Pittsburgh fans say they have seen him go to first on an infield hit in 3⅖ seconds, which is fast traveling.
>
> Quiet, unassuming, as modest even as the great Lajoie, the big fellow is not given to talking about his performances, playing each batter with a sixth sense, he is always on top of a ball hit in his direction, fairly smothering it. Because he plays so close to the ground it makes no difference to him how suddenly or poorly the ball hops; he grabs it, and, with his wonderful right arm, fairly shoots it across the diamond.
>
> But if Wagner shines in the field, he simply radiates gleams of dazzling

brightness at the bat. Wagner stands in the far corner of the box when batting. He swings his bat in a small circle until the pitcher starts his delivery; then, if he likes the ball, he steps forward, swinging his bat at the same time, and when he hits it square that ball has an engagement somewhere else.

Barney Dreyfuss is simply putting dimes in a gold mine to draw out dollars in their places when he pays Hans Wagner $10,000 a year.[3]

Tip Wright's laudatory article succinctly encapsulated Wagner's memorable career. His barrel chest and bowed legs were an intricate part of how he functioned. He was like a piece of complex machinery that performed beautifully and achieved its purpose even if it looked ugly doing so. Those large hands also resembled giant steam shovels, scooping up the baseball and any dirt or stones they came in contact with when making a play. In 1902, Wagner had received a unique glove from veteran shortstop Herman Long of the Boston Beaneaters that he used throughout most of his career. The glove had a hole cut out in the center about twice the size of a baseball. This glove served Wagner well for many baseball campaigns. Whether it was superstition or sentimentality, he hung on to this glove like grim death.[4]

Due to his huge hands, any Honus Wagner model glove had interesting specifications. His glove measured 16 inches around the band, 11 inches long, and 14½ inches around the wrist. The circumference of the thumb was seven inches, while that of the little finger was six inches. Days before Decoration Day in 1913, Pittsburgh baseball writer Ralph S. Davis strolled into the local Spalding's sporting goods outlet. "Uncle Al" Pratt, former manager of the American Association's local Alleghenys team in 1882 and 1883, operated the store. When Davis placed his hand into the Wagner model glove, there was still space left for the paw of an ordinary person. This monstrous fielder's mitt, which resembled a sack rather than a glove, was a special order item at Pratt's Spalding store.[5]

"We don't carry that glove in stock," Mr. Pratt explained to Davis. "It is two sizes larger than our largest stock size, and every time Honus wants a new glove, which is not often, we have one made to order for him. You wouldn't be able to recognize this one after he has had it for a week. He will blacken it up as quickly as possible, and will also cut the entire palm of the hand out, leaving only the fingers and a band around the wrist. He wants no protection for the palm of the hand, but merely a hole there into which the ball will stick easily."[6]

Much in the same way that a piece of equipment eventually wears down because of extensive use each day, the career of even the grandest baseball player in the world declines at some point. Years of giving maximum effort on the baseball diamond began to take its toll on Honus Wagner's body after he and his teammates experienced the glory of winning the 1909 World Series. An injury to his left knee in spring training caused him to miss the first four games of the 1913 season.[7] Wagner appeared in 114 games that year, the lowest total since his rookie season with Louisville in 1897. Suffering a knee injury certainly did not alter the way he played the game. He continued to go after a base because he desperately wanted it. He still adhered to the practice of never trying to save himself and took a chance when the opportunity presented itself.[8] He also did not want to hear any talk from dissenters who believed he no longer was a productive player.

"That's the way it's been going for three seasons," said Wagner in the summer of 1913.

> "The old boy for the boneyard," you hear. Three seasons ago I broke an ankle at Brooklyn. Some fans said: "Cash in, old stiff! Your number's been taken." I beat 'em then and also in 1912 and am going to try wallop the guessers again. It's an old player's lot to hear such talk whenever he is hurt. Gibbie (George Gibson) is getting his. "All in. No chance to play again." That's what he's hearing. Hack may not be able to go much this season, but watch him next race. No use trying to force nature. She kicks on being driven. Rest is the best medicine for us old-timers when our shanks are on the blink.[9]

Although Wagner truly believed he was not ready to "cash in," 1913 was the final year he reached the heralded .300 batting mark for the 16th time, batting an even .300.[10] The Wagner family also suffered a personal tragedy a little more than a month after the season ended. On November 12, 1913, Honus' father Peter Wagner passed away at the age of 75 in the Carnegie family home. Although Peter Wagner had recently contracted pneumonia, his death came as a surprise to the family. The passing of their father meant that Honus, along with fellow bachelor brothers Al and Louis, were the only Wagners who still resided at the home on Railroad Avenue.[11]

Back on the baseball diamond in 1914, Honus Wagner saw his average dip to .252, although he did appear in 150 games and led all National League shortstops in fielding percentage for the third consecutive year.

His team also found themselves in foreign territory as they finished in the second division for the first time during Fred Clarke's tenure as manager. The Pirates limped home in seventh place with a record of 69–85. One reason for Pittsburgh's sudden decline was that Clarke and Barney Dreyfuss failed to bring in quality players to replace old-guard performers who had either retired or were shipped to other teams.

Players such as Marty O'Toole, Ed Konetchy and Mike Mowrey were abject failures who never came close to performing up to the expectations of their star predecessors. A threat from a viable third major league called the Federal League did not help Pittsburgh's fortunes as numerous Pirates were courted throughout the 1914 campaign. Star hurler Claude Hendrix had jumped to the new league prior to the season. Former Pirates pitcher Howard Camnitz, who had been traded to the Philadelphia Phillies on August 20, 1913, joined the Federal League's Pittsburgh Rebels. He also acted as an agent for the league and attempted to lure Pirates players away from Barney Dreyfuss.

Camnitz was the Pirates' ace during their 1909 championship season when he went 25–6 and posted a 1.62 ERA. The fact that Camnitz had been Honus Wagner's teammate and friend for more than eight seasons was irrelevant to Pittsburgh's great shortstop when Camnitz showed up in Hot Springs during the 1914 training session, hoping to steal players for the Federal League. Wagner gave his former teammate a severe reprimand when the two ran into each other in Hot Springs. Wagner was determined to ignore his former teammate as they passed until Camnitz stopped him and insisted on knowing what seemed to be the problem.[12]

> "I'll tell you," said Wagner brusquely. "I had nothing to say when I heard you had jumped, for that was your own business. Even when I heard you were trying to get older men to join I felt that it was strictly up to them. But let me give a tip to you: Let the young fellows alone. They have a reputation to make and a future in front of them. Give them a chance and don't lead them astray. It is every man for himself in this game and everyone knows his own business; but you trouble makers can get a lot of innocent guys in wrong and a decent fellow won't do it. Keep off the kids, Cammy, and we old fellows will think more of you."[13]

It was believed that Honus Wagner's quiet, stern advice proved more effective in convincing Howard Camnitz and the Federal League to back off than Barney Dreyfuss' court injunction.[14] The Federal League

remained in existence until it folded after the 1915 campaign. Wagner experienced a minor resurgence at the plate in 1915 as he appeared in 156 games, batted .274 and drove home 78 runs. The Pirates improved two spots and came home fifth in the National League with a record of 73–81. That was also Fred Clarke's final season as skipper of the Pittsburgh Pirates. After essentially retiring as a player following the 1911 season, Clarke had managed the Pirates from the dugout for the past four years.

At noon on September 8, 1915, it was announced that Fred Clarke had tendered his resignation as Pittsburgh's manager effective at season's end, and planned on retiring to the quiet, tranquil life on his ranch in Winfield, Kansas.[15] As a player, Fred Clarke retired with a .312 batting average and 2,678 hits. Clarke also had impeccable managerial credentials as he posted a record of 1602–1181 during his 19 seasons piloting Louisville and Pittsburgh. He captured four National League pennants with Pittsburgh (1901, 1902, 1903 and 1909) and one world championship when the Pirates defeated Detroit in the 1909 World Series. Although some people believed Honus Wagner might replace Clarke, former pitcher Jimmy Callahan was Barney Dreyfuss' choice to run the Pirates in 1916.

Fred Clarke's decision to retire left Honus Wagner as the final member of that select group of five players who had played on Pittsburgh's four pennant winning teams from 1901 through 1909. Pitcher Babe Adams and catcher George Gibson were also still with the Pirates through the 1915 season. Months after Wagner completed his 19th season playing major league ball, the city of Pittsburgh honored him during a special celebration. On February 24, 1916, Wagner was toasted on his 42nd birthday at the Hot Stove League's "Wagner Day" banquet at the Colonial Annex Hotel in Pittsburgh. More than 300 Stovers and other baseball fans gathered to pay homage to the greatest player who had ever worn a pair of spikes.[16]

Various luminaries were sprinkled throughout this crowd of passionate baseball fans. Barney Dreyfuss was in attendance along with former teammates Tommy Leach and Deacon Phillippe. Lifelong friend James Orris, Stove League president Paul Knox Collins, toastmaster Bill Connelly, state senator Joseph H. Thompson of Beaver County and city councilman John H. Dailey were seated at the speaker's table next to

Wagner. As Connelly finished the speechmaking portion of the banquet before the evening's entertainment features, the crowd began shouting and clamoring for Wagner to say a few words. Awkwardly rising to his feet amid the roar of the crowd, Wagner dithered for a moment before he made a brief comment. "I'm glad to be here," said Wagner. "But just now I'm on third base and I feel like stealing home. I'm much obliged."[17]

While everyone appreciated this short comment from the guest of honor, it was his boss who stole the show. The sentiment expressed by Barney Dreyfuss as he talked about Wagner was shared by every person at the Colonial Annex Hotel.

> I want to call attention to the "other side" of Wagner—the "man" side. We all know his ability as a ball player, but there may be some who do not know that he is a true man in all that the term implies. Wagner was and is one ball player we never have to watch. He is always faithful, always in condition. He has gone out on the diamond literally swathed in bandages—he has played when he should have been in a hospital. And I have yet to hear him complain.
>
> Honus made his reputation as a man just as he did a ball player—by being "on the square" in all his dealings. It wasn't necessary for him to go into the courts [this being a fling, apparently, at some recent handlers] to achieve distinction. Instead he has offered the best he had in him; and the Pittsburgh Club is not unappreciative.[18]

Dreyfuss continued his stirring speech by stating that no matter how long Wagner wanted to remain on the Pirates' payroll, he could do so. "When the time comes when he can no longer play ball, we will find something else for him to do," said Dreyfuss. Pittsburgh's longtime owner concluded his speech by making the analogy that if George Washington was "first in war, first in peace and first in the hearts of his countrymen," then Honus Wagner was "first on the field, first off the field, and first in the hearts of the American baseball fans."[19]

Once all the speeches were completed, everyone was treated to Bill McCullough's minstrel show and various acts from the Davis and Harris theaters. When the festivities for the evening concluded, the toast of Carnegie was surrounded by a multitude of grateful fans. Wagner received numerous congratulations from friends and admirers. Deeply moved emotionally by this outpouring, he offered a sincere, heartfelt response. "This is absolutely the greatest moment of my life," said Wagner. "I have tried to do the best I could at all times, and tonight I feel

that I have been fully repaid for every effort I ever put forth. Gee, this sort of thing makes a fellow feel like life is worth living after all."[20]

Although Honus Wagner avoided the spotlight, he deeply cherished all of the kind words that were offered at this banquet which celebrated his 42nd birthday. A few months prior to this grand celebration, Barney Dreyfuss had schooled a young cub reporter when the subject of baseball's greatest player ever came up during the December National League meetings in New York. Dreyfuss was shocked when it became apparent that this young scribe seemed to be totally unaware of Wagner's great diamond exploits.

"Whenever I want to see the greatest ball player I go out to Carnegie, Pa.," remarked Dreyfuss.

"Carnegie? Carnegie? What's in Carnegie?" asked the cub reporter.

"That's the place that has the honor of housing the greatest ball player that ever wore a pair of spikes," answered Dreyfuss.

"Oh!" exclaimed the young scribe, still not quite understanding Dreyfuss' point.

"There have been other great ball players," continued Dreyfuss, "and there are some great ones now, but I always will feel that Wagner was the greatest. In his prime he could hit, throw, field and run with the best of them. Other players maybe were a little better on the whole average, but one thing you must remember—Wagner was out there trying day after day. We never had to fear that he would get excited during a crucial series and do things that would result to his being suspended for a week or two—suspended just at a time when we needed him most.

"We always can count on Wagner playing 154 games a year unless sick or disabled. We always can depend upon him; always know he would be with us when we needed him. And so, because of this greatest virtue of all, and because of this his terrific hitting, his great fielding, running and throwing, I believe that Wagner always should rank as the greatest player the game has produced."[21]

The game's greatest player was entering his 20th season in the major leagues in 1916. Although Wagner had recommended that Dreyfuss reduce his salary for the upcoming season due to deteriorating skills, Pittsburgh's owner refused. Dreyfuss continued to pay Wagner $10,000 a year, just as he had done for the past four seasons. Dreyfuss also claimed that Wagner would continue to be paid this yearly salary for as long as he remained in the game.[22] Wagner appeared in 123 games for the Pirates in 1916 and batted a respectable .287. His ability to drive home runners did drop precipitously from the previous year as he only

knocked in 39 runs in 1916 after recording 78 RBI in 1915. Still, he finished tied for third on the team in that category with first baseman Wheeler "Doc" Johnston.

Things were not much better for Pittsburgh, which finished in sixth place under new skipper Jimmy Callahan with a 65–89 record thanks to going 1–19 over the final 20 games. Pirates fans were left to ponder an interesting event that occurred as that year came to a close. On the night of December 30, Honus Wagner married Miss Bessie Smith, daughter of former Allegheny county detective John G. Smith. At the conclusion of an intimate ceremony at the parsonage of the St. John's Lutheran Church in Carnegie, Mr. and Mrs. Wagner immediately left for their honeymoon trip.[23] Since Honus had claimed on many occasions that he would not take wedding vows until his baseball career had ended, numerous Pittsburgh rooters expected him to announce his retirement in the near future.

While no retirement affirmation was forthcoming, Wagner was not with the team when Pittsburgh opened the 1917 campaign against the Chicago Cubs at Weeghman Park on April 11. Amid rumors that Barney Dreyfuss had decided to make drastic payroll cuts to every player on Pittsburgh's roster, Wagner was officially classified as a holdout. Both Dreyfuss and Wagner insisted that there was no salary dispute between the two men. Wagner finally agreed to play one final season for the Pirates when he attached his signature to a contract on June 6 that paid him $10,000 for the remainder of the campaign.[24] He was in the lineup the following day when Pittsburgh was defeated by the Brooklyn Robins at Forbes Field, 5–3. Wagner played first base and went 1-for-4.

The 1917 season acted as a summer farewell tour for Honus Wagner. Baseball fans in every National League city relished the opportunity to watch him one final time on the diamond. On August 26, Paterson, New Jersey, held "Wagner Day" when the Pirates came to town to play an exhibition game against the Doherty Silk Sox. Days prior to this special event, Wagner was the guest of millionaire silk manufacturer and team owner Harry Doherty, who took him on a tour of his factory. Before Wagner left to rejoin the Pirates, Doherty presented him with material for a beautiful silk dress for Mrs. Wagner. The city also bestowed upon Wagner a purse of money prior to the exhibition game. Paterson's residents always liked to claim Wagner as one of their own, much to the

chagrin of people from Pittsburgh and Carnegie, since his great baseball career had started there.[25]

On September 3, 1917, Honus Wagner recorded the final hit of his career against Cincinnati Reds hurler Joe Engel in the first game of a Labor Day doubleheader at Forbes Field. Wagner made his final start for Pittsburgh at third base in the nightcap. He batted one final time on September 11 against St. Louis after he had replaced Jake Pitler at second base. Baseball's greatest player made his final appearance as a major leaguer on September 17 when he came into the game against the Boston Braves at Forbes Field as a defensive replacement. Used primarily as a first and third baseman in 1917, Wagner had received an opportunity to man his shortstop position one final time during the latter stages of a contest against the New York Giants on August 29. He appeared in 74 games in 1917 and batted .265.

Wagner's final major league season was bittersweet for the man who always placed team goals above personal glory. The Pirates were undisputed cellar dwellers in 1917 as they finished 20½ games behind the seventh-place Brooklyn Robins. Their 51–103 record left them very worthy of the National League's basement designation. While the Pirates had been absolutely horrible during Wagner's final season, this did nothing to diminish his 21-year career. He finished with a batting average of .328, 3,420 hits, 643 doubles, 252 triples and 101 home runs. He also knocked in 1,732 runs and stole 723 bases. Wagner became the second member of the elite "3,000 Hit Club" when he blasted a double off Phillies pitcher Erskine Mayer on June 9, 1914. An eight-time National League batting champion, he led the circuit in every major offensive category other than home runs at least twice during his career.

While Honus Wagner had blazed a path of glory throughout his spectacular baseball career, the Carnegie citizen found it a bit difficult establishing a new legacy in retirement. Besides doing things that he enjoyed such as hunting, fishing and going for drives in his automobile, he tried his hand at coaching football at Carnegie High School and as a physical instructor and baseball coach at Carnegie Tech.[26] Wagner also made an unsuccessful run for Allegheny County sheriff in 1925 and opened the Honus Wagner Sporting Goods Store in downtown Pittsburgh.[27] After he hung up his spikes as a major leaguer, he continued playing baseball for the "Green Cab" team on local sandlots around Pitts-

burgh.[28] Wagner usually played first base for the Green Cab Company. At the age of 53, in the summer of 1927, he blasted a triple off the right-center field gate at Forbes Field during a game between the Green Cab Company and the Homestead Grays.[29]

Still trying to find his niche in society away from baseball years after the start of the Great Depression, Wagner received the opportunity of a lifetime when the Pirates asked him to return as a coach for the 1933 season. Bill Benswanger, son-in-law of Barney Dreyfuss and president of the organization since the great baseball mogul responsible for building the Pirates dynasty had passed away on February 5, 1932, brought Wagner back into the fold.[30] Wagner was reunited with former teammate George Gibson, who was in his second stint as Pittsburgh's manager. Wagner's primary job his first few seasons as a coach was to teach a youngster named Arky Vaughan how to become a great shortstop. He taught Vaughan the finer points of the position he had perfected during his baseball career. Unfortunately for Vaughan, these instructions were not always clear, and he had a problem explaining how the lessons were going when Gibson asked Vaughan how he was progressing.[31]

"I'm not sure," replied Vaughan. "When I asked Mr. Wagner what to do, he said, 'You just run fast, grab the ball, and throw it to first base ahead of the runner.' But he didn't tell me how."[32]

Honus Wagner's tutelage paid huge dividends as Arky Vaughan quickly became recognized as the National League's top shortstop. Vaughan also established the single-season franchise record for batting average when his .385 mark paced the circuit in 1935. The Waner brothers, Paul and Lloyd, were in the prime of their careers when Wagner rejoined the Pirate organization in 1933. Paul Waner considered Wagner to be a wonderful man who was good-natured, affable and accommodating to everyone. Each member of the Pirates squad adored Wagner, and Pittsburgh's fans were ecstatic that he was back with the team in a coaching capacity. Paul Waner claimed that whenever someone told a good joke or a funny story, Wagner would slap his knee, let out a loud roar, and exclaim: "What about that!"[33] Wagner, in turn, loved watching the Waner brothers play. When asked by a visiting reporter how to rate Paul as a hitter, Wagner offered a concise assessment regarding his batting style and love of the nightlife.[34] "Just say he's a low-ball hitter and a high-ball drinker," responded Wagner as he spit out a chew of tobacco and chuckled.[35]

When Wagner arrived at his first training camp in Paso Robles, California, as a Pirates coach in 1933, he was the most popular member of the team's entourage. School kids throughout Paso Robles flocked to the ballpark to catch a glimpse of Wagner. Many of the youngsters tried to walk bowlegged, while each one enthusiastically announced that he wanted to play shortstop on the California sandlots that summer. Pirates manager George Gibson made the point that Wagner, at the age of 40, had been better than any other shortstop ever. When pressed to respond to Gibson's praise, Wagner changed the subject and started talking about how players from the current era were just as good as when he played.[36] "We've got more good players than we ever had," said Wagner. "That's because there are more strong leagues. The game is stricter and better now. You can't bully the 'empire' (umpire) any more. The boys used to be a rough and ready lot. Now the 'empire' is a real authority and it's all for the best."[37]

Honus Wagner's coaching tenure with the Pittsburgh Pirates ended up exceeding the 18 seasons he had played for his hometown team, lasting 19 years from 1933 to 1951. Although Pittsburgh did not win any National League pennants during those 19 years, a new generation of Pirates fans was exposed to the engaging, colorful tales that had become part of his personality. As time went by, Wagner tended to allow fantasy to creep in as embellishment was a common theme when he delighted an attentive audience with a story regarding his playing days. Veteran pitcher Charles "Red" Lucas was one of his favorite foils when stories were swapped in the dugout. A hurler for Pittsburgh from 1934 to 1938, Lucas was equally capable of exaggerating a recollection to make a point.

Lucas was one of the true wise-crackers during his five years in Pittsburgh and could relate tales for hours. He would sit on the bench and listen to Wagner's whoppers before he told a tale that seemed even more unlikely. Lucas' usual greeting when he arrived at spring training was: "What's Honus been lying about all winter?"[38] Each man would try to outdo the other on any subject. Once, Wagner upstaged Lucas when they discussed the virtues of hunting dogs they had owned.[39]

"Red," Wagner said solemnly. "I had a pointer once that you should have seen. Best in the world. We went out in the hills for those quails one morning and this dog of mine sniffed and took off and we got lost from each other, so I went home. Two years later I was out in those same

hills and I found him. There was nothing left but his skeleton, but it was still right at point. That dog died right there waitin' for me to come up and shoot those quails."

"You win," Lucas grunted. "I can't tie that one."[40]

Wagner loved to indoctrinate new members of Pittsburgh's aggregation with words of wisdom from the world according to Wagner. Zack Taylor became a member of Pittsburgh's coaching staff in 1947. Taylor had been a successful catcher for 16 seasons from 1920–1935 for the Brooklyn Robins, Boston Braves, New York Giants, Chicago Cubs and New York Yankees. He remained on the Pirates coaching staff for one season under managers Billy Herman and Bill Burwell. Wagner wasted no time reminiscing about the good old days in Pittsburgh shortly after the 1947 baseball campaign opened.

"It's easy to get to the park nowadays, ain't it?" Wagner asked Taylor without cracking a smile. "Back in the days when we played in Allegheny, I used to ride to our old Exposition Park on horseback. One day that darn horse wouldn't get on the ferry boat, so I rode him right into the river and made him swim across, with me on top of him."[41]

Wagner did not miss a beat as he segued from riding to Exposition Park on a horse and regaled Taylor with a story regarding the first automobile he had owned. "It was so high I could look into everybody's second-story windows as I drove by. And it had five hundred pounds of tools in it. And whenever we bounced over a trolley track, the tools rattled more'n the car."[42] Al Abrams recalled Wagner's propensity for the tales growing taller as he advanced in age. Abrams was a columnist and sports editor for the *Pittsburgh Post-Gazette* throughout most of Wagner's time as a coach.[43] He had been fortunate enough to watch Wagner play in 1917 and decades later saw the mother of a young player remonstrate with Wagner for telling her son and other youngsters on the team stories which lacked authenticity.[44]

"Why do you tell the boys such outlandish things?" asked the mother. "You know they're not true and they're downright lies."

"Maybe lies, ma'am," Wagner told her, "but, I've never told them a story they couldn't repeat before their mothers."[45]

Al Abrams interacted with Honus Wagner shortly before the baseball icon retired following the 1951 season. Late during that campaign, Abrams went to Forbes Field's clubhouse to gather information for a

column. He was talking to Ralph Kiner when Pittsburgh's slugger nudged the writer and said: "Look at old Honus." Abrams directed his attention toward Wagner, who was standing in the middle of the clubhouse, his eyes first staring to one side of the dressing room, before they slowly moved around in the other direction. It appeared that the former great player was in deep reflection, searching for memories deep within the recesses of his mind.[46]

Kiner and Abrams watched Wagner for ten minutes as he remained motionless except for the blinking of his watery eyes while one hand afflicted with palsy shook uncontrollably. Illness, which had been gripping Wagner for some time, made it impossible for him to continue as a coach beyond 1951. Wagner knew this might be the last time he visited the Pirates clubhouse at Forbes Field. Kiner finally broke the silence. "What memories this place must hold for Honus," Kiner said reverently. When Wagner finally returned to his locker to dress in a baseball uniform for the final time, Abrams approached him in order to chronicle this sentimental moment.

"What were you thinking about?" Abrams asked.

"Did you see me? How about that?" responded Wagner in a booming voice. "I was thinkin' about the first time I came to this clubhouse in June of 1909. Things have changed since then, a lot of changes, but I thought this place and all of Forbes Field was beautiful then.

"I was thinkin' of Cap Clarke, Tommy Leach, George Gibson, Babe Adams, Chief Wilson, Mr. Dreyfuss and the rest. We had fun in those days. That's all I've got left now in baseball, my memories, but they're worth a million bucks to me."[47]

Beyond these lasting memories that Honus Wagner alluded to, there were two events which occurred that insured he would have an enduring legacy as one of the greatest players in baseball history. On February 2, 1936, the Baseball Hall of Fame announced its first class of great players to be inducted when the facility in Cooperstown, New York, opened in 1939. Honus Wagner was immortalized forever, along with Ty Cobb, Babe Ruth, Walter Johnson and Christy Mathewson, as the first group of players to be honored in the Baseball Hall of Fame's hallowed halls. Wagner and 25 other men from the classes of 1936, 1937, 1938 and 1939 were officially inducted during a grand ceremony in Cooperstown on June 12, 1939.[48]

Honus Wagner's major league career spanned 21 seasons with the Louisville Colonels and Pittsburgh Pirates. He retired with a lifetime batting average of .328 and 3,420 hits. Still considered by many to be the greatest shortstop in baseball history, Wagner was part of the inaugural class elected to the Baseball Hall of Fame in 1936. He was also a Pirates coach for 19 seasons from 1933 to 1951 (courtesy National Baseball Hall of Fame Library, Cooperstown, New York).

These 26 greats were honored as 15,000 people attended the ceremony to catch a glimpse of baseball history. Connie Mack had preceded Wagner to the platform before it was his turn to give a speech. Baseball Writers' Association of America president and *Pittsburgh Sun-Telegraph* scribe Charles "Chilly" Doyle introduced Wagner to the crowd. Wagner immediately charmed the gathering by acknowledging Mack and then using some of his down-to-earth humor. "I used to walk 14 miles to see Connie Mack play ball in Pittsburgh, but it was worth it," said Wagner in a slow, friendly drawl. "A nice quiet town you have here. Reminds me of Sleepy Hollow."

Veteran Manhattan reporter Ken Smith from the *New York Mirror* believed Wagner's speech turned the ceremony into a more casual affair. "Instantly the lid was off the formal proceedings," he wrote. "The celebration was back in its homespun ice-cream-and-cake-picnic atmosphere, after the man who towers so far above every shortstop that no one ever dares compare another with him, had spoken."[49]

Honus Wagner's lasting legacy in his hometown of Pittsburgh was cemented during the spring of 1955. A constant reminder of Wagner's greatness was made available for future generations of baseball fans when a statue of him was unveiled on Saturday April 30.[50] Appropriately, this sculpture's initial home was adjacent to the famous ballpark where he had excelled for so many years, unveiled in Schenley Park near the left field bleachers at Forbes Field during a ceremony that took place at 10:30 in the morning. William Benswanger, son-in-law of the late Barney Dreyfuss and one-time Pirates president, acted as the master of ceremonies for the dedication.[51] Former teammates and opposing players in attendance included Fred Clarke, George Gibson and Cy Young.[52]

Members of the Pirates and Cincinnati Reds, playing that afternoon at Forbes Field, attended the ceremony.[53] An estimated crowd of 1,000 people were on hand for the dedication at Schenley Plaza. As Wagner's granddaughter, four-year-old Leslie Ann Blair, pulled the cord unveiling the statue, Wagner's eyes brightened briefly as he sat in an open convertible in front of the speakers' stand. A trace of that renowned smile weakly came across his pale, haggard features. At that precise moment, the sun broke through the morning clouds and radiated its bright rays upon a nine-foot, ten-and-a-half-inch-high bronze casting that immortalized forever a muscular, robust figure from an era long ago who had

written baseball history. Former baseball writer and current commissioner Ford Frick encapsulated the moment as inspirational commendations and superlatives were extended to Wagner by a host of dignitaries.[54] "Men are great, men are strong, men give leadership because they are born to it," said Frick. "Today you honor such a man—a great man, a strong man, a gentle man, a kindly man."[55]

This lasting symbol of Honus Wagner's greatness, which currently resides at PNC Park, became a reality due to the diligent efforts of the Pittsburgh Professional Baseball Association. The statue, done by sculptor Frank Vittor, was an intensive labor of love that took two years to complete. The bronze sculpture caught Wagner in a typical pose, outlining in detail the bulging muscles in his mammoth forearms and the parenthetical nature of his sturdy legs. When the ceremony ended, the automobile with a weary Wagner in the front seat drove away very slowly, leaving behind a lasting image that would keep his memory alive for future generations.[56] Wagner had uttered only one, typical remark as he wiped a tear from his cheek when his statue was unveiled. "How about that," said he as he gazed at his bronze likeness.[57]

This statue unveiling ceremony would be Wagner's final public appearance.[58] On December 6, 1955, John Peter "Honus" Wagner passed away at the age of 81 in his Carnegie home. Wife Bessie and other relatives were at his bedside when Wagner died in his sleep at 12:56 a.m.[59] He had been in failing health for the past several years. He had fallen in his house two months earlier and had been bedridden since he slipped into a coma ten days before his death.[60] Tributes honoring the great shortstop poured in from all areas of the country. One-time Pirates outfielder Ralph Kiner stated that Wagner was the finest man he had ever met.[61] Former St. Louis Browns great George Sisler expressed the sentiment that there should be a separate Hall of Fame for Honus Wagner and another for the rest of Cooperstown's greats.[62]

A stirring tribute was offered by William E. Benswanger, who had been responsible for bringing Wagner back as a coach 16 years after his retirement. "He was the greatest of all ball players and I say that without hesitation or reflections on any of the other fine players down through the years," said Benswanger. "His death, although it wasn't unexpected, brings to mind lots of memories and baseball history."[63]

More than four years before Wagner's death, friend and former

teammate Fred Clarke may have summed up the Wagner mystique best during an interview with Joe King of *The Sporting News*. "At Pittsburgh," Clarke claimed, "we traveled not as Pittsburgh, but as Wagner. Honus got the billing, just as the Yankees went around later with Babe Ruth."[64] While this statement certainly was accurate, Clarke could have expanded beyond the fact that his great team traveled as Wagner. Loved by fans everywhere, Wagner was baseball from alpha to omega throughout his great career. He personified how a man could fight on the diamond in a figurative sense and still play the game in a gentlemanly manner. A man who valued the camaraderie and companionship that existed with teammates he called friends, Wagner was the game when he played, and always was one of its greatest chroniclers during his 40-plus years connected to baseball.

Honus Wagner's love for baseball was as pure and innocent as that of a child playing on the Pittsburgh sandlots. It came as no surprise that Wagner seemed to be in his element participating in pick-up games with youths in Carnegie and having fun as he always did playing baseball. On one occasion, he appeared at the Pittsburgh ballpark with a ragged, five-year-old urchin who embodied the typical street type trying to find his way in one of the area's neighborhoods.[65]

"Who's the kid?" someone questioned Wagner as he entered the ballpark.

"Oh," replied Honus, "he's a pal of mine."[66]

How about that.

Appendix

Career Statistics

The statistics presented here were compiled from *Retrosheet* and *Baseball Reference* since both of these entities, through exhaustive searches, believe these numbers are accurate, although they differ from MLB records.

Career Batting Statistics

	G	AB	R	H	2B	3B	HR	RBI	SB	AVG	OBP	SLG
1897 LOU–NL	62	242	38	81	18	4	2	39	20	.335	.376	.467
1898 LOU–NL	151	588	80	176	29	3	10	105	27	.299	.341	.410
1899 LOU–NL	148	575	100	196	45	13	7	114	37	.341	.395	.501
1900 PIT–NL	135	527	107	201	45	22	4	100	38	.381	.434	.573
1901 PIT–NL	140	549	101	194	37	11	6	126	49	.353	.417	.494
1902 PIT–NL	136	534	105	176	30	16	3	91	42	.330	.394	.463
1903 PIT–NL	129	512	97	182	30	19	5	101	46	.355	.414	.518
1904 PIT–NL	132	490	97	171	44	14	4	75	53	.349	.423	.520
1905 PIT–NL	147	548	114	199	32	14	6	101	57	.363	.427	.505
1906 PIT–NL	142	516	103	175	38	9	2	71	53	.339	.416	.459
1907 PIT–NL	142	515	98	180	38	14	6	82	61	.350	.408	.513
1908 PIT–NL	151	568	100	201	39	19	10	109	53	.354	.415	.542
1909 PIT–NL	137	495	92	168	39	10	5	100	35	.339	.420	.489
1910 PIT–NL	150	556	90	178	34	8	4	81	24	.320	.390	.432
1911 PIT–NL	130	473	87	158	23	16	9	89	20	.334	.423	.507
1912 PIT–NL	145	558	91	181	35	20	7	101	26	.324	.395	.496
1913 PIT–NL	114	413	51	124	18	4	3	56	21	.300	.349	.385
1914 PIT–NL	150	552	60	139	15	9	1	50	23	.252	.317	.317
1915 PIT–NL	156	566	68	155	32	17	6	78	22	.274	.325	.422
1916 PIT–NL	123	432	45	124	15	9	1	39	11	.287	.350	.370
1917 PIT–NL	74	230	15	61	7	1	0	24	5	.265	.337	.304
TOTALS	**2794**	**10439**	**1739**	**3420**	**643**	**252**	**101**	**1732**	**723**	**.328**	**.391**	**.467**

Career World Series Batting Statistics

	G	AB	R	H	2B	3B	HR	RBI	SB	AVG	OBP	SLG
1903 PIT–NL	8	27	2	6	1	0	0	3	3	.222	.323	.259
1909 PIT–NL	7	24	4	8	2	1	0	6	6	.333	.467	.500
TOTALS	**15**	**51**	**6**	**14**	**3**	**1**	**0**	**9**	**9**	**.275**	**.393**	**.373**

Career Pitching Statistics

	W	L	ERA	G	GS	CG	IP	H	R	ER	BB	SO
1900 PIT–NL	0	0	0.00	1	0	0	3.0	3	3	0	4	1
1902 PIT–NL	0	0	0.00	1	0	0	5.1	4	2	0	2	5
TOTALS	**0**	**0**	**0.00**	**2**	**0**	**0**	**8.1**	**7**	**5**	**0**	**6**	**6**

Accomplishments

National League Leader in Batting Average—1900, 1903, 1904, 1906, 1907, 1908, 1909, 1911

National League Leader in On-Base Percentage—1904, 1907, 1908, 1909

National League Leader in Slugging Percentage—1900, 1902, 1904, 1907, 1908, 1909

National League Leader in Runs Scored—1902, 1906

National League Leader in Hits—1908, 1910

National League Leader in Doubles—1900, 1902, 1904, 1906, 1907, 1908, 1909

National League Leader in Triples—1900, 1903, 1908

National League Leader in Runs Batted In—1901, 1902, 1908, 1909

National League Leader in Stolen Bases—1901, 1902, 1904, 1907, 1908

Elected to the Baseball Hall of Fame in 1936

Chapter Notes

Chapter 1

1. Honus Wagner, "A Few Facts About My Life," *Baseball Magazine*, January 1915, 33–34.

2. Dennis DeValeria and Jeanne Burke DeValeria, *Honus Wagner: A Biography* (New York: Henry Holt, 1995), 7–8.

3. Wagner, "A Few Facts About My Life," 34.

4. F. C. Lane, "The Grand Old Man of Baseball," *Baseball Magazine*, January 1915, 39.

5. Les Biederman, "Sports World Mourns Honus Wagner: Death Takes Baseball Idol of Millions," *The Pittsburgh Press*, December 6, 1955, 34.

6. Jack Hernon, "Honus Faithful to Carnegie for 81 Years: He Was Truly a Native Son!" *Pittsburgh Post-Gazette*, December 7, 1955, 38.

7. Les Biederman, "Honus, the Coal Miner, Turns to Baseball: The Wagner Story—No. 2," *The Pittsburgh Press*, December 7, 1955, 52.

8. *Ibid.*

9. Hernon, "Honus Faithful to Carnegie for 81 Years: He Was Truly a Native Son!" 38.

10. Wagner, "A Few Facts About My Life," 34.

11. *Ibid.*

12. DeValeria, *Honus Wagner*, 11.

13. Wagner, "A Few Facts About My Life," 34.

14. Hernon, "Honus Faithful to Carnegie for 81 Years: He Was Truly a Native Son!" 38.

15. Biederman, "Honus, the Coal Miner, Turns to Baseball: The Wagner Story—No. 2," 52.

16. Hernon, "Honus Faithful to Carnegie for 81 Years: He Was Truly a Native Son!" 38.

17. Biederman, "Honus, the Coal Miner, Turns to Baseball: The Wagner Story—No. 2," 52.

18. Daniel R. Levitt, *Ed Barrow: The Bulldog Who Built the Yankees' First Dynasty* (Lincoln: University Of Nebraska Press, 2008), 23.

19. Honus Wagner, "Honus Wagner Says: Of Course, He Had to Start in Minors, Just as Every Other Big Leaguer Did—Newspapers Bring Big Change Since He Was in Kansas City," *The Pittsburgh Press*, April 1, 1937, 30.

20. Levitt, *Ed Barrow*, 23.

21. Chester L. Smith, "The Village Smithy: Honus—Such a Gentle Man," *The Pittsburgh Press*, December 7, 1955, 52.

22. "Wagner's Start: Manager Barrow Tells How He Engaged the Great Pittsburg Star When at the Head of the Paterson Club," *Sporting Life*, May 6, 1905, 5.

23. Chester L. Smith, "The Village Smithy: Took Baseball Job for $125," *The Pittsburgh Press*, December 7, 1955, 52.

24. Edward G. Barrow, "Discovered Hans: Ed Barrow Developed Wagner at Paterson," *The Sporting News*, March 26, 1908, 3.

25. *Ibid.*

26. *Ibid.*

27. *Ibid.*

28. *Ibid.*

29. *Ibid.*

30. Honus (John H.) Wagner, "Honus Wagner's Own Baseball Story: Great Shortstop Tells How He Began Playing Ball on

Old Steubenville Club," *The Pittsburgh Gazette Times*, January 16, 1916, 4.

31. DeValeria, *Honus Wagner*, 41–42.

32. *Ibid.*, 42–43.

33. "Base Ball Caught on the Fly," *The Sporting News*, August 15, 1903, 5.

34. Lane, "The Grand Old Man of Baseball," 40.

35. "Baseball By-Plays," *The Sporting News*, March 8, 1917, 4.

36. Pirate, "Gigantic Deal: Star Colonels Sold to Pittsburg Club," *The Sporting News*, December 16, 1899, 3.

37. DeValeria, *Honus Wagner*, 80–81.

38. Jack Hernon, "Wagner Won First Batting Title in 1900: Honus Beat Flick of Phils on Last Day," *Pittsburgh Post-Gazette*, December 10, 1955, 13.

39. *Ibid.*

40. "Wagner Scored Run that Won the Pennant: Lefty Davis, Clarke, Beaumont and Bransfield Also Prominent in Rally that Ended the Long Struggle," *The Pittsburg Press*, September 28, 1901, 8.

41. Duquesne, "American's Agent: Charge of Disloyalty Made Against Ely," *The Sporting News*, August 3, 1901, 4.

42. DeValeria, *Honus Wagner*, 94.

43. Louis Masur, *Autumn Glory: Baseball's First World Series* (New York: Hill and Wang, 2003), 24.

44. Ralph S. Davis, "Blow to Pirates: Hans Wagner Will Rest for Season," *The Sporting News*, March 19, 1908, 3.

45. Ralph S. Davis, "Hans Wagner Has Signed Contract: Flying Dutchman Entered Fold Yesterday, and Left Last Night to Join Pirates at Cincinnati," *The Pittsburg Press*, April 18, 1908, 5.

46. "M'Graw Rates Hans Wagner the Greatest Player the Game Ever Knew: Great Tribute to Flying Dutchman," *The Pittsburg Press*, July 21, 1912, 2.

47. L. H. Constans, "Honus Wagner: The Champion Batter of All Time and What We Think of Him in Pittsburgh," *Baseball Magazine*, August 1913, 96.

48. David L. Fultz, "The Baseball Players Fraternity: Hans Wagner," *Baseball Magazine*, April 1913, 58.

Chapter 2

1. A. R. Cratty, "Pittsburgh Pennings: Steel City Slow to Awaken to the Grand Old Game," *Sporting Life*, May 13, 1916, 7.

2. James Jerpe, "On and Off the Field," *The Pittsburgh Gazette Times*, July 25, 1915, 6.

3. *Ibid.*

4. Honus (John H.) Wagner, "Honus Wagner's Own Baseball Story: Great Shortstop Tells How He Began Playing Ball on Old Steubenville Club," *The Pittsburgh Gazette Times*, January 16, 1916, 4.

5. "Baseball By-Plays," *The Sporting News*, March 16, 1916, 4.

6. Wagner, "Honus Wagner's Own Baseball Story: Great Shortstop Tells How He Began Playing Ball on Old Steubenville Club," 1.

7. "Baseball By-Plays," *The Sporting News*, March 16, 1916, 4.

8. Jack Hernon, "Wagner Broke into Organized Ball as a Pitcher for Steubenville: Fast Ball his Best Pitch—And Only Delivery," *Pittsburgh Post-Gazette*, December 8, 1955, 27.

9. *Ibid.*

10. *Ibid.*

11. John H. Wagner and John H. Dailey, "Seventh Wagner Series Story: Baseball Skilled Labor, Says Wagner," *The Pittsburg Press*, August 1, 1915, 2.

12. *Ibid.*

13. Frederick G. Lieb, *The Pittsburgh Pirates* (1948; reprint Carbondale: Southern Illinois University Press, 2003), 52.

14. "Wagner Found by Accident: Great Pittsburg Shortstop Among Famous Players Unheard of Before Jumping to Big Show," *Galveston Opera Glass*, January 28, 1911, 5.

15. "How Wagner Broke into National Game," *Indianapolis Sun*, May 7, 1906, 7.

16. *Ibid.*

17. Lieb, *The Pittsburgh Pirates*, 52.

18. "Wagner Found by Accident: Great Pittsburg Shortstop Among Famous Players Unheard of Before Jumping to Big Show," 5.

19. Wagner, "Honus Wagner's Own Baseball Story: Great Shortstop Tells How

He Began Playing Ball on Old Steubenville Club," 4.

20. Hernon, "Wagner Broke into Organized Ball as a Pitcher for Steubenville: Fast Ball His Best Pitch—And Only Delivery," 27.

21. Ralph S. Davis, "Hans Wagner's Days as Regular in Buccaneer Lineup Are Almost Ended: Flying Dutchman Feels Time's Hand," *The Pittsburg Press,* July 6, 1913, 3.

22. *Ibid.*

23. *Ibid.*

24. Wagner, "Honus Wagner's Own Baseball Story: Great Shortstop Tells How He Began Playing Ball on Old Steubenville Club," 4.

25. *Ibid.*

26. Lieb, *The Pittsburgh Pirates,* 58.

27. *Ibid.*

28. "Honus Wagner Was Famous Story Teller," *Beaver Valley Times,* December 6, 1955, 4.

29. Lieb, *The Pittsburgh Pirates,* 58–59.

30. "Baseball By-Plays," *The Sporting News,* March 8, 1917, 4.

31. *Ibid.*

32. *Ibid.*

33. Honus Wagner, "Honus Wagner Says: Clarke, McGraw Called Greatest Managers," *The Pittsburgh Press,* January 18, 1937, 26.

34. Frederick G. Lieb, "N. L. Mourns Honus Wagner, Its Greatest: Won Eight Batting Titles, Played all Posts Except Catcher," *The Sporting News,* December 14, 1955, 19.

35. *Ibid.*

36. Wagner, "Honus Wagner Says: Clarke, McGraw Called Greatest Managers," 6.

37. "Death Claims Honus Wagner, 81; Exploits Live As Baseball Legend: Shortstop Told Many Anecdotes," *The Pittsburgh Press,* December 6, 1955, 1.

38. Wagner, "Honus Wagner Says: Clarke, McGraw Called Greatest Managers," 26.

39. Lieb, "N. L. Mourns Honus Wagner, Its Greatest: Won Eight Batting Titles, Played all Posts Except Catcher," 19.

40. "Death Claims Hans Wagner, 81; Exploits Live as Baseball Legend: Shortstop Told Many Anecdotes," 1.

41. Wagner, "Honus Wagner Says: Clarke, McGraw Called Greatest Managers," 26.

42. "The Scrap Book: Old 'Eagle Eye's' Mean Trick," *The Gettysburg Times,* December 28, 1912, 4.

43. *Ibid.*

44. Wagner, "Honus Wagner's Own Baseball Story: Great Shortstop Tells How He Began Playing Ball on Old Steubenville Club," 4.

45. *Ibid.*

46. "Baseball By-Plays," *The Sporting News,* August 14, 1913, 4.

47. *Ibid.*

48. Wagner, "Honus Wagner's Own Baseball Story: Great Shortstop Tells How He Began Playing Ball on Old Steubenville Club," 4.

49. *Ibid.*

50. J. G. Taylor Spink, "Three and One—Looking Them over with J. G. Taylor Spink: Down Memory Lane with John Peter Wagner," *The Sporting News,* December 27, 1934, .

51. Wagner, "Honus Wagner's Own Baseball Story: Great Shortstop Tells How He Began Playing Ball on Old Steubenville Club," 4.

52. *Ibid.*

53. Bourbon, "Under Arrest: Cleveland Players Heavily Fined at Louisville," *The Sporting News,* July 4, 1896, 1.

54. Wagner, "Honus Wagner's Own Baseball Story: Great Shortstop Tells How He Began Playing Ball on Old Steubenville Club," 4.

55. *Ibid.*

56. Spink, "Three and One—Looking Them over with J. G. Taylor Spink: Down Memory Lane with John Peter Wagner," 4.

57. Wagner, "Honus Wagner's Own Baseball Story: Great Shortstop Tells How He Began Playing Ball on Old Steubenville Club," 4.

58. *Ibid.*

59. *Ibid.*

60. "National League: How They Stand," *The Sporting News,* April 29, 1899, 3.

61. "Baseball By-Plays," *The Sporting News,* October 2, 1913, 4.

62. *Ibid.*

63. "The Diamond: Notes Here and There Concerning the Great National Game," *The Mansfield News*, November 26, 1899, 6.

64. "First Boss Denies He Fined Wagner for Hitting Homer," *The Sporting News*, December 14, 1955, 22.

65. James Jerpe, "On and Off the Field," *Pittsburgh Gazette Times*, September 14, 1913, 3.

66. *Ibid.*

Chapter 3

1. Frederick G. Lieb, "Oilman Clarke Drills into Diamond Memories: From Pirate Heyday, to Present Day, and Still Punching," *The Sporting News*, January 17, 1946, 13.

2. "Baseball By-Plays," *The Sporting News*, November 15, 1923, 4.

3. Honus (John H.) Wagner, "Honus Wagner's Own Baseball Story: Great Shortstop Tells How He Began Playing Ball on Old Steubenville Club," *The Pittsburgh Gazette Times*, January 16, 1916, 4.

4. John H. "Honus" Wagner, "Sixth Story in Wagner Series: Ball Players Affected by Stage Fright," *The Pittsburg Press*, July 25, 1915, 2.

5. *Ibid.*

6. *Ibid.*

7. James Jerpe, "Buccos Again Idle; Play at Home Today: Weatherman is Credited with Checking Pirates' Winning Streak—Clarke Recounts Early Experiences, Anson's Record Nearly Equaled by Wagner," *Pittsburgh Gazette Times*, May 6, 1914, 12.

8. *Ibid.*

9. Frederick G. Lieb, *The Pittsburgh Pirates* (1948; reprint Carbondale: Southern Illinois University Press, 2003), 60.

10. John H. "Honus" Wagner and John H. Dailey, "Third Story in Wagner Series: The 'Nuts' of the National Pastime," *The Pittsburg Press*, July 4, 1915, 1.

11. "Baseball By-Plays," *The Sporting News*, November 2, 1922, 4.

12. Wagner and Dailey, "Third Story In Wagner Series: The 'Nuts' of the National Pastime," 1.

13. *Ibid.*

14. "Baseball By-Plays," *The Sporting News*, November 2, 1922, 4.

15. Wagner and Dailey, "Third Story In Wagner Series: The 'Nuts' of the National Pastime," 1.

16. *Ibid.*

17. "Baseball By-Plays," *The Sporting News*, November 2, 1922, 4.

18. Wagner and Dailey, "Third Story In Wagner Series: The 'Nuts' of the National Pastime," 1.

19. *Ibid.*

20. "Baseball By-Plays," *The Sporting News*, November 2, 1922, 4.

21. *Ibid.*

22. Joe King, "The Wonder Man of Pittsburgh: Life Story Of Fred Clarke, Famed Pirate—Part 3," *The Sporting News*, March 28, 1951, 21.

23. Wagner and Dailey, "Third Story in Wagner Series: The 'Nuts' of the National Pastime," 1.

24. *Ibid.*

25. *Ibid.*

26. "Baseball By-Plays," *The Sporting News*, December 23, 1920, 4.

27. *Ibid.*

28. *Ibid.*

29. "Baseball By-Plays," *The Sporting News*, March 20, 1913, 4.

30. Dennis DeValeria and Jeanne Burke DeValeria, *Honus Wagner: A Biography* (New York: Henry Holt, 1995), 173.

31. *Ibid.*, 173–174.

32. "Baseball By-Plays," *The Sporting News*, March 20, 1913, 4.

33. A. R. Cratty, "In Pittsburg: Weird Gossip about Hans Wagner's Shift," *Sporting Life*, May 2, 1908, 7.

34. *Ibid.*

35. William A. Phelon, "Hans Wagner, a Unique Character: The Dutchman and His Dog—His Love of Hunting and Fishing—His Quaint Oddities of Manner—His Amazing Popularity," *Baseball Magazine*, January 1915, 54.

36. *Ibid.*

37. Edgar G. Brands, "Between Innings: Speaking Of Beer," *The Sporting News*, April 20, 1933, 4.

38. *Ibid.*

39. Joe King, "'The Wonder Man' of Pittsburgh: Life Story of Fred Clarke, Famed Pirate—Part 2," *The Sporting News,* March 21, 1951, 15.

40. Brands, "Between Innings: Speaking of Beer," 4.

41. Hans Wagner and John H. Dailey, "Second Story in Wagner Series: Wagner Tells Story of Remarkable Triple Killing Made on a Pitchout," *The Pittsburg Press,* June 27, 1915, 2.

42. "Baseball By-Plays," *The Sporting News,* December 27, 1923, 4.

43. *Ibid.*

44. Wagner and Dailey, "Third Story in Wagner Series: The 'Nuts' of the National Pastime," 1.

45. *Ibid.*

46. *Ibid.*

47. *Ibid.*

48. Ralph S. Davis, "Clarke Pines for More Active Life: Reason for Giving up His Berth with Pittsburg," *The Sporting News,* September 16, 1915, 2.

49. C. B. Power, "Just by Way of Comment," *The Pittsburgh Gazette Times,* June 1, 1911, 9.

50. *Ibid.*

Chapter 4

1. "Baseball By-Plays," *The Sporting News,* December 7, 1916, 4.

2. *Ibid.*

3. *Ibid.*

4. A. R. Cratty, "Pittsburg Points: Paragraphers Come Close to Creating Trouble," *Sporting Life,* November 25, 1905, 6.

5. *Ibid.*

6. *Ibid.*

7. *Ibid.*

8. "Baseball By-Plays," *The Sporting News,* October 15, 1914, 4.

9. "Baseball By-Plays," *The Sporting News,* January 11, 1917, 4.

10. *Ibid.*

11. "Baseball By-Plays," *The Sporting News,* January 8, 1925, 4.

12. *Ibid.*

13. William A. Phelon, "Hans Wagner, a Unique Character: The Dutchman and His Dog—His Love of Hunting and Fishing—His Quaint Oddities of Manner—His Amazing Popularity," *Baseball Magazine,* January 1915, 55.

14. *Ibid.*

15. "Baseball By-Plays," *The Sporting News,* January 16, 1913, 4.

16. "Characteristic Anecdotes of 'Hans' Wagner: Wagner as a Humorist—His Dislike of the Limelight—His Love Of Athletic Sports—His Generosity—Contradictory Traits—Odd Financial Deals," *Baseball Magazine,* January 1915, 58–59.

17. "Kept Stars off the Stage: Honus Wagner Spurned Tempting Offer to Perform at Last Moment—Batting Act All Ready," *Goshen Daily Democrat,* May 16, 1911, 2.

18. *Ibid.*

19. C. B. Power, "Brooklyn Gets Only One Hit off Steele: The Safety Comes in the Ninth Inning after One Man Is Out," *The Pittsburgh Gazette Times,* August 17, 1911, 7.

20. C. B. Power, "Just By Way of Comment," *The Pittsburgh Gazette Times,* September 4, 1911, 7.

21. *Ibid.*

22. *Ibid.*

23. Bob, "On the Sport Firing Line," *The Syracuse Herald,* April 27, 1916, 36.

24. *Ibid.*

25. John H. (Honus) Wagner, "Fourth Story in Wagner Series: One Pitcher Found Wagner's Weakness," *The Pittsburg Press,* July 11, 1915, 2.

26. *Ibid.*

27. *Ibid.*

28. *Ibid.*

29. "Baseball By-Plays," *The Sporting News,* February 8, 1918, 4.

30. *Ibid.*

31. James Jerpe, "On and Off the Field," *The Pittsburgh Gazette Times,* July 25, 1915, 6.

32. *Ibid.*

33. John H. "Honus" Wagner and John H. Dailey, "Eighth Wagner Series Story: Ball Players Not Always Flush with Coin," *The Pittsburg Press,* August 8, 1915, 3.

34. *Ibid.*

35. *Ibid.*

36. James Jerpe, "On and Off the Field," *The Pittsburgh Gazette Times,* June 17, 1914, 11.

37. John H. "Honus" Wagner and John H. Dailey, "Eleventh Wagner Series Story: Baseball Has Become Second Nature to Hans Wagner, But He Still Enjoys Playing the Game," *The Pittsburg Press,* August 29, 1915, 2.

38. *Ibid.*

39. Phelon, "Hans Wagner, A Unique Character: The Dutchman and his Dog—His Love of Hunting and Fishing—His Quaint Oddities of Manner—His Amazing Popularity," 55.

40. *Ibid.*

Chapter 5

1. "Clarke Says He Won't Play: Not Even Emergency Will Influence Him—Eastman's Father Is Sioux Farmer-Clergyman—Hofman Showing up Well," *The Pittsburgh Gazette Times,* March 14, 1913, 13.

2. Honus Wagner, "Honus Wagner Says: Heap Big Injun Too Smart for Manager Fred Clarke of 1911 Pirates in Walking Race that Turns into Nothing Else but Battle of Wits," *The Pittsburgh Press,* March 18, 1937, 33.

3. *Ibid.*

4. Honus Wagner, "Honus Wagner Says: Too Plump by 30 Pounds for Spring Training in 1898, Hans Isn't Recognized by Barney Dreyfuss; Signals in German Confused Foes, Umpire," *The Pittsburgh Press,* March 4, 1937, 29.

5. *Ibid.*

6. J. Honus Wagner, "Trick Play at Third for Wagner," *The Toledo News-Bee,* March 29, 1933, 10.

7. *Ibid.*

8. Honus Wagner, "Hans Wagner Says: Rube Waddell, One of Greatest Hurlers of All Time, Also Baseball's Most Eccentric—He Liked His Wild West Shows, Raced After Fire Trucks," *The Pittsburgh Press,* February 4, 1937, 29.

9. *Ibid.*

10. *Ibid.*

11. *Ibid.*

12. *Ibid.*

13. Andy Dabilis and Nick Tsiotos, *The 1903 World Series: The Boston Americans, the Pittsburg Pirates, and the "First Championship of the United States"* (Jefferson, NC: McFarland, 2004), 98.

14. Honus (John H.) Wagner, "Wagner's Own Story: Picks the Six Greatest Pitchers He Has Faced on the Diamond," *The Pittsburgh Gazette Times,* January 23, 1916, 4.

15. *Ibid.*

16. Dennis DeValeria and Jeanne Burke DeValeria, *Honus Wagner: A Biography* (New York: Henry Holt, 1995), 206.

17. "'Honus' and 'Jack' Pals," *The Pittsburg Press,* June 16, 1909, 14.

18. J. Honus Wagner, "Wagner's Late Throws to First Made Umpire Hank O'Day Sob in Old Days," *The Toledo News-Bee,* March 24, 1933, 14.

19. Wagner, "Honus Wagner Says: Too Plump by 30 Pounds for Spring Training in 1898, Hans Isn't Recognized by Barney Dreyfuss; Signals in German Confused Foes, Umpire," 29.

20. DeValeria, *Honus Wagner,* 214.

21. Wagner, "Honus Wagner Says: Too Plump by 30 Pounds for Spring Training In 1898, Hans Isn't Recognized by Barney Dreyfuss; Signals in German Confused Foes, Umpire," 29.

22. Wagner, "Wagner's Late Throws to First Made Umpire Hank O'Day Sob in Old Days," 14.

23. Wagner, "Honus Wagner Says: Too Plump by 30 Pounds for Spring Training in 1898, Hans Isn't Recognized by Barney Dreyfuss; Signals in German Confused Foes, Umpire," 29.

24. Wagner, "Wagner's Late Throws to First Made Umpire Hank O'Day Sob in Old Days," 14.

25. Wagner, "Honus Wagner Says: Too Plump by 30 Pounds for Spring Training in 1898, Hans Isn't Recognized by Barney Dreyfuss; Signals in German Confused Foes, Umpire," 29.

26. C. B. Power, "Just by the Way of Comment," *The Pittsburgh Gazette Times,* June 27, 1911, 9.

27. *Ibid.*

28. "Baseball By-Plays," *The Sporting News,* February 28, 1924, 4.

29. *Ibid.*

30. Hans Wagner and John H. Dailey, "Second Story in Wagner Series: Wagner Talks of Remarkable Triple Killing Made on a Pitchout," *The Pittsburg Press,* June 27, 1915, 2.

31. "Rehg's Freshness Subject of Story," *The Pittsburg Press,* April 5, 1913, 8.

32. *Ibid.*

33. *Ibid.*

34. Wagner and Dailey, "Second Story in Wagner Series: Wagner Talks of Remarkable Triple Killing Made on a Pitchout," 2.

35. "Rehg's Freshness Subject of Story," 8.

36. *Ibid.*

37. James Jerpe, "Adams Pitches Fine Ball and Pirates Defeat Reds: Leach and Leifield Sit in Grandstand and See Ex-Comrades Down the Sadly Slumped Cincinnati Pennant Hopes," *The Pittsburgh Gazette Times,* June 1, 1912, 10.

38. "Wagner's Dog Shows His Dislike for the Umpires," *The Pittsburgh Gazette Times,* June 1, 1912, 10.

39. Wagner and Dailey, "Second Story in Wagner Series: Wagner Talks of Remarkable Triple Killing Made on a Pitchout," 2.

40. *Ibid.*

41. "Baseball By-Plays," *The Sporting News,* April 27, 1916, 4.

42. "Battle Of Bushers," *The Jeffersonville Star,* August 5, 1916, 2.

43. Wagner, "Wagner's Own Story: Picks the Six Greatest Pitchers He Has Faced on the Diamond," 4.

44. *Ibid.*

45. Honus (John H.) Wagner, "Wagner Tells of 'Hard Losers' in Baseball: Famous Shortstop Declares the Winners Hate to Lose Games on the Ball Field," *The Pittsburgh Gazette Times,* January 30, 1916, 4.

46. *Ibid.*

47. J. Honus Wagner, "Signal Crossed John McGraw Second Time," *The Toledo News-Bee,* March 30, 1933, 15.

48. *Ibid.*

49. "Jim Scott Sued for Breach of Prom- ise: Wagner Falls for Old Trick—Menke Sport Gossip," *The Lima Daily News,* July 31, 1915, 6.

50. *Ibid.*

51. F. C. Lane, "The Greatest Manager in Organized Baseball: The Talents that Make the Successful Manager—Five Great Names in Baseball—Connie Mack and His Shrewd Policy—The Secret of McGraw's Success—The Greatest of Them All," *Baseball Magazine,* May 1913, 49.

52. *Ibid.*

Chapter 6

1. Honus Wagner, "Honus Wagner Says: Pirate Pinch-Hitter Was Swell Fellow When He Hit but if He Failed—Heaven Help His Missus! Smashed Infielders Out of His Path," *The Pittsburgh Press,* March 23, 1937, 27.

2. James Jerpe, "Old Time Rally Wins from Cubs in Ninth: Fred Clarke Delights Crowd by Batting in a Pinch—Leach's Triple Gives Chicago the Lead, But Pirates Triumph, 5–4," *The Pittsburgh Gazette Times,* May 30, 1913, 14.

3. Russ J. Newland, "Scouting Western Sports," *Reno Evening Gazette,* March 16, 1934, 13.

4. Wagner, "Honus Wagner Says: Pirate Pinch-Hitter Was Swell Fellow When He Hit but if He Failed—Heaven Help His Missus!" 27.

5. "Baseball By-Plays," *The Sporting News,* April 1, 1915, 4.

6. John H. (Honus) Wagner, "Fourth Story in Wagner Series: One Pitcher Found Wagner's Weakness," *The Pittsburg Press,* July 11, 1915, 2.

7. *Ibid.*

8. John H. "Honus" Wagner and John H. Dailey, "Eleventh Wagner Series Story: Baseball Has Become Second Nature to Hans Wagner, But He Still Enjoys Playing the Game," *The Pittsburg Press,* August 29, 1915, 2.

9. *Ibid.*

10. *Ibid.*

11. *Ibid.*

12. *Ibid.*

13. J. Honus Wagner, "Years Ago Honus Wagner Won N.L. Batting Crown in Race with Donlin," *The Toledo News-Bee,* March 23, 1933, 10.

14. *Ibid;* John B. Foster, "Pirate Batting Rally in the Seventh Too Much for 'Matty': Buccaneers Get Revenge on New York Giants Before Biggest Crowd Ever Assembled at Polo Grounds," *The Pittsburgh Press,* July 26, 1908, 16—John B. Foster was the baseball editor for the *New York Herald;* "John Wagner Was in the Spotlight: A Pittsburger Tells of the Doings of the Big Fellow on Saturday," *The Pittsburg Press,* July 27, 1908, 12; "Pirates Still in the Lead: Record Breaking Crowd Sees Team Outplayed," *Boston Sunday Post,* July 26, 1908, 6; A.R. Cratty, "Pirate Points: Mr. Wilson, of Texas, Accepted as a Regular," *Sporting Life,* August 15, 1908, 26; "National League News," *Sporting Life,* August 8, 1908, 19; "Leaders Ready to Tackle Giants in the Third Contest: Pittsburg Boys Expect to Have Another Stirring Struggle With John James McGraw's Boys—John Wagner Overhauls the Leader in the Batting Race," *The Pittsburg Press,* July 27, 1908, 12.

15. Chester L. Smith, "The Village Smithy: Elias a Wagner Booster," *The Pittsburgh Press,* March 9, 1934, 45.

16. *Ibid.*

17. Wagner, "Years Ago Honus Wagner Won N.L. Batting Crown in Race with Donlin," 10.

18. Honus (John H.) Wagner, "Wagner Tells of 'Hard Losers' in Baseball: Famous Shortstop Declares the Winners Hate to Lose Ball Games on the Ball Field," *The Pittsburgh Gazette Times,* January 30, 1916, 4.

19. *Ibid.*

20. James Jerpe, "Max Carey's Home Run Clinches Pirates' Game: Pittsburgh Needed it, As New York Almost Tied up the Score in the Ninth—Hendrix Opposed by Crandall, Final Count is 5 To 4," *The Pittsburgh Gazette Times,* June 16, 1912, 2.

21. John B. Foster, "Home Run by Carey and Donlin's Great Batting Beats New York Giants: Claude Hendrix Fools Champions," *The Pittsburgh Press,* June 16, 1912, 2.

22. John H. (Honus) Wagner, "Fifth Story in Wagner Series: No Luxuries for Ball Players of Other Days," *The Pittsburg Press,* July 18, 1915, 2.

23. "A Real Reason for Honus' Great Diamond Career," *Fort Wayne Journal-Gazette,* January 8, 1913, 6.

24. *Ibid.*

25. Hans Wagner and John H. Dailey, "First Story in Wagner Series: Why I Am Playing Big League Ball at 41," *The Pittsburg Press,* June 20, 1915, 2.

26. *Ibid.*

27. "Honus Wagner Relates Great Tale about Rube," *The Portsmouth Daily Times,* August 22, 1912, 10.

28. *Ibid.*

29. *Ibid.*

30. Honus (John H.) Wagner, "Wagner's Own Story: Picks the Six Greatest Pitchers He Has Faced on the Diamond," *The Pittsburgh Gazette Times,* January 23, 1916, 4.

31. *Ibid.*

32. James Jerpe, "Pirates Lose Game at Long Branch: Ham Hyatt Tries to Pitch and is Charged with the Defeat," *The Pittsburgh Gazette-Times,* August 12, 1912, 7.

33. John H. "Honus" Wagner and John H. Dailey, "Tenth Wagner Series Story: 'When Is a Bonehead?' Asks Wagner," *The Pittsburg Press,* August 22, 1915, 2.

34. "Baseball By-Plays," *The Sporting News,* December 16, 1915, 4.

35. Wagner and Dailey, "Tenth Wagner Series Story: 'When Is a Bonehead?' Asks Wagner," 2.

36. James Jerpe, "Slapnicka Is Puzzle to the Pirate Batters: American Association Champions Defeat Buccos, 5–4, Wagner Gets Ovation," *The Pittsburgh Gazette Times,* October 4, 1913, 8.

37. John H. "Honus" Wagner and John H. Dailey, "Ninth Wagner Series Story: Ball Players Love Their Basehits," *The Pittsburg Press,* August 15, 1915, 3.

38. Jerpe, "Slapnicka Is Puzzle to the Pirate Batters: American Association Champions Defeat Buccos, 5–4, Wagner Gets Ovation," 8.

39. Wagner and Dailey, "Ninth Wagner Series Story: Ball Players Love Their Basehits," 3.

40. Jerpe, "Slapnicka Is Puzzle to the Pi-

rate Batters: American Association Champions Defeat Buccos, 5–4, Wagner Gets Ovation," 8.

41. John H. "Honus" Wagner and John H. Dailey, "Eighth Wagner Series Story: Ball Players Not Always Flush with Coin," *The Pittsburg Press,* August 8, 1915, 2.

42. *Ibid.*

43. Wagner, "Wagner Tells of 'Hard Losers' in Baseball: Famous Shortstop Declares the Winners Hate to Lose Games on the Ball Field," 4.

44. *Ibid.*

Chapter 7

1. Frederick G. Lieb, *The Pittsburgh Pirates* (1948; reprint Carbondale: Southern Illinois University Press, 2003), 66.

2. *Ibid.*

3. *Ibid.,* 66–67.

4. A. R. Cratty, "Pittsburg Points: Champions' Owner Vows that He Is Trying to Have a Quiet Winter," *Sporting Life,* December 3, 1904, 9.

5. *Ibid.*

6. Honus (John H.) Wagner, "Honus Wagner's Own Baseball Story: Great Shortstop Tells How He Began Playing Ball on Old Steubenville Club," *The Pittsburgh Gazette Times,* January 16, 1916, 4.

7. *Ibid.*

8. Andy Dabilis and Nick Tsiotos, *The 1903 World Series: The Boston Americans, the Pittsburg Pirates and the "First Championship of the United States"* (Jefferson, NC: McFarland, 2004), 31.

9. *Ibid.*

10. John H. "Honus" Wagner and John H. Dailey, "Ninth Wagner Series Story: Ball Players Love Their Basehits," *The Pittsburg Press,* August 15, 1915, 3.

11. "Baseball By-Plays," *The Sporting News,* December 25, 1913, 4.

12. *Ibid.*

13. *Ibid.*

14. *Ibid.*

15. *Ibid.*

16. *Ibid.*

17. *Ibid.*

18. James Jerpe, "On and Off the Field," *The Pittsburgh Gazette Times,* April 19, 1913, 14.

19. Hans Wagner and John H. Dailey, "Second Story in Wagner Series: Wagner Tells Story of Remarkable Triple Killing Made on a Pitchout," *The Pittsburg Press,* June 27, 1915, 2.

20. *Ibid.*

21. *Ibid.*

22. Honus (John H.) Wagner, "Wagner Tells of 'Hard Losers' in Baseball: Famous Shortstop Declares the Winners Hate to Lose Games on the Ball Field," *The Pittsburgh Gazette Times,* January 30, 1916, 4.

23. "Little Bits of Baseball," *The Pittsburg Press,* June 16, 1911, 26.

24. C. B. Power, "Just by Way of Comment," *The Pittsburgh Gazette Times,* June 15, 1911, 9.

25. *Ibid.*

26. C. B. Power, "Just By Way Of Comment," *The Pittsburgh Gazette Times,* June 17, 1911, 9.

27. *Ibid.*

28. *Ibid.*

29. *Ibid.*

30. A. R. Cratty, "Pittsburgh Pennings: Steel City Slow to Awaken to the Grand Old Game," *Sporting Life,* May 13, 1916, 7.

31. "News Notes and Highlights," *Sporting Life,* January 13, 1917, 7.

32. A. R. Cratty, "Pittsburg Points: Ed Plank's Success Recalls a War-Time Incident," *Sporting Life,* November 4, 1905, 6.

33. Charles J. Doyle, "Phils Win Exciting Game from Buccos, 3–2: League Leaders Break Tie in Seventh Inning and Mayer Holds Pirate Attack in Check," *The Pittsburgh Gazette Times,* September 12, 1915, 2.

34. "Baseball By-Plays," *The Sporting News,* September 30, 1915, 4.

35. *Ibid.*

36. Doyle, "Phils Win Exciting Game from Buccos, 3–2: League Leaders Break Tie in Seventh Inning and Mayer Holds Pirate Attack in Check," 2.

37. "Baseball By-Plays," *The Sporting News,* October 14, 1915, 4.

38. *Ibid.*

39. "M'Quillan and Mamaux Are Touched Up Freely: Cubs Make Four Runs

off Big Mac First Three Innings and Fisher's Triple with Archer's Single Beats Mamaux—Clarke Sent to Clubhouse," *The Pittsburgh Gazette Times*, September 15, 1914, 10.

40. John H. (Honus) Wagner, "Sixth Story in Wagner Series: Ball Players Affected by Stage Fright," *The Pittsburg Press*, July 25, 1915, 2.

41. *Ibid.*

42. "Baseball By-Plays," *The Sporting News*, March 5, 1925, 4.

43. *Ibid.*

Chapter 8

1. John B. Wiseman, ed., *Joy in Mudville: Essays on Baseball and American Life* (Jefferson, NC: McFarland, 2010), 47.

2. *Ibid.*, 47–48.

3. Honus Wagner, "Honus Wagner Says: 'Tinker-to-Evers-to-Chance,'" *The Pittsburgh Press*, January 4, 1937, 26.

4. *Ibid.* The article doesn't mention why Wagner was dressing in the opponent's clubhouse, but one can imagine that since it was a single Sunday game in Chicago (Pittsburgh commonly played one-day Sunday road games in Chicago due to the state of Pennsylvania prohibiting professional baseball from being played on that day), dressing at the hotel, which was the common practice under this circumstance, may not have been possible if the Pirates were leaving Chicago by train immediately after the game rather than remaining overnight.

5. *Ibid.*

6. *Ibid.*

7. "Baseball By-Plays," *The Sporting News*, April 15, 1915, 4.

8. *Ibid.*

9. Chester L. Smith, "The Village Smithy: More Wagner Stories," *The Pittsburgh Press*, December 9, 1955, 42.

10. *Ibid.*

11. *Ibid.*

12. Frederick G. Lieb, *The Pittsburgh Pirates* (1948; reprint Carbondale: Southern Illinois University Press, 2003), 53.

13. *Ibid.*

14. "Signal for Honus Wagner: Manager McGraw of New York Giants Tells Pitcher Marquard to Give Pittsburger 'Anything,'" *The Oelwein Daily Register*, March 31, 1911, 2.

15. Honus (John H.) Wagner, "Wagner's Own Story: Picks the Six Greatest Pitchers He Has Faced on the Diamond," *The Pittsburgh Gazette Times*, January 23, 1916, 4.

16. James Jerpe, "Great Plays by Old Honus Electrify: Shettsline, Chief Meyers and Others Tell of Greatest Feats," *The Pittsburgh Gazette Times*, July 2, 1916, 4.

17. *Ibid.*

18. Charles J. Doyle, "Jimmie Callahan Is Given His Release: New Leader of Pirates Not Yet Announced by President Dreyfuss," *The Pittsburgh Gazette Times*, July 1, 1917, 2.

19. "Baseball By-Plays," *The Sporting News*, August 2, 1917, 4.

20. *Ibid.*

21. Doyle, "Jimmie Callahan Is Given His Release: New Leader of Pirates Not Yet Announced by President Dreyfuss," 2.

22. Lieb, *The Pittsburgh Pirates*, 54.

23. *Ibid.*

24. James Jerpe, "Cooper Blanks the Cardinals: Pirates' New Lefthander Pitches Excellent Ball, Winning, 8–0—St. Louis Uses Recruits—Simon Works Well Behind the Bat," *The Pittsburgh Gazette Times*, September 7, 1912, 10.

25. "Baseball By-Plays," *The Sporting News*, March 13, 1913, 4.

26. Jerpe, "Cooper Blanks the Cardinals: Pirates' New Lefthander Pitches Excellent Ball, Winning, 8–0—St. Louis Uses Recruits—Simon Works Well Behind the Bat," 10.

27. J.A. Fitzgerald, "The Terrible Story of Nap Rucker's Life: His Name Isn't Napoleon at All, Just Plain George—He Says Brooklyn Is Fine City," *The Pittsburg Press*, September 1, 1912, 1.

28. *Ibid.*

29. Ralph S. Davis, "Record Ball Game Is Protested by the Pittsburg Club: Bargain Bill Is Today's Offering," *The Pittsburg Press*, July 18, 1914, 14.

30. "Baseball By-Plays," *The Sporting News*, April 19, 1923, 4.

31. Frank G. Menke, "Poor Form Is Being Shown Throughout the Winter League: Stallings Once Turned Down the

Great and Only Honus Wagner When a Diamond in the Rough," *The Lima Daily News,* January 4, 1914, 9.

32. *Ibid.*

33. "Baseball By-Plays," *The Sporting News,* April 10, 1919, 4.

34. *Ibid.*

35. "Hans Wagner's 'Rest' an Amusing Stunt," *The Salt Lake Tribune,* February 13, 1916, 4.

36. James Jerpe, "On and Off the Field," *The Pittsburgh Gazette Times,* August 3, 1915, 9.

37. Homer Croy, "Famous Player of Pittsburgh Pirates," *The Cedar Rapids Evening Gazette,* February 22, 1912, 5.

38. James Jerpe, "On and Off the Field," *The Pittsburgh Gazette Times,* August 3, 1915, 9.

39. "Baseball Game Tame: Too Much Candy in National Pastime, Says Gleason," *The Wakefield Advocate,* May 26, 1917, 11.

40. *Ibid.*

41. *Ibid.*

42. *Ibid.*

43. John Shiffert, *Baseball In Philadelphia: A History of the Early Game, 1831–1900* (Jefferson, NC: McFarland, 2006), 250.

44. Jerpe, "Great Plays by Old Honus Electrify: Shettsline, Chief Meyers and Others Tell of Greatest Feats," 4.

45. *Ibid.*

46. "Baseball By-Plays," *The Sporting News,* May 29, 1913, 4.

47. *Ibid.*

Chapter 9

1. Dennis DeValeria and Jeanne Burke DeValeria, *Honus Wagner: A Biography* (New York: Henry Holt, 1995), 98.

2. J. Honus Wagner, "Wagner Liked Basketball, the Pirate Bosses Objected Strenuously to Game," *The Toledo News-Bee,* March 27, 1933, 10.

3. *Ibid.*

4. *Ibid.*

5. A. R. Cratty, "Pittsburg Points: Champions' Camp Shows No Signs of Activity As Yet," *Sporting Life,* March 7, 1903, 3.

6. *Ibid.*

7. James Jerpe, "On and Off the Field," *The Pittsburgh Gazette Times,* August 10, 1915, 9.

8. *Ibid.*

9. J. Honus Wagner, "Plumber Aided Honus in Scrap with Hot Pipe: Old Pirate Shortstop Believes Basketball Great Conditioner," *The Toledo News-Bee,* March 25, 1933, 7.

10. *Ibid.*

11. *Ibid.*

12. "Baseball By-Plays," *The Sporting News,* February 10, 1916, 4.

13. *Ibid.*

14. William A. Phelon, "Hans Wagner, a Unique Character: The Dutchman and His Dog—His Love of Hunting and Fishing—His Quaint Oddities of Manner—His Amazing Popularity," *Baseball Magazine,* January 1915, 52.

15. Charles Dryden, "Dryden Explains Why Wagner Is Still Good: When Not Playing Ball, Hans Fishes, Watching Corks Disappear Instead of Pulling Them out of Bottles," *The Pittsburg Press,* April 29, 1914, 28.

16. *Ibid.*

17. Phelon, "Hans Wagner, A Unique Character: The Dutchman and His Dog—His Love of Hunting and Fishing—His Quaint Oddities of Manner—His Amazing Popularity," 53.

18. *Ibid.*

19. *Ibid.,* p. 52–53.

20. Honus Wagner, "Honus Wagner Says: Claude Hendrix and Pirate Shortstop Go on Fishing Trip, but Hendrix, National League's Free-Style Eating Champion , Uses Bait for His Meal," *The Pittsburgh Press,* March 2, 1937, 26.

21. John H. "Honus" Wagner and John H. Dailey, "Eleventh Wagner Series Story: Baseball Has Become Second Nature to Hans Wagner, but He Still Enjoys Playing the Game," *The Pittsburg Press,* August 29, 1915, 2.

22. Wagner, "Honus Wagner Says: Claude Hendrix and Pirate Shortstop Go on Fishing Trip, but Hendrix, National League's Free-Style Eating Champion, Uses Bait for His Meal," 26.

23. Wagner and Dailey, "Eleventh Wagner Series Story: Baseball Has Become Second Nature to Hans Wagner, but He Still Enjoys Playing the Game," 2.

24. James Jerpe, "On and Off the Field," *The Pittsburgh Gazette Times*, July 12, 1915, 8.

25. Wagner, "Honus Wagner Says: Claude Hendrix and Pirate Shortstop Go on Fishing Trip, but Hendrix, National League's Free-Style Eating Champion, Uses Bait for His Meal," 26.

26. *Ibid.*

27. James Jerpe, "On and Off the Field," *The Pittsburgh Gazette Times*, July 12, 1915, 8.

28. "Baseball By-Plays," *The Sporting News*, December 9, 1915, 4.

29. *Ibid.*

30. *Ibid.*

31. A. R. Cratty, "Pittsburg Points: Veteran Ball Player Settles a Famous Feud," *Sporting Life*, November 21, 1903, 7.

32. *Ibid.*

33. A. R. Cratty, "Pittsburg Points: The McBride Decision Not Relished by President Dreyfuss," *Sporting Life*, December 24, 1904, 7.

34. *Ibid.*

35. "Base Ball Heroes: How Hans Wagner Rescued a Marooned Automobile Party," *Sporting Life*, December 24, 1910, 6.

36. "Wagner Drove Early Ford as Henry Adjusted Engine," *The Sporting News*, December 14, 1955, 22.

37. *Ibid.*

38. "Baseball By-Plays," *The Sporting News*, June 23, 1921, 4.

39. *Ibid.*

40. *Ibid.*

41. "Honus Wagner Gets Car," *Oakland Tribune*, October 28, 1913, 10.

42. *Ibid.*

43. "Characteristic Anecdotes of 'Hans' Wagner: Wagner as a Humorist—His Dislike of the Limelight—His Love of Athletic Sports—His Generosity—Contradictory Traits—Odd Financial Deals," *Baseball Magazine*, January 1915, 59–60.

44. *Ibid.*, 60.

45. "Honus Wagner Is a Modest Teuton," *The Syracuse Herald*, July 1, 1913, 33.

46. *Ibid.*

47. *Ibid.*

48. "Characteristic Anecdotes of 'Hans' Wagner: Wagner as a Humorist—His Dislike of the Limelight—His Love of Athletic Sports—His Generosity—Contradictory Traits—Odd Financial Deals," 58.

49. *Ibid.*

50. *Ibid.*

51. A. R. Cratty, "Pittsburg Points: History Making by the Now Well Shaped Champions," *Sporting Life*, June 13, 1903, 5.

52. A. R. Cratty, "Pittsburg Points: Players Tired of the League Wrangle," *Sporting Life*, February 1, 1902, 9.

53. *Ibid.*

Chapter 10

1. James Jerpe, "Rain Prevents Pirate Game with Bisons: Large Crowd Disappointed at Not Seeing Wagner and Rest of Buccos Perform," *The Pittsburgh Gazette Times*, August 29, 1913, 10.

2. Ralph S. Davis, "Clarke Praises Flying Dutchman: and Pleads for Proper Recognition by Pittsburg Fandom of the Worth of Hans Wagner," *The Pittsburg Press*, August 30, 1913, 10.

3. *Ibid.*

4. "Walter Turner Dies After Illness: World's Leading Pneumatic Engineer and Foremost Inventor Succumbs," *The Pittsburgh Gazette Times*, January 10, 1919, 8.

5. Edgar G. Brands, "Between Innings: $30,000,000 on Hans," *The Sporting News*, February 23, 1933, 4.

6. "Honus Wagner Likes to Help Young Men," *The Cedar Rapids Republican*, March 3, 1915, 9.

7. *Ibid.*

8. "Characteristic Anecdotes of 'Hans' Wagner: Wagner as a Humorist—His Dislike of the Limelight—His Love of Athletic Sports—His Generosity—Contradictory Traits—Odd Financial Deals," *Baseball Magazine*, January 1915, 60.

9. *Ibid.*

10. *Ibid.*

11. William A. Phelon, "Hans Wagner, a Unique Character: The Dutchman and His Dog—His Love of Hunting and Fishing—His Quaint Oddities of Manner—His Amazing Popularity," *Baseball Magazine,* January 1915, p. 54.

12. *Ibid.,* 55.

13. John B. Miller, "Wins by Watching Wagner: Clever Second Baseman of Pittsburg Pirates Gives Big Shortstop Credit for Success," *Goshen Daily Democrat,* November 4, 1910, 6.

14. *Ibid.*

15. C. B. Power, "Brooklyn Gets Only One Hit off Steele: The Safety Comes in the Ninth Inning after One Man Is Out," *The Pittsburgh Gazette Times,* August 17, 1911, 7.

16. Ralph S. Davis, "Alex M'Carthy Is All-Round Player: Little Irishman May be Used Behind the Bat if Gibson Is Injured—Can Play Several Positions," *The Pittsburg Press,* August 19, 1911, 7.

17. *Ibid.*

18. *Ibid.*

19. Honus Wagner, "Along Came Merkle!: Prize 'Bone' Might Never Had Been Heard of Had Not Umpire Called Abby's Hit Foul," *The Pittsburgh Press,* April 15, 1937, 33.

20. Ralph S. Davis, "Pirates Finally Eliminated from Great Race for Pennant: Succumb to Cubs in Final Contest of Season in Presence of Crowd of More than 30,000 Fans," *The Pittsburg Press,* October 5, 1908, 12.

21. Wagner, "Along Came Merkle!: Prize 'Bone' Might Never Had Been Heard of Had Not Umpire Called Abby's Hit Foul," 33.

22. "Cubs Snatch the Pennant from Our Pirates' Grasp; Score, 5 to 2: Brown Too Much for Home Team," *The Pittsburgh Gazette Times,* October 5, 1908, 7.

23. James Jerpe, "On and Off the Field," *The Pittsburgh Gazette Times,* September 14, 1913, 3.

24. "Cubs Snatch the Pennant from Our Pirates' Grasp; Score, 5 to 2: Brown Too Much for Home Team," 7.

25. James Jerpe, "On and Off the Field,"

26. Honus (John H.) Wagner, "Wagner Tells of 'Hard Losers' in Baseball: Famous Shortstop Declares the Winners Hate to Lose Games on the Ball Field," *The Pittsburgh Gazette Times,* January 30, 1916, 4.

27. *Ibid.*

28. Richard Peterson, ed. *The Pirates Reader* (Pittsburgh: University Of Pittsburgh Press, 2003), 83.

29. Jack Hernon, "Honus Stole Show from Ty: Wagner-Cobb Duel Highlight of 1909 World Series!" *Pittsburgh Post-Gazette,* December 12, 1955, 26.

30. "Pirates Slash Tigers in Their Opening Contest: Not Quite Thirty Thousand Witnessed the Game—Young Adams Only Weak at Start—Errors Helped to Beat American Champions," *The Syracuse Herald,* October 9, 1909, 8.

31. Ralph S. Davis, "Pittsburg Points: Fans Eager to See Games in Smoky City," *The Sporting News,* October 14, 1909, 1.

32. *Ibid.*

33. *Ibid.*

34. "Gossip of the Players," *The Sporting News,* November 4, 1909, 4.

35. "Pittsburgh Tenders Glorious Greeting to World Leaders: Champion Pirates Are Acclaimed for Hours by Large Portion of People," *The Pittsburgh Gazette Times,* October 19, 1909, 10.

36. *Ibid.*

37. "Cincinnati Kids Honor Hans Wagner: Carnegie Man Was Center of Admiring Group at Redtown, Does Coin-Scattering Act," *The Pittsburg Press,* August 3, 1910, 12.

38. *Ibid.*

39. Ralph S. Davis, "Baseball's Modest King," *The Pittsburgh Press,* April 18, 1909, 2.

40. *Ibid.*

41. *Ibid.*

42. Edgar G. Brands, "Between Innings: Lesson No. 20 in Ancient History," *The Sporting News,* December 17, 1931, 4.

43. *Ibid.*

44. *Ibid.*

45. "Watch for Real Romance; Hans Meets a Princess: Basehit King and Austrian Royalty Exchange Greetings in Oklahoma;

The Pittsburgh Gazette Times, September 14, 1913, 3.

Wagner a Hero When He Rescues Her Auto from the Mud," *The Pittsburgh Gazette Times*, April 4, 1913, 12.

46. *Ibid.*

47. *Ibid.*

48. *Ibid.*

Chapter 11

1. "Wagner a Dreadnaught, Powerful and Majestic: Cleveland Writer Enthuses in Describing 'Flying Dutchman' after Seeing Him in Action Here," *The Pittsburg Press*, June 11, 1909, 22.

2. Ralph S. Davis, "Cubs Make Season's Bow and Score a Victory: President Taft Sees Cubs Down Pirates in Hard Game," *The Pittsburg Press*, May 30, 1909, 1.

3. "Wagner a Dreadnaught, Powerful and Majestic: Cleveland Writer Enthuses in Describing 'Flying Dutchman' after Seeing Him in Action Here," 22.

4. "A Little History Attached to Wagner's Old Glove," *The Logansport Pharos*, July 14, 1910, 6.

5. Ralph Davis, "Ralph Davis Column," *The Pittsburg Press*, May 28, 1913, 24.

6. *Ibid.*

7. "Wagner Does Not Believe His Diamond Career is Over: Press Representative Has Heart to Heart Chat with Grizzled Hero of Many Frays and Is Told That Pirate Captain Is Not Ready to Quit," *The Pittsburg Press*, July 8, 1913, 24.

8. *Ibid.*

9. *Ibid.*

10. *Ibid.*

11. Dennis DeValeria and Jeanne Burke DeValeria, *Honus Wagner: A Baseball Biography* (New York: Henry Holt, 1995), 258.

12. "Wagner Warned Camnitz: Ex-Pirate Pitcher Was Told to Stay Away from Major League Youngsters," *The Kansas City Star*, April 2, 1914, 8.

13. *Ibid.*

14. *Ibid.*

15. James Jerpe, "Wagner May Succeed Clarke, Resigned: Pirate Leader Ranked with Greatest," *The Pittsburgh Gazette Times*, September 9, 1915, 8.

16. David J. Davies, "Pittsburgh Fans Honor Great Hans Wagner," *Sporting Life*, March 4, 1916, 15.

17. *Ibid.*

18. *Ibid.*

19. *Ibid.*

20. *Ibid.*

21. "Honus Wagner Greatest of All," *Escanaba Morning Press*, January 1, 1916, 11.

22. *Ibid.*

23. "News Notes and Highlights," *Sporting Life*, January 13, 1917, 7.

24. DeValeria, *Honus Wagner*, 272.

25. "Paterson Will Honor 'Old Honus': Veteran Will Be Center of Attraction When Pirates Play Exhibition Game There Tomorrow," *The Pittsburg Press*, August 25, 1917, 14.

26. DeValeria, *Honus Wagner*, 278.

27. *Ibid.*, 284–285.

28. Jack Hernon, "Easy-To-Sign Wagner Changed Pattern in 1909, Held Out Long: Honus Won His Best Pact, $10,000," *Pittsburgh Post-Gazette*, December 13, 1955, 21.

29. Arthur D. Hittner, *The Life Of Baseball's Flying Dutchman* (Jefferson, NC: McFarland, 1996), 245–246.

30. Frederick G. Lieb, *The Pittsburgh Pirates* (1948; reprint Carbondale: Southern Illinois University Press, 2003), 250.

31. David L. Fleitz, *More Ghosts in The Gallery: Another Sixteen Little-Known Greats at Cooperstown* (Jefferson, NC: McFarland, 2007), 188.

32. *Ibid.*

33. Lawrence S. Ritter, *The Glory of Their Times: The Story of the Early Days of Baseball Told by the Men Who Played It* (1966; reprint New York: William Morrow, 1984), 339.

34. Lester J. Biederman, "'Honus' Greatest Thrill: Winning First Batting Title in 1900: The Wagner Story ... No. 3," *The Pittsburgh Press*, December 8, 1955, 52.

35. *Ibid.*

36. "Hans Wagner One Oldtimer Who Believes Baseball Is Better than During His Time," *The Reading Eagle*, March 13, 1933, 10.

37. *Ibid.*

38. Lester Biederman, "'Rosebud' Lucas Released by Pirates: Ancient Righthander

Moundsman Ends Big League Career," *The Pittsburgh Press,* January 16, 1939, 18.

39. Chester L. Smith, "The Village Smithy: Virtually Peerless as Story-Teller," *The Pittsburgh Press,* December 7, 1955, 52.

40. *Ibid.*

41. "Always on Time for a Game, Even If Horse Had to Swim," *The Sporting News,* December 14, 1955, 20.

42. Lieb, *The Pittsburgh Pirates,* 59.

43. "Al Abrams Dies, Covered Sports Here 51 Years: Heart Attack Fatal," *The Pittsburgh Press,* March 4, 1977, A-3.

44. Al Abrams, "Sidelights on Sports: The Honus Wagner I Knew," *Pittsburgh Post-Gazette,* December 7, 1955, 38.

45. *Ibid.*

46. *Ibid.*

47. *Ibid.*

48. George Kirksey, "Connie Mack Is Hit of Baseball Show," *The Pittsburgh Press,* June 13, 1939, 22.

49. Smith, "The Village Smithy: Virtually Peerless as Story-Teller," 52.

50. Jimmy Jordan, "Honus Wagner Statue to be Unveiled Today: Baseball Players and Fans to Attend Ceremonies this Morning in Schenley Park," *Pittsburgh Post-Gazette,* April 30, 1955, 13.

51. *Ibid.*

52. Pat Livingston, "Lasting Tribute Paid to Wagner: 1000 Attend Dedication of Statue," *The Pittsburgh Press,* May 1, 1955, 1.

53. Jordan, "Honus Wagner Statue to be Unveiled Today: Baseball Players and Fans to Attend Ceremonies this Morning in Schenley Park," 13.

54. Livingston, "Lasting Tribute Paid to Wagner: 1000 Attend Dedication of Statue," 1.

55. *Ibid.*

56. *Ibid.*

57. "Bucs' John Wagner Dies in Sleep at 81: Greatest Shortstop Had .329 Average for 21 Seasons," *The Free Lance-Star,* December 6, 1955, 10.

58. *Ibid.*

59. "Honus Wagner, Ex-Pittsburgh Star, Passes," *The Times-News,* December 6, 1955, 10.

60. "Bucs' John Wagner Dies in Sleep at 81: Greatest Shortstop Had .329 Average for 21 Seasons," 11.

61. Jack Hernon, "Glowing Tribute Paid Wagner at Chicago Meeting," *The Sporting News,* December 14, 1955, 22.

62. Jack Hernon, "Honus Stole Show from Ty: Wagner-Cobb Duel Highlight of 1909 World Series!" *Pittsburgh Post-Gazette,* December 12, 1955, 26.

63. "Sports World Mourns Honus Wagner: Loss to City, Baseball, Friends Say," *The Pittsburgh Press,* December 6, 1955, 34.

64. Joe King, "'The Wonder Man' of Pittsburgh: Life Story of Fred Clarke, Famed Pirate, Part 2," *The Sporting News,* March 21, 1951, 16.

65. "Characteristic Anecdotes of 'Hans' Wagner: Wagner as a Humorist—His Dislike of the Limelight—His Love of Athletic Sports—His Generosity—Contradictory Traits—Odd Financial Deals," *Baseball Magazine,* January 1915, 61.

66. *Ibid.*

Bibliography

Books

Churchill, April, and Dorothy Kizer-Dennis. *Postcard History Series: Claremore*. Charleston, SC: Arcadia Publishing, 2007.

Dabilis, Andy, and Nick Tsiotos. *The 1903 World Series: The Boston Americans, the Pittsburg Pirates and the "First Championship of the United States."* Jefferson, NC: McFarland, 2004.

DeValeria, Dennis. and Jeanne Burke DeValeria. *Honus Wagner: A Biography.* New York: Henry Holt, 1995.

Finoli, David, and Bill Ranier. *The Pittsburgh Pirates Encyclopedia.* Urbana, IL: Sports Publishing, 2003.

_____, and Bill Ranier. *When Cobb Met Wagner: The Seven-Game World Series of 1909.* Jefferson, NC: McFarland, 2011.

Fleitz, David L. *Ghosts in the Gallery at Cooperstown: Sixteen Little-Known Members of the Hall of Fame.* Jefferson, NC: McFarland, 2004.

_____. *More Ghosts in the Gallery: Another Sixteen Little-Known Greats at Cooperstown.* Jefferson, NC: McFarland, 2007.

Hageman, William. *Honus: The Life and Times of a Baseball Hero.* Urbana, IL: Sports Publishing, 1996.

Hittner, Arthur D. *The Life of Baseball's "Flying Dutchman."* Jefferson, NC: McFarland, 1996.

Levitt, Daniel R. *Ed Barrow: The Bulldog Who Built the Yankees' First Dynasty.* Lincoln: University of Nebraska Press, 2008.

Levy, Alan H. *Rube Waddell: The Zany, Brilliant Life of a Strikeout Artist.* Jefferson, NC: McFarland, 2000.

Lieb, Frederick G. *The Baltimore Orioles: The History of a Colorful Team in Baltimore and St. Louis.* 1955. Reprint, Carbondale: Southern Illinois University Press, 2005.

_____. *The Pittsburgh Pirates.* 1948. Reprint, Carbondale: Southern Illinois University Press, 2003.

Martin, Alfred M., and Alfred T. Martin. *The Negro Leagues in New Jersey: A History.* Jefferson, NC: McFarland, 2008.

Masur, Louis P. *Autumn Glory: Baseball's First World Series.* New York: Hill and Wang, 2003.

McCollistor, John. *Bucs: The Story of the Pittsburgh Pirates.* Lenexa, KS: Addax, 1998.

McIntire, A.H., ed. *The Electric Journal Vol. XII.* Pittsburgh: Electric Journal, 1915.

Neyer, Rob. *Rob Neyer's Big Book of Baseball Legends: The Truth, the Lies and Everything Else.* New York: Fireside, 2008.

Parker, Clifton Blue. *Big and Little Poison: Paul and Lloyd Waner, Baseball Brothers.* Jefferson, NC: McFarland, 2003.

Peterson, Richard, ed. *The Pirates Reader.* Pittsburgh: University of Pittsburgh Press, 2003.

Porter, David L., ed. *Biographical Dictionary of American Sports: Baseball, Revised and Expanded Edition—G-P.* Westport, CT: Greenwood Press, 2000.

Prout, Henry G. *A Life of George Westinghouse.* New York: Scribner, 1921.

Ritter, Lawrence S. *The Glory of Their Times: The Story of the Early Days of Baseball Told by the Men Who Played It.* 1966. Reprint, New York: William Morrow, 1984.

Shiffert, John. *Baseball in Philadelphia: A History of the Early Game, 1831–1900.* Jefferson, NC: McFarland, 2006.

Singletary, Wes. *The Right Time: John Henry "Pop" Lloyd and Black Baseball.* Jefferson, NC: McFarland, 2011.

Skipper, John C. *Umpires: Classic Baseball Stories from the Men Who Made the Calls.* Jefferson, NC: McFarland, 1997.

Stump, Al. *Cobb: A Biography.* Chapel Hill, NC: Algonquin, 1996.

Waldo, Ronald T. *Fred Clarke: A Biography of the Baseball Hall of Fame Player-Manager.* Jefferson, NC: McFarland, 2011.

Wiseman, John B., ed. *Joy in Mudville: Essays on Baseball and American Life.* Jefferson, NC: McFarland, 2010.

Newspapers and Magazines

Atlanta Constitution

Baltimore American

Baseball Magazine

Beaver Valley Times (Beaver, PA)

The Cedar Rapids Evening Gazette (Cedar Rapids, IA)

The Cedar Rapids Republican (Cedar Rapids, IA)

The Duluth Evening Herald

Escanaba Morning Press (Escanaba, MI)

Evening Press (Sheboygan, WI)

Fort Wayne Journal-Gazette (Fort Wayne, IN)

The Free Lance-Star (Fredericksburg, VA)

Galveston Daily News (Galveston, TX)

Galveston Opera Glass (Galveston, TX)

The Gettysburg Times (Gettysburg, PA)

Goshen Daily Democrat (Goshen, IN)

The Indianapolis Sun

The Jeffersonville Star (Jeffersonville, IN)

The Kansas City Star

Lebanon Semi-Weekly News (Lebanon, PA)

The Lethbridge Daily Herald (Lethbridge, Alberta)

The Lima Daily News (Lima, OH)

The Logansport Pharos (Logansport, IN)

The Lowell Sun (Lowell, MA)

The Mansfield News (Mansfield, OH)

New Castle News (New Castle, PA)

The New York Dramatic Mirror

Oakland Tribune

The Oelwein Daily Register (Oelwein, IA)

Ogden City Evening Standard (Ogden City, UT)

The Pittsburg Press

The Pittsburgh Gazette Times

Pittsburgh Post-Gazette

Portsmouth Daily Herald (Portsmouth, NH)

The Portsmouth Daily Times (Portsmouth, NH)

The Reading Eagle (Reading, PA)

Reno Evening Gazette

The St. Paul Globe

The Salt Lake Tribune

San Antonio Light and Gazette

Sheridan News (Sheridan, IN)

Sporting Life

The Sporting News

Syracuse Herald

The Times-News (Hendersonville, NC)

The Toledo News-Bee

The Wakefield Advocate (Wakefield, MI)

Washington Post

Waterloo Evening Courier (Waterloo, IA)

Websites

books.google.com

news.google.com

www.baseballalmanac.com

www.baseballhall.org

www.baseball-reference.com

www.carnegieborough.com

www.fultonhistory.com

www.la84foundation.org

www.loc.gov

www.newspaperarchive.com

www.paperofrecord.com

www.retrosheet.org

www.sabr.org

Index

Numbers in **_bold italics_** indicate pages with photographs.